The Insect Guide

ORDERS AND MAJOR FAMILIES
OF NORTH AMERICAN INSECTS

BY

Ralph B. Swain, Ph.D.

BUREAU OF ENTOMOLOGY
AND PLANT QUARANTINE,
U.S. DEPT. OF AGRICULTURE

ILLUSTRATED BY

SuZan N. Swain

1948
DOUBLEDAY & COMPANY, INC., and
THE AMERICAN GARDEN GUILD, INC.

MOUTH	ANTENNAE	TARSAL SEGMENTS	CERCI	HABITAT
Chewing	Apparently none	One	Absent	Terrestrial and semiaquatic
Chewing	Long, many-segmented	Two or three	Present	Terrestrial and semiaquatic
Chewing	Long, many-segmented	One	Present	Terrestrial and semiaquatic
Chewing	Mostly short, four-to six-segmented	Fused with tibia as one segment	Absent	Terrestrial and semiaquatic
Chewing	Thread-like, short to long, many-segmented	Variable, none to five	Present	Terrestrial
Chewing	Thread-like, many-segmented	Three	Present	Terrestrial
Chewing	Thread-like, many-segmented	Three	Present	Aquatic as nymphs
Chewing	Bead-like, short or long	Four or five	Present	Terrestrial
Chewing	Thread-like	Three	Present	Terrestrial and semiaquatic
Chewing	Thread-like, short or long	Two or three	Absent	Terrestrial
Chewing	Bead-like	Two	Present	Terrestrial and semiaquatic
Chewing	Thread-like or club-like, short, three-to five-segmented	One or two	Absent	Terrestrial
Piercing-sucking	Bristle-like, short, three-to five-segmented	One	Absent	Terrestrial

CONTINUED INSIDE BACK COVER

The Insect Guide

To Alfred and Elizabeth Satterthwait
whose inspiring example and loving helpfulness have
meant so much to so many young students of nature

CONTENTS

ORDER AND FAMILY

CONTENTS

INTRODUCTION

About 670,000 different kinds of insects have been described since the days of Linnaeus, the inventor of our present system of naming insects, and the total number of species that eventually will be discovered and described is conservatively estimated to be 2,000,000. In short, there are more species of insects than of all other animals taken together.

Since there are so many insects that no one can know all of them or a very considerable part of them, any volume or limited series of volumes treating of individual kinds must be highly selective. While admitting that it is impossible for the general reader to become acquainted with more than a comparatively few insect species, the writer believes that it is within the power of any interested person, whether trained in the sciences or not, to learn to recognize the larger groups of insects. It is the purpose of this book to present the insects of North America north of Mexico, in pictures and in non-technical language, at the family rather than at the species level, and to describe as fully as space permits the "niches" they fill in animal and plant communities.

The broad view is usually the more inspiring one—the outlook from a mountaintop, putting rivers and hills, towns and highways in more understandable perspective, always requites the climber. So let us look at the world of insects, seeing only the larger elements of its composition, and hope that in so doing some who hitherto have been appalled and confused by the sheer numbers and diversity of insects will have a pleasurable experience akin to that of the mountaineer who has achieved the summit.

Is It an Insect?

One who wishes to distinguish different kinds of insects first must know how to tell them from the various animals with which they commonly are confused. Almost any small creature with more than 4 legs mistakenly may be called an insect or "bug," and the immature stages of many insects too often are miscalled "worms." One may use the word "cutworm" for the wormlike young (larvae) of certain moths, but no insects should be called just plain "worms," for there are 4 major groups (phyla) of animals properly called worms—the round worms (Nemathelmínthes), the flat worms (Platyhelmínthes), the hair worms (Nematomórpha), and the earthworms or annulated worms (Annélida). Slender, legless insect larvae probably are confused most frequently with the worms of the last-named phylum. As the reader will discover, only a small fraction of the total number of insects are truly "bugs."

The great division of the animal kingdom to which insects belong is called the phylum Arthrópoda—a word from the Greek meaning, literally, "jointed legs" and, appropriately, arthropods are characterized by their possession of jointed appendages. The entire body, in fact, is jointed, being composed of a linear series of segments, some of which bear paired appendages. The outer covering of arthropods is a limy or horny shell composed of many different plates of varying thicknesses and hardnesses and constituting both an external skeleton to which muscles are attached and a protective armor for the softer parts of the body.

Adult insects differ from other arthropods in having usually 2 pairs of wings, 3 distinct major body divisions—head, thorax, and abdomen—and never more than 3 pairs of legs, a pair to each thoracic segment. With the exception of male strepsipterons, insects with a single pair of wings always lack the hind pair. The following table summarizes for ready comparison the distinguishing features of 6 principal classes of arthropods and the succeeding 2 plates illustrate typical examples of each class of insect relatives.

HOW INSECTS DIFFER FROM

CLASSES AND EXAMPLES	MAJOR BODY DIVISIONS	PAIRS OF WALKING LEGS
PALEÓSTRACHA Horseshoe or king crab	two: cephalo-thorax* and abdomen	five
CRUSTÀCEA Crayfish, crabs, sowbugs, barnacles, etc.	Variable, usually two: cephalo-thorax and abdomen	five or more
ARÁCHNIDA Spiders, ticks, mites, chiggers, scorpions, daddy- long legs, etc.	two: cephalo-thorax and abdomen	four
DIPLÓPODA Millipedes	two: head and body	two per segment
CHILÓPODA Centipedes	two: head and body	one per segment
INSÉCTA Bugs, beetles, butterflies, bees, etc.	three: head, thorax, and abdomen	three

*The fused head and thorax.

OTHER CLASSES OF ARTHROPODS

NUMBER OF ANTENNAE	BREATHING ORGANS	OTHER CHARACTERISTICS
none	gills	Marine: Atlantic and Gulf coasts. Leg bases modified for chewing.
two pairs	gills or body surface	Chiefly salt- and fresh-water dwellers; some terrestrial.
none	tracheae and book-lungs	Land dwellers except for certain mites.
one pair, short	tracheae	Land dwellers. Vegetarian. Body cylindrical, rolling up into a spiral when disturbed. No poison glands.
one pair, long	tracheae	Land dwellers. Predacious on other arthropods and small animals. Body flattened. A pair of poison fangs on first body segment.
one pair	tracheae	Mostly land dwellers or fresh-water forms, but some live in salt water. One or two pairs of wings.

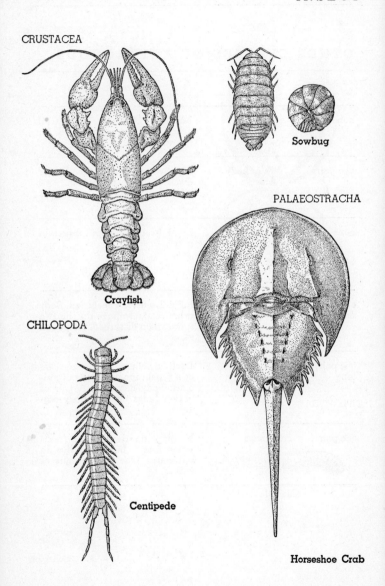

INSECT

CRUSTACEA

Sowbug

PALAEOSTRACHA

Crayfish

CHILOPODA

Centipede

Horseshoe Crab

RELATIVES

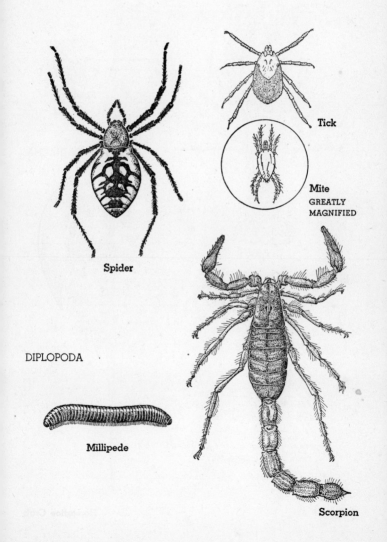

ARACHNIDA

Tick

Mite
GREATLY
MAGNIFIED

Spider

DIPLOPODA

Millipede

Scorpion

About Insects in General

PREHISTORIC

According to the record of the rocks, insects preceded man on this planet by quite some time, and pessimists contend that the former will be the last to leave it. Paleontologists have recognized some 11,500 species of insects among the impressions in coal, peat, lignite, shale, and the often beautifully preserved specimens in amber. About 75 per cent of these ancient species belong to orders and families existing today. The oldest insects still living are the roaches, whose ancestors of carboniferous times (some 200,000,000 years ago) differed very little from present-day forms.

INSECTS AND PLANTS

Through the ages, insects and the higher plants evolved together and long ago became interdependent. The relationships between flowering plants and insects in the absence of man are, for the most part, "friendly" and mutually beneficial, wherein plants afford food and often shelter to insects and the insects do an effective and specialized job of cross-pollinating the flowers. The color, forms, and odors which we admire in flowers serve to attract different kinds of insects whose mouth parts or other body structures peculiarly adapt them as pollinators. This interdependence is so great that without insects countless species of plants undoubtedly would disappear. The large populations of so-called pest insects which build up in response to our intensive agricultural practices and other man-made disturbances of nature cause us much anxiety but usually do not threaten the existence of a plant species over even a very small area. Complete harmony does not prevail, for insects transmit virus, fungous, and bacterial diseases to their food plants; and fungi and bacteria, in turn, afflict insects with disease. Also, some plants—the pitcher plant, the sun dew, and Venus' fly trap, for example, utilize insects as food.

INSECTS AND OTHER ANIMALS

A large proportion of each major group of animals is dependent upon insects as a direct or indirect source of food. Insects are the basic food source of many of our birds, which too often are judged to be "good" or "bad," according to their tastes in insects. The structural adaptations of birds as insect-catching organisms are truly remarkable. Swallows, nighthawks, and members of the flycatcher family subsist altogether upon flying insects, and woodpeckers are especially adapted for feeding on wood-boring insects. The brown creeper and numerous vireos and warblers scour the trunks, branches, and leaves of trees for scales, aphids, and other insects. Towhees, wrens, and thrushes work the ground surface, searching under dead leaves and plant debris for the insects living there. Even sparrows and other birds that are primarily seed eaters consume many insects. Among water birds, the food of grebes has been found to be 25 to 50 per cent insect. Some wading birds are predominantly insectivorous and others take a fair proportion of insects along with worms, crustaceans, and other aquatic invertebrates. Practically all nestling land birds receive a diet consisting largely of insects, regardless of their food habits as adults, some consuming their own weight daily of this sort of food. Hundreds of bird species would become extinct at once if their insect food were eliminated, and the eradication of all insects in any land area eventually would cause the death or exodus of most or all of the birds.

Among mammals, the shrews, moles, bats, skunks, badgers, bears, various squirrels, mice, and rats, and the armadillo are the more important insect eaters. Lizards probably are the chief reptilian predators upon insects, but various snakes and even clumsy box tortoises take insects, at least occasionally. All amphibians spend at least the first part of their lives in fresh water, where they find aquatic insects a major food source. Adult toads and frogs are almost completely insectivorous, and that a toad is desirable in the garden is acknowledged quite generally.

Insects form a considerable or even a major part of the diet of practically all our fresh-water fishes, and the actual existence of many of the game and other edible fishes of stream and lake is dependent upon an abundant supply of insects. Spiders and scorpions prey upon insects, and mites of many species are either external parasites of young or adult insects or predators upon their eggs. The usual relationship of round worms and one-celled animals (Protozóa) to insects is probably that of parasite to host.

INSECTS AND MAN

With the exception of the honey bee, the silkworm, and a few other species, insects too generally are thought to be one of the plagues—but nothing could be further from the truth. Insects have a definite and necessary place in the system of nature that includes man. Having developed with plants, as has been pointed out, they are essential to the reproduction of many plant species upon which man depends as food for himself and for his domesticated animals. The conservationist concerned with the perpetuation or increase of birds, mammals, or fishes must preserve the food of the insectivorous species or else change their food habits, a rather impossible alternative. More directly, we are utilizing insects in the fight against noxious insects and even plants. Various insects and their eggs were (and still are to some extent) eaten by our aborigines.

Anglers, of course, use insects as models for numerous dry and wet flies. These lures may not resemble any particular species of insect, but such names as Red Ant, Mosquito, Western Bee, Black Gnat, and White Miller, indicate the general type of insect the fly is supposed to represent. Flies patterned after European insects (many of which are in use here) or after no insect at all may catch the fish, but many a good fisherman keeps close tab on the seasonal variation in the food of his prey and uses flies to fit the occasion.

The insect menace is not so terrifying as it was some decades ago. Insect injury to agriculture, stored products, wooden con-

xxviii   **THE INSECT GUIDE**

struction, and the health of man amounts to staggering totals in dollars and cents, and we cannot know when some new pest will come to our shores or develop from native talent. But it may be asserted with considerable safety that civilized man is capable of repulsing any and all insect assaults upon his person or possessions. As the science of applied entomology advances, and we now are witnessing its period of most spectacular progress, the more effective and inexpensive will insect control become.

It is possible, even probable, that, from the financial standpoint, conditions will get worse before they get better, for some of the contemplated pest-eradication programs, which recently discovered insecticides may make possible, will involve very large initial expenditures. A government entomologist, J. R. Parker, reports that in 1889, not more than $75,000 of public funds were spent on insect control and entomology in general, but that today the annual cost of entomological teaching, research, quarantine, and control paid out of state and federal funds alone is more than $15,000,000. This is, of course, a very small fraction of the annual total monetary loss occasioned by pest insects, a loss which cannot be precisely calculated but which must certainly amount to several billions of dollars.

Beyond an appreciation of the fact that biologically we are dependent upon them in many ways, there is an aspect of man's relationship with insects which is distinctly pleasurable and to which the final chapter and much of each page of this book have been devoted—the enjoyment of insects for what they are, truly, "the greatest show on earth."

STRUCTURE

Those parts of the anatomy to which it is necessary to refer in describing family characteristics of insects are labeled in the diagrammatic drawings on pages xxx and xxxi. Where a choice was possible, the simpler anatomical term has been used. Many of them are familiar. The word "tarsus," for example, suggests foot; "femur" and "tibia" are used in human anatomy, and although the insect leg is a far cry from the human, the reasonableness of applying those names to certain parts of the insect leg is obvious after a little study and comparison.

The theoretical common ancestor of the insects was a worm-like animal of 21 body segments. In modern insects the first 6 segments have been fused into a head with its mouth parts; the next 3 have become joined together into a so-called thorax, with appendages specialized as organs of locomotion (legs and wings). There are no longer more than 11 abdominal segments, as a rule, and this number usually is found only in the early developmental stages, seldom in the adult insect.

In the flexible regions of the body, the segments are joined by a band or fold of pliable skin which allows one segmental ring to telescope over the one behind it. Where segments have become more or less fused, there usually remains a line of division called a suture. Actually the individual chitinous rings are composed of separate plates, usually 4, sometimes more, sometimes less. The sutures and subdivisions of segments are most important to the systematic entomologist or to anyone using a "key" in order to determine the genus and species of an insect, but we shall not name them or refer to them in this book. For our purposes, the general conformation of the body, the nature of the wings, if present, the specialization of the legs and mouth parts and other of the more conspicuous body features, together with food habits and characteristic behavior, will serve to define and distinguish insect families.

The typical insect leg is composed of 5 parts: a basal coxa, a usually inconspicuous trochanter, a rather long and muscular femur, a usually slender tibia about as long as the femur, and a terminal, jointed tarsus or "foot" composed of 5 or fewer segments.

A brief description of the mouth parts of a grasshopper will assist the reader to understand the labels used in the diagrams of various types of insect mouth parts. The labrum is the single, wide "upper lip" which hangs down in front of the powerful mandibles. The mandibles are a pair of stout, toothed cutting and grinding organs, which are rather similar in function to the human jaws but work from side to side instead of up and down. A smaller pair of secondary jaws, equipped with jointed appendages called maxillary palps, lie just behind the mandibles. The "lower lip" is a broad flap of tissue, divided at its apex into 2 large lobes and bearing on each side a 3-segmented labial palp. As the diagrams show, specialization has

PARTS OF AN INSECT

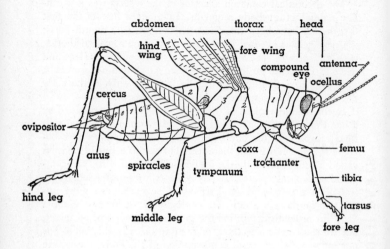

ADULT GRASSHOPPER

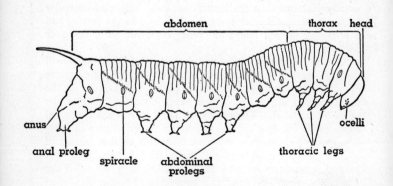

MOTH LARVA

TYPES OF MOUTH PARTS

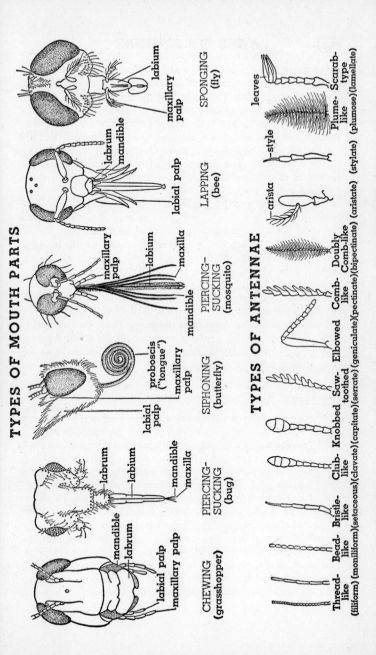

CHEWING (grasshopper)

labial palp
maxillary palp
mandible
labrum
labrum
labium
mandible

PIERCING–SUCKING (bug)

labrum
labium
mandible
maxilla

SIPHONING (butterfly)

proboscis ("tongue")
maxillary palp
labial palp

PIERCING–SUCKING (mosquito)

maxillary palp
labrum
mandible
labium
maxilla
mandible

LAPPING (bee)

labrum
mandible
labial palp

SPONGING (fly)

labium
maxillary palp

TYPES OF ANTENNAE

Thread-like (filiform)

Bead-like (moniliform)

Bristle-like (setaceous)

Club-like (clavate)

Knobbed (capitate)

Saw-toothed (serrate)

Elbowed (geniculate)

Comb-like (pectinate)

Doubly Comb-like (bipectinate)

arista

Aristate

style

Stylate

leaves

Scarab-type (lamellate)

Plume-like (plumose)

led to great modifications of this rather primitive structural plan.

Insects breathe by means of a complicated system of larger and smaller air tubes (tracheae and tracheoles) whose minute branchlets penetrate to all parts of the body, carrying oxygen directly to the cells. The external openings of the system are the spiracles, or breathing pores, usually placed one on each side of the second and third thoracic segments and the first 6 or 8 abdominal segments. The aquatic young of many insects breathe by means of gills, which with a few exceptions are filled with tracheae rather than blood passages. Some aquatic larvae, internal parasites, and very primitive insects breathe directly through the body wall.

Insects perceive light and darkness and, to some extent, color by means of the faceted compound eyes and ocelli (simple eyes). Hearing sometimes is well developed. In the grasshoppers and crickets, for example, part of the hearing organ is a large membrane on the side of the first abdominal segment or a smaller one on the fore leg. The tactile sense seems to be located primarily in the antennae, mouth parts, tarsi (feet), and cerci, as are also the organs of chemical perception. These last are somewhat analogous to our noses and permit insects when hearing and seeing cannot avail to sense the presence of food, host or prey species, and the opposite sex.

GROWTH AND DEVELOPMENT

Because its skeleton is external and stretching is possible only at the folds between the chitinous plates, an insect grows for a while, then sheds its tight old garment and appears in a new and larger one capable of further stretching. All insects cast their skeletons (molt) a number of times during their growth from egg to adult. In the most primitive insects (a silverfish would be an example) the general body form does not change appreciably during this process—the insect leaves the egg in an advanced stage of body development and differs from the adult chiefly in size and in being sexually immature. Immature insects of this sort are simply called "young" for lack of a more descriptive term, and their development is said to be direct. A more advanced type of development (simple or gradual) is exhibited by the grasshopper, whose young, called a "nymph," is like the adult in most respects—it has both compound and simple eyes, eats the same food, and behaves in much the same way; the wings, however, are represented by short, pouch-like extensions from the thorax wall, and the sexual organs are not fully developed. The change from mature nymph to winged adult, especially in the gilled aquatic nymphs (naiads) of stoneflies, dragonflies, and Mayflies, is a considerable transformation but is said to be incomplete. Complete transformation (metamorphosis) occurs in the beetles, butterflies, and other "higher" insects, where the change from the young, called a "larva," to the adult is a truly remarkable metamorphosis. There is almost no suggestion in the larva of the form of the adult—no trace of wings in the caterpillar that will become a moth, not even compound eyes—hence we say that metamorphosis is complete. In this complex type of development a transition stage (pupal period) intervenes between the larval and adult stages. The pupa is usually in a cell in soil or plant tissues, or in a silken cocoon fashioned by the larva, or may be inside the unshed skin of the larva. The drawings which precede this page show diagrammatically these 3 general types of insect development.

BEHAVIOR

Some of the most remarkable behavior patterns in all of nature are found among insects. Why do certain moths always lay their eggs in a particular location or on a particular species of plant? How do creatures with such tiny brains and without education weave such elegant and intricate cocoons? We label such behavior and innate knowledge "instinct," but that makes it no less marvelous. Although we are surrounded by insects at all times, we know very little about the private lives of most of them. The persistent observation of the commonest roach or ant always yields an abundance of new and interesting facts. When all the insects shall have been described, named, and catalogued, the study of their behavior will never cease to afford the joy of original discovery to both professional and amateur.

TYPES OF INSECT DEVELOPMENT

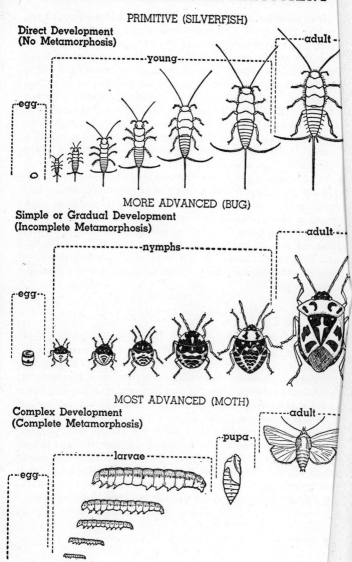

PRIMITIVE (SILVERFISH)

Direct Development
(No Metamorphosis)

young

egg

adult

MORE ADVANCED (BUG)

Simple or Gradual Development
(Incomplete Metamorphosis)

nymphs

egg

adult

MOST ADVANCED (MOTH)

Complex Development
(Complete Metamorphosis)

egg

larvae

pupa

adult

How to Use This Book

COVERAGE

This book is intended to serve as a guide to the principal families of insects anywhere in North America north of Mexico, a vast territory almost coinciding with one of the 6 great "faunal regions" of the earth (Greenland is the chief omission). Since, with the exception of the northernmost, practically uninhabited portions of the continent, no large area lacks representatives of almost every family considered, it usually is unnecessary to define the range of the families. The known distribution of each insect species used as a family representative is given in rather loose terms, for the exact limits of distribution are known for none. Where a species is said to be "widely distributed in our region" it may be assumed that its occurrence in the northern half of Canada and in Alaska is either unknown or rather doubtful.

NAMES

The English names of orders, families, and species of insects used in this book have been chosen carefully and include those approved by the American Association of Economic Entomologists. It will be noted that when the words *fly, louse, bug,* and *worm* are used in any but a scientifically exact sense they are combined or hyphenated with the modifying part of the name. For example: a firefly is not a fly but a beetle, and a webworm is not a worm but a moth larva. Thus the true may be separated readily from the false so far as names are concerned.

For a well-known widely distributed insect there are often

several or even many common names, but it has not been thought desirable to list these synonyms. In fact, things would be much simpler if one common name could be approved and generally accepted for each insect. Actually, insects may have more synonymous scientific names than common ones; but, only one of them is in proper current usage and the others are generally met only in the older literature.

There is little agreement among entomologists, and may not be for generations, as to the number, constitution, and names of such large groupings as the orders of insects, the major subdivisions of the class Insécta; indeed, changes will continue to be made as long as our knowledge of insect relationships remains imperfect. Common names, therefore, are really more permanent than many of the unfamiliar-sounding Latinized names. English names are used for families throughout this book, but it has been necessary to form some of them by the rather artificial device of adding the suffix *id* to the stem of the scientific name. Thus, wasps of the family Bracónidae, for which there is no really descriptive common name, are called "braconids." The common names of insects only rarely are translations of the Latinized scientific names, which, in general, would be unsuited to the purpose.

Each of the 26 insect orders recognized in this book is composed of from one to several hundred families. An insect family, of which more than 900 now are recognized, comprises from one to hundreds of genera—each genus consisting of one to many individual kinds or species of insects. A family, being a larger category, is relatively more stable than a genus, although frequently more difficult to define. The technical family name consists of a Greek or Latin stem with the suffix *idae;* the first letter is always capitalized. The generic and specific names, the first and last names, respectively, of an insect, are italicized in print and the first letter of the generic name is always capitalized; sometimes a third name (subspecific or varietal) is added. Although taxonomic entomologists usually append the name of the man who first described an insect, placing it in parentheses if a subsequent shift in genus has been made, we have considered it unnecessary here.

Immense numbers of insect species sometimes are included in a single family. Still, the family concept is a useful one to the farmer and home gardener as well as to the student. For example, frequently one need not know the exact species of an injurious insect in order to prescribe the correct insecticidal treatment. So far as chemical control is concerned, aphids, regardless of species, are treated much alike, as are different kinds of cutworms, grasshoppers, scale insects, etc. This, however, does not minimize the importance or necessity of specific determinations of pest insects where control by cultural practices or biological means is to be attempted or where certain preventive measures are to be employed.

The sequence of orders and families in the text and illustrations is from lowest or most primitive to highest or most specialized. This is a natural arrangement, which places related insects closer together than would an alphabetical or other artificial scheme.

ILLUSTRATIONS

The plates grouped at the center of this book are intended to be a simple, visual guide, or key, to the orders and principal families of insects. For the most part, only a single example of each family has been illustrated, and, so far as possible, a typical species has been chosen—one which exhibits a maximum number of family characteristics. The name with each figure is not that of a particular kind of insect but of a group, usually of a family, but sometimes of an important aggregation of insects of less than family rank. In the text, each insect figured is identified to species, but in the picture guide it is intended to be simply a typical example of a larger group of species. The bold-face number by each figure is the same as that numbering the family discussions in the text. It will be advantageous for the reader to use the index as little as possible and learn to hunt, somewhat leisurely, through the text and plates for the family description or illustration he wants. Plate numbers are omitted purposely so that the reader must follow the numbers to find a particular illustration. In doing this, it is hoped that more time will be spent looking at the figures. The names in large capitals are the common names of the orders.

In most instances, only the adults of the insects have been

illustrated, but the artist has shown some immature insects of special structural interest. The adults are identified more easily than are immature forms, and, in a book of this scope, it is impossible to deal adequately with the identification of the immature stages of each family.

Because most insects are small, it has been necessary to show many of them enlarged. Some of our very beautiful and curious species are quite uninteresting without magnification simply because they cannot be seen in sufficient detail. A hand lens is at least as important to the student of insects as a field glass to the student of birds. Where feasible, a line paralleling the longest axis of the insect represents its natural size, otherwise the figure following a times sign ($\times \frac{1}{2}$, $\times 1$, $\times 10$, etc.) indicates the amount of reduction or magnification, if any.

On the end pages of this book we have summarized in tabular form, for quick reference, some of the important, distinguishing features of the adults of the various insect orders.

HOW TO IDENTIFY

Become familiar with the illustrations and with the discussion on insect structure in a preceding section; then, when you have an insect you are curious about, leaf through the plates until you have found one which agrees in general with your specimen Check general body contours, wings, antennae, legs, and mouth parts. Color is of minor importance as a rule. Then turn to the family write-up in the text and check the word description. Remember that the insect you have is probably not the species illustrated. If it is obviously different and you wish to know exactly what it is, use the references to find a book which will give you further help. If you have no insects to identify, read the concluding section of the book, which contains suggestions for locating some.

In collecting insects for identification, be sure to take one or more adults, if you can recognize them, or at least some of the largest individuals present. It may be necessary to cage the insects and rear them to adulthood, or simply to wait and take the adults at a later date. *Dead,* properly packed specimens (see the final portion of this book) can be sent to entomologists in state, federal, or private employment, who are always glad to assist with the determination of insect names to the extent of their time and taxonomic ability. State entomologists, county agents, the departments of entomology or zoology at state colleges or universities, natural history museums, the Bureau of Entomology and Plant Quarantine (United States Department of Agriculture) at Washington, D.C., and commercial pest-control operators receive and answer thousands of requests for information about insects. Most of this information and advice is given without charge as a public service. It is well to remember that with the limited number of persons to provide the answers this service can be overtaxed quite easily—so, emergencies excepted, libraries and other local sources of information should be exhausted before appealing for help to the already overburdened institutional and government entomologists.

A helpful source for one desiring to contact other insect enthusiasts is *The Naturalists' Directory* (see References), which lists the names and addresses of many amateur and professional entomologists and the kinds of insects they like to collect, exchange, or correspond about. The addresses of many of the living authors of reference books listed in the bibliography will be found in *American Men of Science*.

Remember that living insects in any stage of development must not be sent through the mails or otherwise transported from state to state or county to county. The danger of accidentally extending the range of a serious insect pest is too great.

Acknowledgments

It is impossible to acknowledge properly the writer's indebtedness to the published works of others—entomologists, ornithologists, and naturalists in general—from which so much of the material in this book has been drawn. Artist and writer are obliged, altogether hopelessly, to the many friends, old and new, who, with so much kindness and patience, critically examined our illustrations and manuscript, the correctness of which, in large measure, is due to their helpfulness. Errors of any kind are entirely the responsibility of the writer.

Most of the insects which served as models for our illustrations were generously made available by the American Museum of Natural History, New York City, and the United States National Museum, Washington, D.C. We are grateful to Monte A. Cazier, Chairman of the Department of Insects and Spiders at the former institution, and to all of the staff members of that department, particularly Charles D. Michener, C. Howard Curran, J. McDunnough, and Willis J. Gertsch, and to John C. Armstrong of the Department of Living Invertebrates, for assistance with the selection of specimens, for criticisms of certain illustrations, and for many other favors.

All of the illustrations and the entire manuscript were reviewed in the Division of Insect Identification of the Bureau of Entomology and Plant Quarantine, United States Department of Agriculture. Our warmest thanks go to C. F. W. Muesebeck, chief of that division, for his personal help and encouragement, and to the specialists who reviewed various portions of the text and certain illustrations: Grace Glance, Thysanura and Collembola; Ashley B. Gurney, Orthoptera, Ephemeroptera,

Dermaptera, Plecoptera, Embioptera, Corrodentia, Neuroptera, and Mecoptera; Thomas E. Snyder, Isoptera; J. C. Crawford, Thysanoptera; Paul W. Oman, Louise M. Russell, Preston W. Mason, and Reece I. Sailer, Hemiptera; Carl Heinrich, Hahn W. Capps, and William D. Field, Lepidoptera; William H. Anderson, L. L. Buchanan, Herbert S. Barber, and Warren S. Fisher, Coleoptera; C. F. W. Muesebeck, Marion R. Smith, Henry K. Townes, Karl V. Krombein, and A. B. Gahan, Hymenoptera; Alan Stone, Curtis W. Sabrosky, Charles T. Greene, Diptera. H. K. Townes also reviewed the references and made numerous suggestions. Certain of the beetle and butterfly plates and correlative portions of the manuscript were reviewed by Edward E. Chapin, Curator of the Division of Insects of the National Museum.

Small numbers of insects or other materials for illustration were furnished kindly by Reginald H. Painter, Kansas State College; Henry Dietrich, Cornell University; Halbert M. Harris, Iowa State College; Nellie M. Payne, American Cyanamid Company; Harlow B. Mills and Herbert H. Ross, Illinois State Natural History Survey; J. Speed Rogers, University of Michigan; C. H. Hadley, Bureau of Entomology and Plant Quarantine at Moorestown, N.J.; Albro T. Gaul, New York City; Robert P. Owen, Seattle, and Phil Rau, Kirkwood, Mo. Maurice T. James loaned a number of fly specimens from the museum of the Colorado State College and also reviewed the text on flies. Brayton Eddy, Curator of Insects and Reptiles of the New York Zoological Society, supplied a number of living insect specimens.

The writer is appreciative of the privilege of using the library of the American Museum of Natural History and is grateful for the many courtesies shown him by Hazel Gay, Librarian, and by the entire staff.

Harold O. Akeson executed the end papers (with the exception of the insect figures). Rachel Akeson and Charlotte Dooley assisted with the typing of the manuscript and the latter also shared the task of proof reading and indexing. The accent markings of the scientific names throughout the book were edited by Eric F. B. Fries of the City College of New York.

The writer is most grateful to P. N. Annand, Chief of the Bureau of Entomology and Plant Quarantine, and to his superiors in the Division of Foreign Plant Quarantines for permission to write this book as an unofficial, personal-time project, and for their friendly interest and support.

We are especially indebted to friend Richard H. Pough, author of the popular *Audubon Bird Guides,* for inducing us to undertake this book and for his many helpful suggestions, and to Clara Claasen, Sabra Mallett, and all the editorial and art staff members of Doubleday and Company, who have done so much to help make its preparation a pleasant task.

RALPH B. SWAIN
SuZan N. SWAIN

January 1948
East Orange, N.J.

Symbols and Special Terms

♂ —male

♀ —female

|———| actual length of an insect's body, exclusive of antennae and tail appendages, or its actual wing expanse

x—a number following a times sign indicates the amount of magnification or reduction, if any, in an illustration. For example, **x1** means natural size, **x½** means half natural size, **x10** means 10 times natural size.

The adjectives listed below, when used before the word "insect," have been given definite meanings so that range in size may be indicated without constantly resorting to figures. When used in any other connection, the words have their usual rather loose and comparative meanings. For example, a large ant may be a small insect, etc.

Large	more than 1 inch long
Medium	more than ½ to 1 inch long
Small	more than ¼ inch to ½ inch long
Very small	more than ⅛ to ¼ inch long
Minute	less than ⅛ inch long

Some Aids to the Pronunciation of Scientific Names

The use of grave and acute accents to indicate the proper pronunciation of scientific names used in this book follows the method which seems to have been introduced by Asa Gray, the great American botanist, and was used in recent years by Brues and Melander in their *Classification of Insects.*

A grave accent is placed over a long vowel in an accented syllable: gràting, Odonàta; adòre, *Calosòma.*

An acute accent is placed over a short vowel in an accented syllable: áccent, *Ágrion;* próper, Trichóptera.

In all diphthongs, the accent mark is placed over the second vowel. The diphthongs *ae* and *oe* are equivalent to the vowel *e* and are usually pronounced like long *e* as in Caesar; *ai* is usually like long *a* as in ail; *eu* like long *u* in eulogy; *ei* like long *i* as in eider; *oi* as it is in coin; *au* as in August. In *oi* and *au* the accent is rather arbitrarily made grave.

The letters *c* and *g* are soft (as in cell, ginger) before the soft vowels *e, i, y,* and the diphthongs *ae* and *oe;* they are hard (as in cat, gone) before the hard vowels *a, o, u,* and the diphthong *oi.* *Ch* is always pronounced like the letter *k.*

The Insect Guide

PROTURONS
Order Protùra

A group of minute, primitive insects; wingless and eyeless, with rudimentary antennae and chewing mouth parts so far retracted within the head that feeding may be a sucking rather than a biting process. The first pair of legs, which serves in a sensory, not a locomotor, capacity, is held above the head and manipulated much like antennae. There is a pair of leg-like appendages on each of the first 3 abdominal segments. Externally, the young differ from the adults chiefly in size, hence development is said to be direct; actually, a segment is added to the body with each successive molt, so that first-stage young

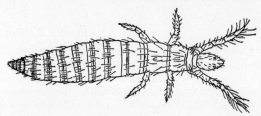

have 9 abdominal segments, while adults have 12. Proturons live in moist places—under stones and bark, in rotten wood, and in soils rich in humus; their life histories are almost unknown. The 23 species so far described from our region are contained in 2 families. The figure above (redrawn from Ewing, 1940) is of a widely distributed species *Aceréntulus bárberi* which is less than 1/16 inch long. This minor order is omitted from the picture guide.

SILVERFISH AND ALLIES
Order Thysanùra

Small, wingless insects, with 3 long conspicuous bristles at the end of the body and with very long, many-segmented antennae. Usually, the entire body surface is covered with minute, silvery scales which rub off easily. The chewing mouth parts are set in a cavity in the head. The young molt 6 or more times before becoming adult; they exhibit no metamorphosis but develop directly from young to adult. There are but 2 families in this primitive order—the machilids (family Machílidae), which live under bark, stones, and in forest litter, feeding on decayed vegetable matter, and the familiar silverfish or bristletails of the family described below.

1 Silverfish   *Family Lepismátidae*

ADULTS: As described for the order, differing from those of the only other family in lacking ocelli, and in being eyeless, or in having small, widely separated compound eyes instead of large ones placed close together. They frequent basements and dark crevices in houses and are usually seen at night on walls or floors near water pipes. The eggs are laid singly or in small groups in concealed places.

YOUNG: Like the adults in form and habit. They may take several months to 2 years to complete their development.

IMPORTANCE: Injurious to books, wallpapers, and fabrics by consuming pastes, glues, sizing, and starch.

EXAMPLE: Common Silverfish   *Lepísma saccharìna*

Common throughout our region and much of the world.

IAPYGIDS AND ALLIES
Order Entótrophi

A small and little-known group of primitive insects, very small or minute in size, which once was included with the silverfish order (Thysanùra). These insects are wingless, eyeless dwellers in dark, damp places, under the bark of logs, in leaf mold and rich humus soils. The color is generally white or gray and the body may be clothed with scattered hairs; there are no scales. At the end of the body is a pair of either slender filaments or forcep-like appendages (cerci). The mouth parts are

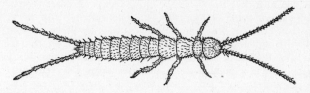

of the biting type. Development is direct. They feed upon fungi and other plant material both living and dead, and possibly upon animals smaller than themselves. Our species are divided between 2 families, neither of which will be described. The figure above (redrawn from Essig, 1942) is of a typical species, *Campòdea fólsomi*. The order is not represented by a figure in the picture guide.

SPRINGTAILS
Order Collémbola

Like the silverfish, these are wingless, primitive insects without metamorphosis, the immature stages resembling the adults in appearance. They are very small or minute, usually less than ⅟₁₆ inch long, with chewing or sucking mouth parts and usually 8, sometimes fewer, simple eyes (not faceted) on each side of the head. Ocelli are absent. Their bodies are scaly, hairy, or naked, and grayish, whitish, metallic-hued, or even brightly colored. The ability of most of these tiny creatures to jump is due to their possession of a spring-like mechanism (furcula) on the underside of the abdomen. This spring is formed by a pair of partially fused appendages arising on either the fourth or fifth abdominal segment and fitting into a catch on the underside of the third. Under the first abdominal segment of every springtail is a unique, short, tube-like organ believed to have a respiratory function. These structures may be seen with a hand lens, but exact studies require a microscope and special techniques for mounting specimens on glass slides.

Springtails occur under damp leaves, the bark of logs, and moist, dark situations throughout our region and almost everywhere in the world, including the polar areas. Some species congregate on the surface of snow and are called "snowfleas"; others are abundant on surfaces of ponds, feeding on algae and diatoms; still others live on sea beaches, where at high tide they are submerged in salt water. A number of springtails are luminous.

Most of these insects are unimportant economically, but a few are sporadically abundant enough to damage seedlings in greenhouses and potted plants and mushrooms in commercial plantings. A Puerto Rican species is vector of a virus disease of sugar cane. The springtails which collect on water surfaces sometimes figure prominently in the diets of fishes.

2 Springtails *Family Entomobrÿidae*

ADULTS: Typical of the order. The smooth, cylindrical bodies are covered with scales and (or) hairs of various types and have 6 abdominal segments. The mouth parts are situated at the front of the head and the antennae, usually 4-segmented, are near them. This is the largest family in number of species in our region.

YOUNG: Very like the adults. The life histories of most springtails are practically unknown.

IMPORTANCE: Seldom of economic importance, but occasionally pests of seedlings in fields and greenhouses.

EXAMPLE: Marsh Springtail   *Isotomùrus palústris*

A large species occurring throughout North America and much of the north temperate Old World. It lives in moist surface litter, moss, or soil and is often found on the surfaces of ponds.

3 Springtails *Family Sminthùridae*

ADULTS: Having more or less globular instead of cylindrical bodies and with mouth parts below the head. The antennae arise from the upper part of the head. Excellent jumpers, occurring in moist places, often upon fresh-water surfaces.

YOUNG: Similar to the adults.

IMPORTANCE: A few plant-feeding species occasionally are abundant enough to damage field and garden crops of vegetables and flowers, but most are harmless to agriculture.

EXAMPLE: Garden Springtail   *Bourletiélla horténsis*

Common in the eastern United States; nearly cosmopolitan. This is one of the springtails capable of doing appreciable injury to cultivated plants.

ROACHES, GRASSHOPPERS, CRICKETS, AND ALLIES
Order Orthóptera

A large order containing some of the greatest scourges of mankind—the locusts of the Bible and our own West, the Mormon cricket, and those plagues of housewives, the roaches, as well as the somewhat more respectable katydids and crickets. These are elongate insects, usually with a pair of leathery fore wings, called tegmina (singular—tegmen), concealing a pair of large, membranous hind wings, which are folded fanwise. They are largely vegetarian, but a few are predacious. The mouth parts are below the head and formed for biting and chewing. The thread-like antennae are usually long and many-segmented. In the large cricket and grasshopper families, the last pair of legs is uniformly longer and better developed than the others and is used for jumping, or, in some of the less agile species, for plunging along in a semi-hop. The first thoracic segment is prominent, and a pair of anal appendages (cerci), usually quite short, is always present.

In the preceding orders there was no metamorphosis; here, metamorphosis is incomplete; that is, the transformation from young to adult is gradual, but there is a decided change in appearance when the "wing pads" that have been enlarging during the growth of the nymph suddenly become the wings of the adult and capable of flight. Until we come to the nerve-winged insects of the order Neuróptera, incomplete metamorphosis as here described will be the rule.

The short- and long-horned grasshopper families (7, 9), which together contain most of the jumping members of the order, are one of the great natural food sources for birds, composing almost 10 per cent of their insect food as determined by actual stomach examinations.

The Grylloblátidae is the only family of the order which has not been represented by an illustration in this guide. It contains 5 described species, 3 in our western mountains and 2 in the mountains of Japan, at elevations usually exceeding 4000 feet. They are wingless and bear some resemblance to silverfish but have only 2 tail filaments. They live in soil, moss, or among stones, and are collected rarely.

4 Roaches   *Family Bláttidae*

ADULTS: Medium to large, flat-bodied insects with a greatly developed first thoracic segment, which, when viewed from above, almost or completely hides the head. The compound eyes are large and the slender, tapering antennae are somewhat longer than the body. A few of our roaches are wingless; the others have 2 pairs of wings; the fore pair, leathery and pigmented with shades of brown or yellow, are folded flat across the back. They are quick-running on fairly long, spiny legs, whose large basal segments (coxae) cover the underside of the thorax and base of the abdomen. The leg spines are used to comb and clean the body, but the legs themselves and the antennae are cleaned in the mouth; roaches probably spend more time cleaning their bodies than do cats. They are nocturnal, hiding in crevices, cupboards, or between walls during the day and coming out at night to feed on unprotected food or garbage. The eggs of most species are contained in an elongate case, which is carried about protruding from the body of the female for a period, sometimes of several days, before being glued with a mouth secretion to the wall of a dark cranny, or placed in a cavity hollowed out by the mandibles of the insect herself. Debris is often plastered over the egg case.

YOUNG: The nymphs are like the adults in appearance and habits, but are wingless. There are 5 to 7 nymphal stages.

IMPORTANCE: Roaches are problems in houses, restaurants, and food stores of all kinds. They are not only unsightly, they leave a disagreeable odor behind them and some may chew holes in starched curtains and linens. It has not been demonstrated that roaches spread disease. Although there are roaches native to almost every part of the world, our most important domestic species are believed to be immigrants from Africa.

EXAMPLE: American Roach   *Periplanèta americàna*

This species formerly was thought to have come to us from Mexico and Central America, but the eminent orthopterist, J. A. G. Rehn, has accumulated what appears to be proof positive that the original home of this species is tropical West Africa. Hence it is likely that slave ships or other vessels brought this evidently misnamed species to the Caribbean and our mainland. It is now widely established in the southern United States and in heated buildings far northward.

5 Walkingsticks   *Family Phasmátidae*

ADULTS: Our commoner species look like twigs with legs, while some of the tropical forms resemble leaves in shape and color. These are very long insects with the second and third thoracic segments together often equaling or approaching half the body length. The compound eyes are small, the antennae fairly long, and the mouth parts are of the biting type. The legs are long, quite slender, and about equal. Our species are wingless with the exception of one in Florida. Walkingsticks spend their active lives in trees, bushes, or among grasses, feeding upon foliage. They have the power of regeneration to some extent, and a lost leg may be replaced, at least partially, at a succeeding molt. The paired tail appendages (cerci) are very small. Only the mantids could be confused with the walkingsticks, and the absence of grasping fore legs in the latter distinguishes them. The eggs of these tree dwellers are dropped to the ground singly, where they rest among fallen leaves until hatching time the following spring or summer.

YOUNG: Quite like the adults. There are usually 5 or 6 nymphal stages.

IMPORTANCE: Walkingsticks are seldom pests. The species illustrated sometimes causes local defoliation of oaks, wild cherry,

and some other deciduous trees in late summer, but no significant injury to the trees results.

EXAMPLE: Common Walkingstick
Diapheromèra femoràta

This is the best-known species from Texas, the Rocky Mountains, and Manitoba eastward to northern Florida, Maine,
and central Ontario. Gray to green in color, usually yellow-
ing with age. Despite its camouflaging shape and colors, this
insect is eaten by the common grackle and more than 15
other bird species, also by its near relatives, the mantids (6),
and various lizards and rodents.

6 Mantids   *Family Mántidae*

ADULTS: Large, much elongated, slow-moving insects with fore
legs fitted for seizing and holding insect prey rather than
for locomotion. The mouth, with biting mandibles, is on the
underside of the small, triangular head. The compound eyes
are prominent and the simple eyes form a small 3-cornered
crown between them. The antennae are long. The first thoracic segment, which bears the grasping fore legs, is very
much longer than the others. There is a pair of short, segmented tail appendages. The 4 walking legs are long and
slender and about equal in length. Protectively colored, mantids easily go unnoticed on green foliage or gray bark. They
are completely predacious, feeding upon almost any sort of
insect they can capture, frequently waiting at flowers for their
prey. The eggs, enclosed in large masses of brownish froth,
which dries to a papery consistency, are laid on twigs. The
egg masses of the various species have characteristic shapes.
Mantids are cannabalistic, and it is not possible to keep more
than one living specimen in a single cage for very long. As
with spiders, the female is very likely to devour the male after
mating.
YOUNG: Resembling the adults and having similar feeding
habits but attacking smaller insects, such as aphids, during
the early stages. They, too, are quite cannabalistic.
IMPORTANCE: Valuable predators for the most part. Although
they take numerous honey bees and other parasitic or plant-
pollinating members of the wasp and bee order (Hymen-

óptera), their effect upon the populations of those insects probably is small. The Chinese mantid (*Tenódera aridifòlia sinénsis*), a native of China and Japan, and the European mantid (*Mántis religiòsa*), common throughout the tropical and warm-temperate regions of the Old World, have both been introduced accidentally into the eastern United States and, later, purposely colonized quite generally as beneficial insects.

EXAMPLE: Carolina Mantid   *Stagmomántis carolìna*

A native species occurring in the southern United States west to Arizona.

7   Short-horned Grasshoppers   *Family Acrídidae*

This large family includes the very important migratory species, popularly called "locusts," and the non-migratory grasshoppers.

ADULTS: The various species are very similar in general appearance and easily distinguished from the members of other orthopteran families. The short antennae, less than half the body length, separate this family from all the other jumping Orthóptera excepting the pygmy locusts and pygmy sand crickets, and the absence of a greatly elongated first thoracic segment or digging fore legs distinguishes it from them. Some species are strong flyers, others customarily fly only short distances, and a few short-winged forms are flightless. Grasshoppers "fiddle" by drawing the femora of the hind legs across thickened veins on the fore wings, and make rattling sounds in flight by vibrating the hind wings against the fore wings. Large hearing organs are present in both sexes. The visible portion of an "ear," the tympanum, looks like an oval window and is found on each side of the first abdominal segment under the wings. In late summer and fall the females lay eggs, cemented together in groups of from 20 to 100, in holes drilled in the soil with their abdomens. One species lays its eggs in dead wood rather than in soil. The winter is passed in the egg stage except in the far South, where adults of some species are found throughout the year.

YOUNG: Development to the adult through from 5 to 8 nymphal stages usually requires 2 or 3 months. The nymphs resemble the adults, except for the absence of wings, and are almost equally destructive.

IMPORTANCE: The temperate and warmer regions of the whole world are periodically afflicted by some kind of grasshopper. In our region, more particularly in the arid West, annual losses of millions of dollars are attributed to the ravages of these insects, against which some of the largest co-operative insect-control programs are directed. Grasshoppers may exhibit definite food preferences; most are grass feeders, but some eat the foliage of various weeds and shrubs. The migrating swarms are likely to destroy all green things in their paths.

The species occurring in large numbers in pasture and range lands are major items in the diets of the sparrowhawk, a bird which could more appropriately be called the "grasshopper hawk," and by other hawks, including the Swainson's, marsh, and red-shouldered hawks, and by screech and barn owls. Grasshoppers are afflicted by tiny red mites which cling to the bodies of the nymphs and adults and feed on the eggs in the soil. Several species of nematode worms and the well-known hairsnake (*Górdius*), as well as several flesh and tachina flies, are parasitic upon adults or nymphs, and certain bee flies and blister beetles feed as larvae upon the eggs. A number of different species of wasps paralyze grasshoppers by stinging them and then store them in their nests as food for the young. Skunks, snakes, and toads feed upon the adults; skunks, shrews, mice, and moles feed upon the eggs in the soil.

EXAMPLE: Two-striped Grasshopper
Melánoplus bivittàtus

One of the important destructive grasshoppers in the Great Plains of North America.

8 Pygmy Locusts   *Family Tetrígidae*

ADULTS: Mostly small insects, our largest species less than ¾ inch long, with a head narrower than the thorax and bearing large, almost globular eyes. The most remarkable feature is the greatly enlarged first thoracic segment, which

extends back over the hind wings to or beyond the tip of the
abdomen and forward, below, to shield the mouth parts like
a muffler. The fore wings are reduced to tiny plates; the
hind wings are well developed, but these insects seldom fly
and some are said to be flightless. They jump when disturbed, always alighting upon soil, never upon vegetation.
The legs are short, the hind femora being greatly enlarged
to contain powerful jumping muscles. Hearing organs are
lacking in this unmusical family. These insects are often
called "grouse locusts," and when at rest they do resemble
sitting birds in body outline. They are protectively colored
and almost invisible on sand or soil. Those species which
live near water can swim quite well. The adults pass the
winter under forest litter and in sod. The eggs, a dozen or
more glued together in a mass, are laid in the ground in
the spring.

YOUNG: Resemble the adults. There are 4 or 5 nymphal stages.
Some nymphs of each species probably hibernate, and alternation of hibernating generations is the rule in some species.

IMPORTANCE: Of slight or no economic importance since they
are seldom numerous; they feed on mosses, algae, fungi,
lichens, decayed vegetable matter, and some higher plants,
chiefly young grasses and sprouting seeds, in very moist or
very dry uncultivated areas. They are the prey of ants, certain
bugs, and a few birds and amphibians.

EXAMPLE: Pygmy Locust   *Tètrix ornàtum*

Widely distributed from the Rockies eastward; a species in
which color and pattern are quite variable.

9 Long-horned Grasshoppers   *Family Tettigonìidae*

ADULTS: The members of this family have antennae nearly as
long or longer than the body. Cave crickets and crickets
(*10, 11*) are the only other orthopterons with such long antennae, but the former differ in lacking hearing organs and
in having shorter ovipositors, and the latter in having flattened
bodies. The ovipositors (egg-laying organs) of the females are
large, long, and shaped like sickles or sabers. This family includes the katydids—narrow-bodied, usually green, the crea-

tures responsible in the eastern half of the United States for
the familiar summer-night sound of "Katy did, Katy she did,"
and the Mormon and coulee crickets—western species, not
laterally compressed, but robust, clumsy-looking insects with
wings much too short for flight. In the latter 2 species, the
hind margin of the first thoracic segment is produced backward over the rest of the thorax and the first one or several
abdominal segments, a feature accounting for the popular
name of "shield-bearer." A slit-like hearing organ is situated
on each of the fore tibiae. Most species are plant feeders, but
some are at least partly predacious upon other insects, and
cannibalism is not unusual. Katydid eggs are flat, oval, and
are placed on the surfaces or along the margins of leaves,
inserted into leaf edges carefully split by the sharp ovipositors,
arranged in rows along twigs, or placed in crevices of tree
bark. Mormon cricket eggs are laid in soil in small clusters
stuck together with a gluey substance.

YOUNG: The nymphal food habits are like those of the adults.
There are 7 nymphal stages as a rule.

IMPORTANCE: The Mormon cricket is by far the most serious
agricultural pest in the family. It is a gregarious, migrating
species, moving in enormous bands, often spread over several
square miles of rangeland, and threatening with destruction
every sort of crop encountered, a destruction which may be
total in the absence of defensive or offensive measures. The
spectacular depredations of this insect upon the fields of
isolated ranchers in the intermountain West and its heavy toll
of range forage plants have made it the object of large-scale
federal and state control programs.

EXAMPLE 9a: Fork-tailed Bush Katydid
                                    Scuddèria furcàta

Common in the eastern half of the United States. One of the
smaller katydids, easily startled to flight from the tall weeds
and grasses or bushes in which it remains during the day.

EXAMPLE 9b: Mormon Cricket   *Ánabrus símplex*

Ranging from western Minnesota and Colorado west to the
Sierra Nevada Mountains of California and the Cascade
Range of Oregon and Washington. During the critical early

days of the Mormon settlement at Salt Lake City, the crops, whose loss would have meant starvation and defeat, were threatened with complete destruction by droves of these insects. Sea gulls, probably the California gull (*Làrus califórnicus*), came to gorge on the pests and were credited, as agents of the Lord, with saving the crops. An impressive monument to the birds stands today in Temple Square in the Mormon capital. Adult Mormon crickets are preyed upon by various gulls and hawks, the sage thrasher, Brewer's blackbird, and many others. The western meadowlark, sage thrasher, and various shrews and mice are avid eaters of the eggs; their most effective destroyer is a tiny wasp, *Sparaìson pilòsum*, of the family Sceliónidae (*132*). The adults are preyed upon by several flesh flies (*172*) and by a big black wasp of the family Sphécidae (*140*). Aborigines of the intermountain area of the United States used the insects, dried and roasted, as food. An imaginative cook might find even more palatable ways of preparing them.

10 Cave Crickets and Allies *Family Gryllacrídidae*

ADULTS: This family includes the large, narrow-bodied, hump-backed, long-legged cave or camel crickets and the robust, burrowing Jerusalem crickets. They are wingless or nearly so. With their long antennae, some of them suggest long-horned grasshoppers, but they differ in lacking hearing organs on the fore tibiae and in having generally smaller, sometimes inconspicuous ovipositors. Cave crickets live in caves, sometimes far from their mouths, under stones and logs, in cellars, cisterns, and other moist places. Jerusalem crickets, found only in the western and southern parts of our region, have legs adapted for tunneling in sandy soil. All are carnivorous or mostly so. Sound-producing organs may be present.

YOUNG: Resemble the adults.

IMPORTANCE: Cave crickets are of little economic importance; some are nuisances in cellars and greenhouses. Jerusalem crickets possibly are useful as predators upon other insects but are not numerous enough to be significant controls on any species.

EXAMPLE 10a: Jerusalem Cricket   *Stenopelmàtus fúscus*

Occurs in the prairie and plains regions west of the Mississippi River.

EXAMPLE 10b: Cave Cricket   *Ceuthóphilus gracílipes*

A common species in eastern North America.

11   Crickets   *Family Grýllidae*

ADULTS: The tree crickets, representing 1 of 2 general body types in this family, are much flattened, in male insects the outline gradually widening from front to rear, resulting in a narrow wedge form. The ground-dwelling crickets, such as the common field cricket, one of our examples, are large-headed, almost parallel-sided, and more cylindrical than flattened. The antennae are always long and thread-like, often longer than the body. They are nocturnal and among the best known of insect singers, the males making music by vibrating the fore wings together. The auditory organs are on the tibiae of the fore legs. Crickets feed on plant foliage but are partially carnivorous, eating other insects and small invertebrates; they are also somewhat cannabalistic. A very few of the tiniest species, less than ¼ inch long, live in ant nests, apparently deriving nourishment by cleaning the bodies of the ants and the walls of the galleries. Tree crickets and some others insert their eggs in rows in twigs and plant stems; the field cricket lays its eggs in the soil.

YOUNG: Very like the adults.

IMPORTANCE: Field crickets, during occasional outbreaks, are extremely damaging, cutting the stems of seedling plants at ground level, stripping the grain from the heads of cereal grasses, and eating great holes in the fruits of garden and truck crops such as tomatoes, strawberries, peas, and cucumbers. Tree crickets spread a canker disease in apple twigs and raspberry canes by their egg laying. They feed on aphids, scale insects, and decaying plant tissue.

EXAMPLE 11a: Common Field Cricket
Ácheta assímilis

Throughout southern Canada and the United States.

Example 11b: Snowy Tree Cricket   *Oecánthus níveus*

Occurs from New England and Ontario to Minnesota and
Utah and southward to Georgia and Texas. Although the
male is an excellent singer, the female has no auditory organs
with which to hear him. She is attracted to him chemically,
there being a gland on the top of his third thoracic segment
whose exudate she tastes while copulating.

12 Mole Crickets   *Family Gryllotálpidae*

Adults: Resemble moles as nearly as insects can. The narrow
body is covered with fine, short hairs which give the insect
a furry appearance, and the tibiae of the fore legs are short,
wide, shovel-shaped digging organs. The fore wings are very
short, covering little of the hind wings with which mole
crickets fly very well. At night mole crickets may leave their
burrows and fly to the lights of towns. Most of their existence
is spent well underground in permanent galleries, but when
the soil is moist they make temporary burrows so close to the
surface that it is pushed up like the roofs of mole tunnels. The
eggs are laid in loose masses in cells 3 to 10 inches underground.

Young: The nymphs resemble the adults in appearance and
have similar feeding habits.

Importance: Destructive chiefly in Florida, Georgia, South
Carolina, and some other southeastern states. Seedling plants
are cut off below the soil surface or even uprooted by the
burrowing insects. Turnips, peanuts, and potatoes sometimes
are heavily damaged. Grass roots are eaten, too, and lawns
may be ruined. Strawberries and other fruits lying in contact
with soil may be eaten on warm damp nights when the insects are tunneling at the soil surface or when they may leave
their burrows altogether.

Example: Northern Mole Cricket
Gryllotálpa hexadáctyla

In the southern United States only in damp heavy soils, but
widely distributed in the northern United States and Canada.
The female places all her eggs in a single cell in the soil and

bestows some parental concern upon them and the early stages of the young.

13 Pygmy Sand Crickets   *Family Tridactýlidae*

ADULTS: Small or very small, burrowing insects, much like mole crickets but less than ⅜ inch long. The hind legs are powerfully developed for jumping and have a single tarsal segment or none at all, but attached to the extremities of the hind tibiae are sets of narrow plates which are used in jumping from water and sand surfaces. The fore legs, which are modified for digging, have 2-segmented tarsi. The fore wings are very short and the hind wings extend beyond the end of the body. Neither sound-producing nor hearing organs are present.

YOUNG: Similar to the adults.

IMPORTANCE: These insects are of no economic importance. They are said to be vegetarian, but very little is known of their food habits. Toad bugs (*34*), which frequent much the same situations, have been seen to feed upon them.

EXAMPLE: Pygmy Sand Cricket   *Tridáctylus apiciàlis*

In damp situations near water, throughout our region.

EARWIGS
Order Dermáptera

The members of this small order are recognized by the forcep-like tail appendages (modified cerci), without which they might be confused with the rove beetles (*94*), insects which they resemble in general body shape and in having short fore wings that do not nearly cover the abdomen. Earwigs originally were placed in the beetle order (Coleóptera), then in the roach and grasshopper order (Orthóptera), before being dignified with an order of their own. The derivation of the common name is obscure. Although these insects may at various times have found their way into human ears, it was not with intent to destroy the hearing or enter the brain of the sleeper as has been believed. The hind wing when spread is seen to be shaped like a human ear, but this is not necessarily the reason for the name. Three families of earwigs are represented at present in our fauna. The description of one of these, the Forficùlidae, will serve to characterize earwigs in general.

14 Earwigs   *Family Forficùlidae*

ADULTS: Elongate, flat-bodied, with biting mouth parts at the front of the head, which is shaped somewhat like a heart with the apex to the fore. The heavy, bead-like antennae may exceed half the length of the body. The leathery, veinless fore wings meet in a straight line down the center of the back and are less than half the length of the abdomen, leaving exposed the tips of the hind wings, which are folded lengthwise and crosswise. Most earwigs do not fly or fly infrequently; some are wingless. One common species of another family (*Làbia mìnor*) often flies to lights at night. Glands situated on the second and third abdominal segments exude a liquid smelling of creosote and probably are defensive in function, but the terminal forceps can give a strong nip and would seem to be the more effective weapon. It has been written that the forceps, in some species, may be used to tuck away the hind wings after alighting from a flight. The males have more strongly developed forceps than the females. Earwigs are nocturnal, hiding under bark, in cracks of buildings, and under debris during the day. They are primarily scavengers but may attack insect larvae, snails and other slow-moving animals, and young, succulent foliage, flowers, and ripe fruit. The females of several species are known to brood the little groups of smooth white eggs which they lay in cells in the soil or in almost any protected place. Soon after the eggs have hatched, the mother ceases attendance.

YOUNG: Much like the adults. There are 4 or 5 nymphal stages, and metamorphosis is incomplete.

IMPORTANCE: Earwigs are more often abundant in the coastal areas of our continent. Like roaches, they constantly enter our ports with all sorts of cargo. Our pest species are almost all introduced. Living in garbage dumps and in damp situations in human dwellings, earwigs may become a nuisance by their mere presence. They are occasional pests out of doors, where they feed on plants, chiefly mosses, lichens, algae, grasses, and, in some species, upon insects either dead or alive. A few species appear to be somewhat useful as predators on other insects.

EXAMPLE: European Earwig   *Forfícula auriculària*

Now cosmopolitan, this species has become established in our region only since about 1912. It is a pest in houses and sometimes in gardens. It is most abundant on the Pacific coast of Washington and Oregon but is established at widely separated points in the northern United States and southern Canada. Two of its parasites, species of European tachina flies (*173*), have been introduced.

STONEFLIES
Order Plecóptera

Adult stoneflies, usually found resting on streamside vegetation, may scurry away when alarmed, instead of taking wing. Since they are clever at hiding, sweeping or beating foliage at the water's edge with a net is the best way to capture them. Occasionally stoneflies are seen at lights. The eggs, several thousand from a single female, are deposited in the water.

The immature stages, the nymphs or naiads, are aquatic, living under stones, leaves, and other debris, chiefly in currents. They have been described as "the dominant invertebrates of mountain streams." The tracheal gills, if external, are either tufts or single filaments at the sides of the thorax and abdomen or about the anus. If external gills are lacking, respiration takes place in gills inside the rectum. Metamorphosis is incomplete, so much so that in several genera the gills are carried over into the adult stage. From 1 to 3 years are required for development from egg to adult. The nymphs of one species which completes its life cycle in a single year molts 22 times.

There are 9 North American families of stoneflies, comprising 30 genera and something over 200 species.

15 Stoneflies   *Family Pérlidae*

ADULTS: Yellowish, greenish, or brownish soft-bodied insects with 2 pairs of long, somewhat transparent wings which fold flat over the back. The blunt head is widest at the eyes and bears 2 or 3 ocelli. The long, many-segmented antennae, set wide apart, taper gradually to the tips. The mouth parts are of the biting type, but most stoneflies apparently do not eat or take a little plant food. At the end of the abdomen are 2 conspicuous appendages (cerci). The males in some genera have on the lower side of the ninth abdominal segment a percussion disk, which they strike rapidly against a hard surface to produce rapping sounds.

YOUNG: The cerci of the nymphs are much longer than those of the adults. Some nymphs are predacious on other small, aquatic animals, such as Mayfly nymphs, and the larvae of midges; others are plant feeders.

IMPORTANCE: Stonefly nymphs are eaten by the young of the larger dragonflies and by salamanders, frogs, and turtles. The adults have been found in the stomachs of some 40 different kinds of birds. Both adults and nymphs are major articles of food in the diets of fishes, particularly trout, bass, crappie, and other of our best fresh-water game fishes. The adults of a large species of the West, *Pteronárcys califórnica* (family Pteronárcidae), once were used as food by Indians and are still used as live bait for trout by fishermen. This insect reaches a length of 3½ inches as a nymph and 1¾ inches as a female adult. Anglers usually refer to stonefly adults as "browns" and imitate their shapes in both dry and wet flies.

EXAMPLE: Stonefly   *Neophasganóphora capitàta*

Occurs throughout North America east of the Rocky Mountains. One of the diurnal species, most active on sunny days; rarely attracted to lights. The nymphs, which are more abundant in the larger creeks and rivers, require at least 2 and perhaps 3 years to complete their development.

TERMITES
Order Isóptera

Termites, often miscalled "white ants," are the only truly social insects outside the order Hymenóptera (wasps, ants, and bees). They do bear a superficial resemblance to ants but are readily distinguished by the fact that the abdomen is joined very broadly to the thorax, there being no constriction or "waist" as there is in all ants. There are 2 pairs of almost equal membranous wings in the winged forms and a pair of short, terminal abdominal appendages (cerci). The bodies of termites are quite soft and, with the exception of the swarming sexual forms, almost without pigment.

Ordinarily there are 4 different castes in a termite colony. The winged males and females, the potential kings and queens of new colonies, appear in early summer or spring in vast numbers, often issuing at the same hour from numerous colonies in one locality. They are dark in color, have functional, pigmented compound eyes, and wings about twice the body length, which they hold flat over the back. The sexes pair off during the swarming flight and alight on the ground together, perhaps at a great distance from their original colonies. It is probably good genetics for each member of the royal pair to come from a different colony, and this is made possible by the synchronized swarming flights. Shortly after descending to earth the wings of king and queen are shed at a suture, or line of breakage, just above the wing attachment. The pair then is ready to start a new colony. The queen turns to serious egg production, eventually becoming an enormous egg-laying machine tended by her progeny.

The most numerous offspring of the queen belong to the worker caste, pale, soft, eyeless creatures of the dark. Those that tend the queen are privileged to lick a delectable exudate from the pores of her body; others build and extend the colony. To a third caste belong the soldiers, blind also, but with very large heads and long, powerful mandibles, the defenders of the colony if it should be broken into. In some species, soldier forms of the kind described are replaced with "nasuti," soldiers with heads drawn out into what look like long noses, from which a liquid can be secreted for defensive purposes or as a cement for the tunnel walls of earth, excrement, and partly digested wood. If one or both of the primary royal pair should die, the gap is filled from the ranks of a fourth caste of secondary reproductive individuals—insects, which never leave the colony, are pale in color, have compound eyes with some pigment, and wing buds that never develop into wings. A substitute queen is not capable of laying as many eggs as the primary queen, so several of them may take over the job. Sometimes there is even a third reproductive caste whose members lack even wing buds.

Except for the brief swarming season of the primary sexual forms, termites are always confined to their tunnels. In the case of our common destructive species, the queen and the nest itself may be in the ground, but galleries connect it with the source of food—a dead tree, fence post, or the timbers of a house. To reach the sills and flooring of a house, termites may build a covered runway of earth, wood, excrement, and saliva up the surface of stone, brick, or cement foundations for a distance of 2 or 3 feet, or may erect slender turrets of the same materials.

In order to use cellulose as food, termites must tolerate in their alimentary tracts a population of protozoa, one-celled organisms which can digest that relatively inert and indigestible material which makes up the cell walls of wood. These "guests," which multiply rapidly, are themselves digested by their hosts. The habit of exchanging food from mouth to mouth and of eating freshly voided feces insures the transfer of protozoa from one termite to another. Certain fungi found in the tunnels seem to be associated with termites, perhaps as food, perhaps in making wood more digestible before it is eaten.

Termites have achieved their greatest development in the tropics, where some species build mounds 10 or more feet high, sometimes containing fungus gardens, or great oval masses of cemented wood pulp on the trunks or branches of trees. Some termite colonies are contained entirely in wood. The queens, seldom seen, may live for 10 years or so and produce millions of eggs during a lifetime. Fried or roasted termite queens are a delicacy to certain African natives. Termites, of course, are well protected from parasites and predators by their tunnel-dwelling habit; but during the swarming flights, adults are eaten by nighthawks, English sparrows, domestic fowl, toads, lizards, spiders, and predacious insects.

16 Termites   *Family Rhinotermítidae*

This is 1 of 3 families of termites represented in our region.

ADULTS: As described for the order. The nests of most species are in the ground. In the Kalotermítidae, on the other hand, the colony is entirely in dry or moist wood, either above or below the ground surface. Attacks on living wood are not common. There are about 10 species in the important genus *Reticulitérmes* in our region, the most destructive of which is our example.

YOUNG: Metamorphosis is incomplete; there are 6 nymphal stages, requiring 2 years for completion. Worker nymphs from the second stage on contribute to the building and maintenance of the colony. Even in their last stage of development workers remain juveniles in so many respects that it seems inappropriate to consider them adults. As one student has put it, the termite society depends upon "child" labor, while the ant society depends upon adult labor. This is an interesting contrast. In the social Hymenóptera the young of worker bees and wasps, as well as ants, are helpless larvae that cannot even feed themselves, to say nothing of contributing to the upkeep of their homes.

IMPORTANCE: The annual bill for repair to termite-damaged structures is tremendous. It is estimated that 40 million dollars of injury is sustained each year in the United States, almost 80 per cent of it in the South. At great expense, cross-ties, telephone poles, and fence posts now are usually treated with some termite-repelling solution before being placed in the ground.

EXAMPLE: Common Termite   *Reticulitérmes flávipes*

Occurs from Brownsville, Texas, eastward into Florida and northward to Lake Superior and southern Maine.

EMBIIDS
Order Embióptera

A small order of largely tropical and subtropical gregarious insects represented in our region by 3 families. Collectors in California and the extreme southern portion of the United States are the only ones likely to come upon embiids. These insects are remarkable for the very long and narrow thorax which often approaches the length of the abdomen. The males of most species have wings—2 pairs, which are held flat over the body; the females are wingless. The short cerci are 2-segmented. In the adult males the tip of the abdomen is not symmetrical but is skewed slightly to the left. A habit of lining the covered runways through turf, under bark and rocks, and in surface litter with silk spun from specialized hairs situated on the enlarged first tarsal segment of the fore legs is characteristic of the order and is the reason for the popular name of "webspinners." The mouth parts are of the biting type; the food is believed to be only dead vegetable matter. Some species are known to be parthenogenetic (reproduce without mating).

17 Embiids   *Family Oligotómidae*

ADULTS: Typical of the order. This family has no species native to North America, although 2 other families do. The life histories of embiids are largely a mystery, but the adults are said to care for the eggs, which are deposited in small groups in the silken tunnels under a canopy of silk. They are said to be able to run backward about as rapidly as they can run forward.

YOUNG: Development is gradual (incomplete metamorphosis). Even the first-stage nymphs can spin silk, and there is little but size to assist in distinguishing the nymphs from the wingless adult females.

IMPORTANCE: Embiids are of no economic importance, at least not in our region.

EXAMPLE: Embiid   *Oligótoma saundérsii*

Occurs in most of the tropical and subtropical areas of the world. Introduced in Florida and Texas.

PSOCIDS, BOOKLICE, AND ALLIES
Order Corrodéntia

Minute or very small insects with large heads and 2 pairs of wings, the hind pair the smaller, held roof-like over the body; or wingless. The biting mouth parts are at the front of the head but are scarcely visible from above. The antennae are thread-like and of various lengths. The first thoracic segment is very small, sometimes neck-like, and the other 2 frequently are fused. Metamorphosis is incomplete.

18 Psocids   *Family Psócidae*

ADULTS: In our species there are 4 membranous wings with a few longitudinal veins, almost no cross veins, and scattered hairs or even scales. The tarsi are 2-segmented. Psocids are more or less social, living in family groups of various sizes. All stages of the insect are often sheltered under a net of silk spun from the mouth glands of the adults. They are found most frequently on plants, especially on the bark of trees and shrubs, but also on a number of greenhouse plants, and in ground litter. They feed on lichens, algae, fungi, and dead plant and animal matter, the cadavers of insects figuring in the diets of some species.

YOUNG: Like the adults, but wingless.

IMPORTANCE: Very small. Chimney swifts are known to take the adults in flight.

EXAMPLE: Psocid   *Psòcus confratérnus*

Widely distributed in our region.

19 Booklice and Allies   *Family Trogìidae*

ADULTS: Typically wingless and minute with relatively large
heads and wide femora. The eyes are small and ocelli are
wanting. The antennae are about as long as the body. There
are 3 tarsal segments.

YOUNG: Very like the adults, but with only 2 tarsal segments.

IMPORTANCE: Booklice damage books by feeding on glue, paste,
and paper; they destroy dried plant, insect, and other specimens in museums, and are often abundant in packaged cereal
foods. They and their allies are thought to feed on molds to
some extent.

EXAMPLE: Common Booklouse   *Lipóscelis divinatòrius*

This is the minute, yellowish speck which everyone with
reasonably good eyesight has seen wandering about rather
hesitantly on the pages of old books. Cosmopolitan. Parthenogenesis has been observed in this species. In heated
buildings these insects breed continuously. They produce faint
tapping noises by beating their bodies against the surface on
which they rest.

ZORAPTERONS
Order Zoráptera

A very small order of minute, predacious, and possibly scavenging insects, closely related to the psocids and book-lice. They are mostly tropical or subtropical. There is a single family, Zorotýpidae, containing 1 genus of 19 species, only 2 of which occur in our region. The mouth parts are of the biting type; the antennae are bead-like and 9-segmented. Winged and wingless adults of both sexes occur in a single species.

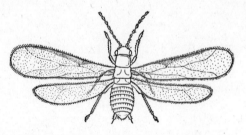

Wingless individuals have no ocelli and no eyes (or mere vestiges of eyes). The winged insects shed their wings, suggestive of termites. There is a pair of cerci—quite short in our species. Metamorphosis is incomplete. The only North American species that we know much about, *Zorótypus hubbárdi,* ranges through much of the southern United States, is gregarious, and lives in decaying wood and under bark. The figure above (modified from Caudell, 1920) is of a winged female of this species.

BITING LICE
Order Mallóphaga

Small to minute insects, flat, broad-headed, wingless external parasites of warm-blooded animals. Birds, rodents, and domesticated animals are the principal classes of hosts in our region. The biting mouth parts are on the underside of the head. The antennae are 3- to 5-segmented and quite short. Ocelli are wanting and the compound eyes are not well developed. The tarsi are 1- or 2-segmented. These insects feed upon hair and feathers and the outer layers of skin of the host. They do not consume flesh but are often numerous enough to become very irritating and even cause death. The eggs are laid singly, glued to the hairs or feathers of the host. Metamorphosis is incomplete.

20 Bird Lice   *Family Philoptéridae*

ADULTS: Typical of the order. This is the largest family of biting lice; all its members are parasites upon birds. The insects are quite host-specific, one species living on only one or a very few closely related bird species.

YOUNG: Very like the adults; the food habits are the same.

IMPORTANCE: Infested domestic fowl lose weight and lay fewer eggs as a result of the irritation caused by biting lice.

EXAMPLE: Slender Pigeon Louse *Columbicola colúmbae*

Very common on adult and young pigeons throughout our region.

SUCKING LICE
Order Anoplùra

A small order of wingless, minute, or very small, flat-bodied insects, all external parasites on mammals, including bats, moles, lions, sea lions, and man. The stylets and sucking tube, which are thrust into the skin of the host while the insects are feeding, can be retracted within the head. The legs are short with a single tarsal segment ending in a large claw used for clinging to the hairs of the host. There are no ocelli, and the compound eyes, when present, are small. The most important species, the human louse (known also as the head or body louse, according to the situation in which it is found), is the only species of the family Pediculidae found in this country, and people exercising a reasonable amount of body care usually are unacquainted with it. The infestation by this louse is called pediculosis. It is important chiefly as a transmitter of typhus fever, trench fever, and European relapsing fever.

21 Sucking Lice   *Family Haematopínidae*

ADULTS: Like the adults and young of the other North American families of sucking lice, these bear a superficial resemblance to a crab when seen through a magnifying lens, owing to the strongly flattened body and the powerfully clawed, crab-like legs. This family is our most important one, containing parasites of the horse, hog, sheep, goat, dog, and of cattle and numerous wild rodents. All species are bloodsucking. The eggs, or nits, are glued to the hairs of the host.

YOUNG: Resembling the adults in appearance. There are usually 3 nymphal stages; metamorphosis is incomplete. The entire life cycles of these insects are completed upon the host animals.

IMPORTANCE: A source of much annoyance to the hosts and sometimes numerous enough to cause serious illness and death.

EXAMPLE: Hog Louse   *Haematopinus adventicius*

Everywhere in our region on swine. Cosmopolitan. This is the largest of our sucking lice, approaching ¼ inch in length. Eggs are laid throughout the year, there being from 6 to 12 generations annually.

THRIPS
Order Thysanóptera

An order of minute but important insects which usually can be recognized by the 2 pairs of very slender, almost linear wings, edged with fringes of long hairs. The mouth parts are developed for piercing and sucking or for rasping. The antennae, of medium length, are 6- to 9-segmented and bear setae; the compound eyes are fairly large. The winged species have 3 simple eyes (ocelli); wingless forms have none. The legs are unique in being cup-shaped at the extremities; from these depressions bladder-like adhesive organs can be extruded. There are no claws. An old name for the order—"Physópoda"—meant, literally, "bladder-feet." The word *Thríps* was Linnaeus's generic name for the only 4 species that he knew. (The singular and plural forms of the word are the same.) He grouped them with the bugs, from which we have long since separated them. The wings, which are folded flat over the body when at rest, have few or no veins. The abdomen of the female ends in an ovipositor or in a tubular last segment. The eggs are inserted in plant tissues by those species with ovipositors. The others lay them on plant surfaces, in cracks and crevices in bark, etc. Some thrips are parthenogenetic. There are 2 to 4 larval stages and 1 to 7 generations a year. Metamorphosis is incomplete, but the last 1 or 2 larval stages are non-feeding inactive ones corresponding somewhat to the pupal periods of insects having complete metamorphosis.

Some thrips are predacious on mites and small insects, including other thrips; others feed on the foliage and flowers of plants to which they may transmit virus diseases. Still others feed on sap, fungi, and decaying vegetation. The important known enemies of thrips include the insidious flower bug (*31*), the larvae of lacewings (*54, 55*) and lady beetles (*106*), and young toads.

22 Thrips *Family Thrípidae*

ADULTS: Have the characters described for the order.
YOUNG: Similar to the adults, but wingless.
IMPORTANCE: This family contains the tobacco or onion thrips (*Thríps tabàci*), the greenhouse thrips (*Helìothrips haemor-rhoidàlis*), the gladiolus thrips (*Taenìothrips símplex*), and many other important plant-feeding species.

EXAMPLE: Wheat Thrips *Frankliniélla trítici*

Generally distributed in North America, feeding on a great variety of grasses, wild and cereal, and upon many truck crops, trees, and shrubs. In Florida it is a serious pest of citrus, feeding on buds, flowers, and young fruits and causing the dropping of flowers and fruits or the dwarfing of the latter. First described as a wheat pest, this species is often called the flower thrips because it occurs in the flowers of most wild and cultivated plants. The smooth, brownish rings and blotches seen so often on oranges and grapefruits are caused mostly by the feeding scars of this and other thrips upon the small developing fruits.

BUGS, APHIDS, SCALES, AND ALLIES
Order Hemíptera

A vast group of insects, differing greatly in appearance, but with one feature in common—piercing-sucking mouth parts, consisting of a jointed beak or rostrum (labium) enclosing the bristle-like mandibles and maxillae, the stylets which do the actual penetrating of plant or animal tissues. The inner pair of stylets, the maxillae, are grooved and so fitted that they form both a sucking tube and a salivary injection tube. Most hemipterons have wings, and the winged ones, with the exception of male scale insects, have 2 pairs. Development is gradual except among the whiteflies and in some psyllids, where it is complex. There are 2 major suborders of the Hemíptera, one including the true bugs, the other such bug allies as leafhoppers, aphids, scales, and others. These 2 groups differ so greatly that it seems better to treat them separately.

BUGS
Suborder Heteróptera

The bugs are rather handsome insects, with long, slim legs upon which they move slowly and somewhat majestically. Their bodies usually are smooth, but occasionally are hairy or spiny. The jointed beak, rising from the front of the head, is held below the body, between the legs, when not in use. The 4- to

5-segmented antennae are usually half to two thirds the length of the body. Typically, the head extends forward of the eyes and, together with the first thoracic segment, forms a rough triangle and gives bugs a "broad-shouldered" appearance. The second thoracic segment, above, forms a prominent, equilateral triangle (scutellum) separating the wing bases. The fore wing is distinctive for the suborder in that the basal half or two thirds is thickened and leathery while the remainder is membranous. Most bugs feed upon plant juices, some prey on other insects and spiders, and a few parasitize mammals—either living, as the bed bug, in the habitation of the host, or attaching themselves permanently to the body of the host, as do the bat bugs of the family Polycténidae.

23 Stink Bugs and Allies — Family Pentatómidae

ADULTS: Probably the best known of all bugs. They are mostly small or medium in size and shield-shaped in body outline. The term "shield bug," however, is usually reserved for those pentatomids in which the scutellum is so greatly enlarged that it covers most of the abdomen. The antennae are usually 5-segmented. The eyes are relatively small and there are only 2 ocelli. Glands at the sides of the thorax emit the strong, memorable odors that give the group its popular name. The legs are smooth, spiny, or covered with short hairs. The eggs, usually shaped like squat barrels, are often beautifully ornamented; they are equipped with hinged covers and are laid in small clusters, side by side and upright, glued to each other and to a leaf surface.

YOUNG: Similar to the adults in form and habit, usually passing through 5 nymphal stages.

IMPORTANCE: With a few notable exceptions our pentatomids are plant feeders, some being important pests of cultivated plants. A few are predacious on the young of moths and butterflies and leaf beetles. Birds, apparently disregarding their scent, feed freely upon them. Stink bugs of several species are used as human food in Mexico, India, and Africa.

EXAMPLE 23a: Ground Bug — *Pangaèus bilineàtus*

Widely distributed in eastern North America. Together with

its close relatives, this insect is burrowing in habit. The fore and middle legs of some ground bugs are more obviously adapted for digging. A small, related group of shiny, black bugs, frequently mistaken for beetles, are the "negro bugs"; they are sometimes placed in a separate family, as are the ground bugs.

EXAMPLE 23b: Shield Bug   *Eurygáster alternàtus*

Found throughout our region except in the extreme north and south. Note that the scutellum, the dorsal portion of the second thoracic segment, almost completely covers the abdomen.

EXAMPLE 23c: Southern Green Stink Bug
Nézara virídula

An important pest of tomatoes, okra, and other vegetables in the southeastern United States from Virginia to Florida and Louisiana.

EXAMPLE 23d: Harlequin Bug   *Murgántia histriónica*

One of many economically important insects that have spread northward from Mexico and Central America; it now ranges from Texas, where it was discovered in 1864, to South Dakota and eastward to Massachusetts and Florida. It is a pest, chiefly in the southern half of its range, on cabbage, radish, and most other cultivated plants of the mustard family. English sparrows have been known to control harlequin bug populations locally.

24 Squash Bugs and Allies   *Family Corèidae*

ADULTS: Our better-known species are small or medium-sized insects, elongate, with rather large compound eyes and 4-segmented antennae. The membranous portion of the fore wing is traversed by numerous parallel, longitudinal veins; this distinguishes them from the members of the chinch bug family (25), which have few longitudinal veins on the membrane and those somewhat twisting and not parallel. In some species, for example the "leaf-footed bugs" of the genus *Leptoglóssus,* the legs are variously enlarged and beset with spines. The odor of the squash bug is strong and rather offensive at close

range. The winter is passed as an adult by many species.
There is usually a single generation annually. The eggs are
laid upon the host plants.

YOUNG: There are usually 5 nymphal stages. The earliest
nymphs have much heavier antennae, relatively, than the
adults.

IMPORTANCE: The common squash bug, our example and the
best-known representative of this family, feeds on the various
cultivated cucurbits—squash, pumpkin, and related plants—
causing leaves and stems to wilt and die. The beautiful red-
and-black boxelder bug, which feeds on ash and maple too,
damages the seeds, flowers, and the tender twigs and foliage
of its host plants and also may be a nuisance in the Middle
and Far West by its habit of entering houses in the fall to
seek warm winter quarters. All coreids are plant feeders.

EXAMPLE: Squash Bug *Anasa tristis*

Everywhere in the United States and southern Canada on
plants of the squash family. Because of its odor, this insect
is widely thought to be immune to attack by birds, but this
is not the case. It has been found in the stomachs of 6 different kinds of birds, and that is probably not the total
number of its avian predators. Its most effective natural enemy
is a tachina fly, *Trichópoda pénnipes,* which lays its eggs on
the nymph or adult.

25 Chinch Bugs and Allies *Family Lygaèidae*

ADULTS: Averaging smaller than the members of the preceding
family. The compound eyes are large, and the 4-segmented antennae arise low on the sides of the head. The legs are comparatively short. Only 4 or 5 unbranched, meandering, longitudinal veins appear on the membrane of the fore wing. Both
short-winged and long-winged forms may occur in the same
species. The adults of most species hibernate.

YOUNG: There are usually 5 nymphal stages.

IMPORTANCE: The chinch bug is one of the most serious pests of
corn and small grains, its sucking of the juices causing wilting and death. Although the lygaeids of economic importance
are plant feeders, many are predators upon other insects.

EXAMPLE: Chinch Bug   *Blíssus leucópterus*

Found everywhere in the United States except the Northwest; and in southern Canada from Ontario eastward.

26 Lace Bugs   *Family Tíngidae*

ADULTS: Very small or minute, usually less than ⅛ inch long. The fore wings, at rest, extend stiffly beyond the body at sides and rear and do look like lace, being coarsely reticulate with hundreds of sunken, membranous areas. Lateral and dorsal extensions of the thorax, when present, are likewise reticulate. The edges of the lacy covering often have a fringe of tiny spines. Lace bugs live on the undersides of the leaves of many different broad-leaved trees and shrubs. The eggs, encased in little cones of a brownish, hardened gummy substance, often are glued to the midribs of leaves. The winter usually is passed in the adult stage among fallen leaves.

YOUNG: The very spiny nymphs cover the lower leaf surfaces with a sticky excrement to which their cast skins adhere. There are 5 nymphal stages.

IMPORTANCE: Lace bugs are exclusively plant feeders, causing the foliage of their hosts to brown and die.

EXAMPLE: Sycamore Lace Bug   *Corythùcha ciliàta*

One of the more important species, economically, responsible for the unseasonal browning of sycamore trees all over the United States and southern Canada.

27 Ambush Bugs   *Family Phymátidae*

ADULTS: A small family (25 known species in our region) of oddly shaped insects, usually ⅜ inch or less in length. They are slow-moving predators on other insects, their fore legs modified as powerful grasping organs. As their popular name suggests, these insects, whose spiny armor, color patterns, and body outlines do camouflage them, lie in wait on flowers and foliage for their prey, which they seize, pierce with their beaks, and drain of body juices.

YOUNG: Much like the adults in form and habit.

IMPORTANCE: Ambush bugs exercise little if any choice as to food. It is thus unavoidable that those which frequent flowers kill a certain number of honey bees and other useful insects. However, their importance as predators is rather small, for they are not especially numerous.

EXAMPLE: Ambush Bug   *Phẏmata pennsylvánica*

One or more of the 3 subspecies of this insect occurs in almost every part of the United States with the exception of California.

28 Assassin Bugs   *Family Reduvìidae*

ADULTS: Predators with large eyes midway or far back on the sides of the long, narrow heads. The ocelli, when present, are 2 in number and are placed behind the eyes. The 4-segmented antennae are slender. The tip of the short, apparently 3-segmented beak is received in a furrow between the bases of the fore legs. Rubbing the beak against the many fine striations in this furrow produces a sound. The fore legs may be used for seizing prey but are not conspicuously modified for that function. The tarsi are 1- to 3-segmented. The first thoracic segment is large. Wings are usually present and lie in a concavity on top of the abdomen, but sometimes they are very short and in some species they are absent altogether.

YOUNG: The nymphs, which have the predatory instincts of the adults, are often camouflaged with debris which clings to their hairy, sticky bodies.

IMPORTANCE: Adults and nymphs feed on both beneficial and injurious insects. The species frequenting flowers kill many honey bees. One of the common "kissing bugs" (*Redùvius personàtus*) enters houses and will feed on bed bugs. Several South American species transmit Chagas' disease to humans, and at least 2 species occurring in the southwestern United States are known to infect wood rats with the causal agent of this disease (*Trypanosòma crùzi*). The bites of reduviids are usually painless, but some are painful or with subsequent local reactions and in any case should be avoided.

EXAMPLE: Giant Wheel Bug   *Arìlus cristàtus*

Found in the southern United States from New Mexico and

Oklahoma to Pennsylvania and Florida. A valuable predator of leaf-eating caterpillars and the adults of the Japanese beetle.

29 Damsel Bugs   *Family Nàbidae*

ADULTS: Wholly predacious insects with fore legs modified for grasping the prey, which consists of small insects. The beak is long and usually 4-segmented. Both head and first thoracic segment are narrow and long. The eyes are large and ocelli are present. The middle and hind legs are slender with 3-segmented tarsi. The long antennae are 4- or 5-segmented.
YOUNG: Similar to the adults, but wingless.
IMPORTANCE: Nabids are almost entirely beneficial in habit, preying upon small insects such as plant bugs, aphids and other homopterons, and caterpillars injurious to cultivated plants and pasture vegetation.

EXAMPLE: Damsel Bug   *Nàbis férus*

Found throughout the United States and eastern Canada. It is also native to Mexico and the temperate Old World.

30 Bed Bugs and Allies   *Family Cimícidae*

A small family of vampire insects whose love for the close society of humans during the hours of darkness is not requited. The common bed bug is by far the best-known and most abundant species, and the descriptive material which follows applies to it. The rare, blind, wingless bat parasites of the family Polycténidae are close relatives of the bed bugs.
ADULTS: Flat, wingless, hairy, with 4-segmented antennae of which the last 2 segments are much more slender than the others. The head, with conspicuous protruding eyes, is sunken in a wide notch in the rim of the first thoracic segment; there are no ocelli. During the day bed bugs hide under mattresses, behind loosened wallpaper, baseboards, and in other dark crevices. They may exist without feeding for a year or so under otherwise favorable conditions. Besides man, bed bugs feed upon various rodents, cattle and horses, and poultry. The elongate, white eggs, $\frac{1}{32}$ inch long, with a little raised cap at one end, are glued a few at a time to the surfaces of the

hiding places. "Bed bug odor" is due to the oily secretion from a pair of glands which open on the underside of the third thoracic segment.

YOUNG: Quite similar to the adults and likewise bloodsucking. Development from egg to adult requires 4 to 6 weeks; there are 5 nymphal stages.

IMPORTANCE: The common bed bug is not a proven disease carrier; its bite, however, is in many instances followed by intense itching, swelling, and reddening of the skin. A southwestern species of another genus attacks poultry and is occasionally a nuisance in houses. Species of still other genera feed on swallows, martins, and chimney swifts; they live in the nests over winter, awaiting the spring return of the migrants. Bats are attacked by several cimicids.

EXAMPLE: Common Bed Bug   *Cìmex lectulàrius*

In houses and buildings throughout our region and the world.

31 Flower Bugs   *Family Anthocóridae*

ADULTS: These tiny bugs (less than ⅛ inch long) are predators upon smaller insects and mites in flowers, on other parts of plants, or on the ground. They are squarish bugs with a "cuneus," a marginal, triangular segment of the fore wing between the membranous and thickened portions, which is found also in the plant bugs (*32*). The large eyes are far back on the head; the beak is 3-segmented.

YOUNG: Similar to the adults in general appearance and habits.

IMPORTANCE: Because they are so numerous, they are fairly important checks upon thrips, many kinds of scale insects, aphids, and other small homopterons, most of which are injurious plant feeders.

EXAMPLE: Insidious Flower Bug   *Òrius insidiòsus*

Found in the United States from Texas and Colorado eastward and in Quebec and Ontario.

32 Plant Bugs   *Family Mìridae*

ADULTS: This is the largest family of bugs. Mostly very small insects with no ocelli, but fairly large eyes. Both the antennae and beak are 4-segmented. The membranous portion of the fore wing has 2 large, basal cells and a single longitudinal vein. The marginal, triangular area of the fore wing, the cuneus, found in the preceding family, is a conspicuous feature of the plant bugs. In the same species, individuals may be long- or short-winged. The males usually are long-winged in species with short-winged females. The narrow, slightly curved eggs are inserted into the tissues of the food plants. The winter usually is passed in the adult stage.

YOUNG: The nymphs pass through 5 developmental stages and are much like the adults in appearance and habits.

IMPORTANCE: The best-known species are plant feeders, causing serious injury to many cultivated and uncultivated plants, but some are predacious. Certain of the plant feeders are especially destructive, for while feeding they apparently inject a toxic substance which deforms or kills the host tissues. The vegetative growth and seed production of alfalfa, many grasses, and other forage plants is adversely affected by plant bug populations. The food habits of the predators are little known; some feed on aphids. An Australian species, which has been introduced into Hawaii as a biological control agent, feeds only upon the eggs of a destructive sugarcane leafhopper.

EXAMPLE 32a: Tarnished Plant Bug   *Lỳgus oblineàtus*

A very common, destructive bug throughout all but the western coastal area of the United States and in much of Canada. It feeds on the leaves of a wide variety of garden and field crops and on buds and young fruits of apple, peach, pear, and berry plants, causing deformity, discoloration, fruit drop, and even death. It spreads several virus diseases—spindle tuber of potato, potato mosaic, and spinach blight.

EXAMPLE 32b: Garden Fleahopper   *Hálticus bracteàtus*

Occurs from New York to Utah and southward. It feeds on many different truck crops and ornamentals, spotting and killing the leaves. Both the short- and long-winged females of this species have been illustrated; the male is long-winged and narrower in body outline.

33 Water Striders *Family Gérridae*

ADULTS: Elongate and flattened with short, grasping fore legs and very long, slender middle and hind legs which they hold out from the body like long oars on a small boat. They spend their active life on the surface of water. Above they are dull, dark brown; below, silvery white with minute, velvety, water-repellent hairs. The short antennae are 4-segmented. The eyes are conspicuously large; ocelli are present. About half the length of the body is occupied by the thorax, the first segment of which is much the longest. Wings may or may not be present, and if present may be very short. These insects do not fly when disturbed but skate away with a speed that makes them difficult to capture. Winged individuals fly at night. Our forms inhabit fresh and brackish water, chiefly the former, but the family contains a few marine species which may be found far from land in tropical waters. The eggs are placed in the tissues of aquatic plants or attached to plant stems in sticky masses. The winter and periods of drought, during which ponds and streams may dry up, are passed by the adults ashore under rocks, logs, and debris.

YOUNG: Very like the adults. They live on the water from time of hatching.

IMPORTANCE: Water striders feed upon insects and other very small creatures which fall into the water or which for one reason or another are upon aquatic vegetation. Dead as well as living food is acceptable.

EXAMPLE: Water Strider *Gérris marginàtus*
Abundant in the northern United States and in Canada from Manitoba eastward.

34 Toad Bugs *Family Gelastocóridae*

ADULTS: Very small hopping insects, mostly about ¼ inch long, frequenters of the shores of lake and stream at water's edge. Their robust, warty, gray- and greenish-mottled bodies with great protruding eyes strongly suggest tiny toads. They are protectively colored and easily might be overlooked if they did not jump. There are no ocelli and the antennae are hidden below the head. The beak is quite short. The fore legs are short and heavy, fitted for grasping the prey, which is thought to consist of other insects. Rather unexplainably, the habits of these interesting little bugs have received very little study.

YOUNG: Similar to the adults.

IMPORTANCE: Probably of very little, if any.

   EXAMPLE: Toad Bug   *Gelastócoris oculàtus*

Found in the United States from Arizona and Colorado to Florida and New York.

35 Waterscorpions   *Family Nèpidae*

ADULTS: Wholly aquatic, either much elongated and almost stick-like or long-oval, with short, stout fore legs for seizing prey and very long, slender middle and hind legs. The bodies vary from a little less than an inch to about 2 inches in length. The fore legs suggest the large claws of a scorpion, and the long breathing tube at the end of the body vaguely resembles a scorpion's tail. The first thoracic segment is long and, in some species, neck-like. The tarsi are 1-segmented. Most of the time they are bottom crawlers; they can swim but not with ease and occasionally they must come to the surface of the water to breathe. They have well-developed wings but seldom fly, and then only at night. They insert their eggs into the stems of aquatic plants or crevices in submerged logs. These eggs are peculiar in bearing from 2 to 7 thread-like extensions which lie in the water and probably have a respiratory function.

YOUNG: Very like the adults.

IMPORTANCE: Waterscorpions are predacious upon the eggs and other stages of aquatic insects and other small invertebrates and upon small fishes and fish eggs.

   EXAMPLE: Waterscorpion   *Ránatra fúsca*

Found in fresh water from Quebec and Ontario to Florida, Texas, and California.

36 Giant Water Bugs   *Family Belostomátidae*

This family, small in number of species, contains the largest members of the entire suborder of bugs—*Lethócerus grándis* of the American tropics attains a length of 4 inches or more, and our example sometimes attains 2 inches.

ADULTS: Large, brown, flat-bodied, with powerful grasping fore legs and hind legs formed for vigorous swimming. They live in fresh-water ponds and lakes and the estuaries and quiet waters of streams and rivers, preying upon a great variety of insects, snails, frogs, and other amphibians and even small fishes. At night they frequently fly to the strong lights of towns, sometimes in numbers sufficient to create a nuisance. The bites of these bugs are quite severe, being rendered more painful by the injection of a powerful digestive fluid. The eggs are laid on submerged objects or, in some species, upon the backs of the males.

YOUNG: The nymphs resemble the adults in appearance and habit.

IMPORTANCE: These fine predators feed upon young fishes, tadpoles, snails; in fact, any water-dwelling animal that they can subdue. They may be seriously abundant in fishponds. They are themselves eaten by ducks and herons. In China a giant water bug is cooked and eaten as a delicacy.

EXAMPLE: Electric Light Bug   *Lethócerus americànus*

Occurs throughout the United States and southern Canada.

37 Backswimmers   *Family Notonéctidae*

ADULTS: The commoner species, which are about ½ inch long, have enormous compound eyes and no ocelli. Each pair of legs is adapted for a different function: the fore legs for seizing aquatic arthropods, small fishes, and tadpoles, upon which these insects feed; the middle pair for holding onto things; and the hind pair for oars, which they resemble, being long, flattened, and usually fringed with stiff hairs to increase the surface used in swimming. The habit of swimming on the back is common to all species. The bite from the beak of one of these bugs is quite painful, as many a swimmer knows, and care must be exercised in handling living specimens with the fingers. The adults carry underwater a small supply of air, which adheres to the hairs in 2 large grooves on the lower side of the abdomen. They are night flyers, jumping out of the water, landing belly down, and then taking off on powerful wings. The eggs are placed in plant tissues or glued to plants.

YOUNG: Resembling the adults except for the absence of wings. Nymphs (and adults) hibernate at the bottom of ponds or may remain active all winter.

IMPORTANCE: These insects destroy small fishes and compete with them for food. However, they are in turn eaten by larger fishes and are abundant enough to be an important source of fish food.

EXAMPLE: Backswimmer   *Notonécta undulàta*

One or another of the 6 varieties of this species can be found everywhere in the United States and southern Canada.

38 Water Boatmen   *Family Coríxidae*

ADULTS: Aquatic, swimming rather jerkily below the water surface; present everywhere in fresh and brackish waters. They are somewhat like the members of the preceding family in general body outline but are flatter, with smaller, triangular eyes and the front of the head wider. Air is carried on the body surface and under the wings. The food consists of algae and other minute vegetable and animal organisms. They are night flyers, like the backswimmers, and may collect in large numbers at lights. The males of some species are said to make sounds by rubbing a series of pegs on the fore femora against the sides of the head. The eggs are attached to plants and other submerged objects, including crayfishes, by short stalks. There is only one generation a year in our region, and the winter is passed as an adult.

YOUNG: Similar in habits and appearance to the adults. The first 3 of the 5 nymphal stages do not come to the water's surface to get air, but take it directly through the skin from the water.

IMPORTANCE: An important article in the diets of many fresh-water fishes. In certain Mexican lakes, the eggs of both water boatmen and backswimmers are so numerous that they are collected from water plants, dried, and turned into a flour for human consumption. All stages of both these insects are collected, dried, and ground for commercial fish foods.

EXAMPLE: Water Boatman   *Arctocoríxa interrúpta*

Everywhere in the United States except the Southeast and Gulf states.

LEAFHOPPERS, APHIDS, SCALES, AND ALLIES
Suborder Homóptera

A very large and economically important aggregation of insects, exhibiting amazing strangeness of form and behavior, and sometimes, as in the leafhopper family, great beauty of color and pattern. While homopterons differ exceedingly among themselves, they are easily distinguished from the bugs of the suborder Heteróptera, the only other group of insects with similar mouth parts, by the fact that the jointed beak arises at the base rather than at the front of the head. The wings, moreover, are seldom divided into leathery and membranous portions. With the exception of the males of the scale insects and the sexual forms of some aphids, which do not feed at all, the insects in this suborder live upon the juices they suck from plants. The penetrating mouth stylets of scale insects and some other homopterons are so very long—sometimes exceeding the body length—that when withdrawn from the tissues of a plant they are looped in a sac inside the insect.

39 Planthoppers *Family Fulgóridae*

This very large family, in the sense considered here, is increasingly treated as a group of smaller families.

ADULTS: Typically there are 2 ocelli in depressions below and near the eyes. The antennae are of 2 basal segments tipped with a filament; they arise below and behind the eyes. These insects sometimes are confused with leafhoppers, treehoppers, and froghoppers, but may be distinguished readily by the position of the antennae and the fact that the hind tibiae have only a few small spurs. They are excellent jumpers. The heads of comparatively few of our species are prolonged forward as great, horn-like processes, but the "lanternfly" of Brazil, with a head shaped like a peanut shell, is a member of this family. In the tropics, fulgorids run to great extremes in form and color.

YOUNG: The nymphs are somewhat like the adults in appearance and habit but do not move about very much and may be almost hidden beneath a heavy, white coating of powdery wax.

IMPORTANCE: Our species are not known to be particularly important economically.

EXAMPLE 39a: Common Scolops   *Scòlops súlcipes*

Found abundantly throughout the United States and southern Canada among grasses and other low-growing vegetation.

EXAMPLE 39b: Planthopper   *Órmenis septentrionàlis*

Common throughout most of the United States east of the Great Plains, especially on shrubs and woody vines.

40 Cicadas   *Family Cicàdidae*

There are about 75 species of cicadas distributed among 16 genera in our region.

ADULTS: Large, robust insects of rather uniform appearance, with broad heads and protruding eyes. The wings, the fore pair much the larger, are usually transparent, with few cross veins, and are held roof-like over the body. There are 3 ocelli in a triangle between the eyes, and the antennae are short, consisting of a stout basal segment and a 5- or 6-segmented filament. The male "harvestflies," as these insects are often called, are responsible for the sad, sustained whirring sound which fills the air on late summer days. The sound-producing and amplifying organs are internal, concealed beneath 2 large plates below the third thoracic segment. A pair of vibrating membranes operated by powerful muscles make the sounds—really a type of drumming. The legs are short, the femora of the first pair heavy and usually armed with spines below. Cicadas insert their eggs in the branches of broad-leaved trees, in the stems of various weeds, and in grass stems.

YOUNG: Upon hatching, they crawl or fall to the ground, burrow into it, and commence feeding upon the roots of trees, shrubs, and other plants. The shortest known life cycle requires 4 years and most are much longer. Some of the species of the genus *Tibicen* are believed to require more than 20 years to complete development. The mature nymph leaves the soil by night in the late spring or summer and, climbing partly up a tree trunk, takes a secure hold. The skin then splits down the center of the back and the adult emerges, leaving the nymphal skin attached to the bark.

IMPORTANCE: When numerous, cicadas may damage forest, shade, and orchard trees by ovipositing in the branches, which, as a result, are often splintered and weakened so that the wind breaks them. Greatest damage is done to young trees in orchards and nurseries. The species which come out in definite broods, such as the periodical cicada, are the worst offenders. Gulls and terns, grackles, English sparrows, and numerous other birds have been seen to gather to feast on the periodical cicada. The cicada-killer wasp (*140c*) stings even the largest cicadas and drags them to its burrow as food for its young.

EXAMPLE: Periodical Cicada   *Magicicàda septéndecim*

Throughout the United States from Kansas and Oklahoma eastward. This species actually spends from 13 to 17 years (according to latitude) as a burrowing, root-feeding nymph. The population is divided into a number of "broods," whose times of emergence as adults entomologists can predict with great accuracy.

41 Treehoppers   *Family Membrácidae*

ADULTS: Distinguished by the remarkable development of the first thoracic segment, which is produced over the head and much of the abdomen, and may take all sorts of weird shapes, some of them apparently protective in function. For example, some treehoppers, brown in color, are shaped like small thorns and could be mistaken for them by you and me. Whether this similarity is a defense against any natural enemies is not certainly known. The antennae arise between and slightly below the eyes. There are 2 ocelli between the eyes. The females insert their eggs in the midribs of leaves, in the buds, bark, or wood of trees and shrubs, or in the stems of herbaceous plants. Treehoppers quite aptly have been called the brownies of the insect world.

YOUNG: May be as strange-looking as the adults. The pronotum, or upper part of the first thoracic segment, often is remarkably developed even if not as in the adult. Large, much-branched spines sometimes adorn the bodies. The nymphs of some species feed on weeds and grasses, although the overwintering eggs are placed beneath the bark of trees.

IMPORTANCE: The buffalo treehopper, our example, and several other species are sometimes minor pests in orchards, where the twigs and small branches of apple and other fruit trees are badly stunted as a result of their egg-laying punctures. Herbaceous plants of various sorts may be seriously injured by the feeding of adults and nymphs. Most species, however, are of no economic importance.

EXAMPLE: Buffalo Treehopper   *Cerèsa bùbalus*

Common in eastern Canada and the entire United States. It is a pest of apple, pear, cherry, and other fruit and shade trees.

42 Spittlebugs   *Family Cercópidae*

ADULTS: Mostly drab-colored insects; our species usually brown, gray, or black, sometimes marked with yellow. They are rather robust, often nearly as wide as long. The antennae and the 2 ocelli are situated between the eyes. The hind tibiae are smooth, with only 1 or 2 heavy spines on their outer sides and clusters of smaller ones at their extremities. These insects are often called "froghoppers," and, at rest on a leaf or plant stem, they do have a froggy look. Spittlebugs do not fly very much and are not easily disturbed when feeding. They insert their eggs in plant stems or place them between stem and leaf sheath in grasses, and sometimes cover them with a protective, frothy material. The egg-laying habits of most species are unknown at present.

YOUNG: The nymphs, soon after commencing to feed, become enveloped in a froth which is continuously emitted from the anus as a liquid film. Probably everyone has seen these masses of so-called "frog spit" or "cuckoo spit" on the stems or leaves of grasses and weeds and other plants. Some species feed on the roots of plants. The larvae of a drosophilid fly (*163*) live in the spittle as harmless "guests" of the nymphs.

IMPORTANCE: Most spittlebugs are of little or no economic importance, but some species of the genus *Aphróphora,* especially the pine spittlebug (*A. parallèla*) and the Saratoga spittlebug (*A. saratogénsis*), are pests of pine. In parts of the eastern United States the pine spittlebug becomes numerous enough to kill young trees. The meadow spittlebug, *Philaènus leucophthálmus,* is frequently a pest of strawberries, alfalfa, and other truck or forage crops. Birds consume the adult insects but apparently do not feed upon the well-protected nymphs. The eggs of one species are known to be parasitized by a tiny mymarid wasp.

EXAMPLE: Spittlebug   *Aphróphora quadrinotàta*

One of the most abundant and widespread species in eastern North America, living on grasses and other low-growing vegetation; adults and nymphs have been found feeding on grape. Ordinarily a nymph is not visible through the spittle that covers it. Our illustration shows a nymph from which the spittle has been partially removed.

43 Leafhoppers   *Family Cicadéllidae*

A large family of generally beautiful and frequently important insects which, according to the latest check list, comprises 175 genera and about 2000 species in our region.

ADULTS: Characteristically slender-bodied, with the front margin of the head, as seen from above, either triangular or broadly curved, the large eyes being at or below the basal angles. The small, hair-like antennae are situated in front of and between the eyes. The 2 ocelli are between the eyes along the front margin of the head. Leafhoppers may be distinguished readily from all other closely related homopterons by the double row of spines along the undersides of the hind tibiae. If you will watch a leafhopper closely while it is feeding actively you will probably see tiny drops of clear liquid forcibly expelled with considerable regularity from the tip of its abdomen. The writer has observed the red-banded leafhopper fire away at the rate of a shot a second for a good 2 minutes. Many of the larger leafhoppers are called "sharpshooters" because of this behavior. The liquid is simply the unused part of the plant sap which is flowing steadily into the insect, with the addition of some body wastes. The material is sweetish and is called honeydew; sweet-loving insects of all kinds, especially flies, bees, wasps, and ants, are attracted to it. Leafhoppers fly readily on being disturbed, although at first they may sidle to the opposite side of a stem or leaf. Many species are attracted to lights at night. The winter is passed by the adults and sometimes by nymphs under dead leaves on the ground, or in dried grass clumps, and also by the eggs in plant tissues. Leafhopper eggs are inserted under the epidermis or outer skin of plant stems, petioles, or leaves; they are elongate, cylindrical, and lie side by side with the head end of the egg nearest the incision in the plant skin.

YOUNG: Much like the adults in general shape and in food habits, but lacking the often attractively colored wings; they haven't the fine appearance of the adults. Ordinarily there are 4 or 5 nymphal stages.

IMPORTANCE: Leafhoppers severely damage plants by merely sucking their juices, causing wilting and discoloration, and also by transmitting virus, fungus, and bacterial diseases. One of the most important of the pest species is the beet leafhopper, *Eutéttix tenéllus,* which transmits the virus of "curlytop" to sugar beets. Peach yellows and aster yellows are other virus diseases that are spread by leafhoppers.

EXAMPLE 43a: Red-banded Leafhopper
Graphocéphala coccínea

A very common species, occurring throughout eastern Canada and the United States east of the Rocky Mountains on many different garden flowers and vegetables, shrubs, and succulent weeds.

EXAMPLE 43b: Blue Dodger   *Oncometòpia undàta*

Widespread in eastern Canada and in the United States west and southwest to New Mexico. Occurs on the stems of sunflower, okra, and many other tall herbaceous plants. This big leafhopper is one of the species popularly called "sharp-shooters." "Dodger" seems to the writer the more descriptive name for this species. It usually sidles quickly to the opposite side of a plant stem from a collector, but if approached cautiously may be picked up between the fingers before it can fly away.

44 Psyllids   *Family Psýllidae*

ADULTS: Minute to very small, about the size of the commoner aphids; they have 2 pairs of membranous wings and resemble cicadas in miniature. Their hind legs are stout, permitting them to jump and fly short distances when disturbed. The 9- to many-segmented antennae are almost half the length of the body and are almost constantly in motion; the tarsi are 2-segmented. In Australia, psyllids known as lerp insects produce encrustations of honeydew or "lerp" on eucalyptus branches. This sweet substance is eaten by the aborigines. The eggs, often short-stalked, are laid upon the leaves or stems that will nourish the young, or in crevices under tree bark if they are to overwinter. The adults of some species hibernate.

YOUNG: Oval to almost circular in outline, flat, with very large wing pads and sometimes with fringed body margins. Some secrete a waxy covering. Heavy infestations produce copious honeydew, which covers the food plant and supports a growth of unsightly mold. There are usually 5 nymphal stages and several generations a year. Although development in the psyllids is typically gradual, it is complex in some species—that is, there may be a transition period preceding the adult stage when the insect is called a pupa. In these species the young are considered larvae rather than nymphs.

IMPORTANCE: Some serious economic pests are found in this small family. The pear psylla (*Psýlla pyrícola*), unintentionally introduced from Europe early in the last century and now widely distributed in pear-growing areas, causes foliage burn and the dropping of leaves and undeveloped pears. Nuthatches feed on this species. The apple sucker (*P. màli*), another European species infesting the developing buds and fruits of apple and a few other plants, has become established in New Brunswick, Canada. The species causing the cupping of the terminal leaves of boxwood is *P. búxi,* the box-wood psyllid, well known in the East. Our example is one of the species important because it transmits a virus disease to its food plants. A few psyllids cause galls in flower heads and on leaves of trees.

EXAMPLE: Potato (or Tomato) Psyllid
Paratrìoza cockerélli

Occurs from the Great Plains west to the Pacific Coast. It is a vector of psyllid yellows, a virus disease of potato and tomato. The original wild hosts are various species of the nightshade family (*Solanàceae*). Peppers and eggplant are additional cultivated host plants. About 300 yellow, stalked eggs are laid by a single female along the leaf margins. The nymphs at first are orange, later becoming light green. Lady beetles (*106*) prey upon them but never effect control. Serious dwarfing, discoloration, and reduction in yield are caused the infested plants.

45 Whiteflies   *Family Aleyródidae*

ADULTS: Minute insects, with both body and wings coated with a white, waxy powder. The wings are held flat or slightly sloped over the back; they have a much-reduced venation. Whiteflies live on the undersides of the leaves of many different plants. When an infested bush or tree is shaken, the insects may swarm out in a cloud, then rapidly settle down again. The female sometimes lays 10 to 20 short-stalked eggs in a circle about her feeding site, or may scatter them. From 100 to 200 eggs may be laid by a single insect in her lifetime.

YOUNG: Complex development occurs in certain psyllids; it is found throughout this family. On hatching, the young, called a larva, crawls a short distance and settles down to feed. At the first molt it loses legs and antennae and becomes a flat, scale-like creature, often with a fringe of waxy filaments either appressed to the leaf surface or descending steeply to it. They may be covered with wax in the form of rods, plates, and cottony masses, or they may be naked. The larvae produce copious honeydew, which is ejected from a conspicuous opening on the upper surface of the body—the vasiform orifice—a unique structure into which the anus empties. The last stage of development of the immature insect, the pupa, differs in being larger and usually more distinctly segmented. The adult leaves the pupal skin by a T-shaped opening on the back.

IMPORTANCE: Most whiteflies are of little importance, but some that infest citrus trees are pests, especially for the honeydew that covers the leaves and fruits and is soon blackened with molds—necessitating the washing of the fruit before marketing it. The citrus blackfly (*Aleurocánthus wóglumi*), a serious pest of the tropics, which is established in the West Indies, has immature stages that are black, fringed with white filaments; it is the subject of quarantines aimed at keeping it from our citrus areas. Whiteflies are attacked by several species of fungi. In Florida these fungi are so effective that they are capable of controlling whitefly infestations and are artificially propagated and disseminated for that purpose.

   EXAMPLE: Greenhouse Whitefly
                      Trialeuròdes vaporariòrum

Everywhere in greenhouses and out of doors southward. Cosmopolitan. This species attacks a great variety of plants and, if abundant enough, may weaken or kill them.

46 Aphids   *Family Áphidae*

A very large family of winged or wingless insects with complex life histories and considerable economic importance, particularly as vectors of virus diseases of plants. They are closely related to the chermids and phylloxeras of the family Chérmidae with which they were formerly included in the single family Áphidae. Chermids live on the foliage, twigs, and trunks, of coniferous trees, often enclosed in galls. The phylloxeras, which number many makers of galls on deciduous trees, are notable principally for the infamous grape phylloxera (*Phylloxèra vitifóliae*), a native of eastern North America, which came close to destroying the wine industry of France. The species has winged and wingless and parthenogenetic and sexual forms. Some individuals cause the formation of galls on grape leaves; others feed on the roots, causing nodules and eventually killing the vine. Grafting of susceptible foreign vines upon wild, native, resistant stocks

has been the means of saving grape culture here and throughout the world.

ADULTS: Minute, delicate, exclusively plant-feeding insects, with
small heads and relatively large abdomens. The antennae
have 3 to 6 segments, the last of which may be wide, basally,
with a narrow, almost hair-like tip. Alternation of host plants
is usual; the migrating females and some males are winged.
The wings are few-veined and the hind pair is the smaller. A
pair of oil- or wax-secreting organs, the cornicles, is present
in many species on the fifth abdominal segment. These structures may be produced as long tubes or reduced to slightly
elevated rings. The tarsi are usually 2-segmented. The woolly
apple aphid (*Eriósoma lanígerum*) is probably the best
known of the species which cover themselves with masses of
waxy thread; it feeds on the roots, trunk, and branches of
apple, producing galls or swellings, and curls the leaves of
elm—the alternate host plant. A number of common galls on
leaves, stems, and other plant parts are caused by the aphids
or aphid relatives which are found feeding inside them.
Aphids, while feeding upon the juices of plants, are continuously voiding droplets of honeydew from the anus (not the
cornicles). This substance, rich in plant sugars, is eagerly fed
upon by flies, ants, and many other insects; bees use it as they
do flower nectar—to make honey. Certain aphids, popularly
known as "ant-cows," are tended by ants in return for honeydew. Ants protect them and carry them from one food plant
to another. Aphids hatching from overwintering eggs are
females, often wingless, producing living young without
mating (parthenogenesis). The succeeding summer generations are also parthenogenetic females, but one of them may
consist of winged individuals which will fly to other plants of
the same species or to "secondary" hosts—plants of different,
often quite distantly related, species. A fall generation of
winged females may migrate back to the primary host plant
and produce a sexual generation (males and females). The
overwintering eggs, produced by fertilized females, are very
small, oval, and glistening black and are placed in the shallow crevices in the bark of the host trees and shrubs, especially about the buds. There may be as many as 13 generations
of aphids a year.

YOUNG: The nymphs are quite similar to the adults in appearance and habits.

IMPORTANCE: Aphids are serious pests of plants owing to their feeding injuries and to their transmission of virus, bacterial, and fungus diseases. Mosaic diseases (virus-caused) of sugar cane, clovers, beans, peas, tobacco, cucurbits, and crucifers, the bacterial black rot of cabbage, and perennial canker (fungus-caused) are some of the diseases for which aphids are the only or more important vectors. Aphids are destroyed by the larvae of syrphid flies, lacewings, and lady beetles, and such birds as the flycatchers, chickadees, warblers, and vireos; kinglets and chickadees eat the overwintering eggs. There are some effective wasp parasites of aphids and several fungus diseases. The honeydew is often a nuisance on sidewalks and parked cars but is collected avidly by honey bees. The fall flights of myriad aphids sometimes create a public nuisance.

EXAMPLE: Green Peach Aphid *Mȳzus pérsicae*

Introduced long ago from Europe, now found throughout our region and much of the world. The overwintering eggs are laid principally on peach, plum, and cherry. The summer wingless generations are parthenogenetic and live on a great variety of truck and garden crops, such as spinach, cabbage, potato, and on ornamental shrubs and herbaceous plants. The virus leaf roll of potato and tomato and the viruses of bean and tobacco mosaic are transmitted by this species, as are more than 20 other virus diseases of plants.

47 Scale Insects *Family Cóccidae*

A very large family of highly specialized insects. They are mostly very small to minute and would be rather inconspicuous if they did not live together, frequently in populous colonies. Twigs, leaves, and the skins of fruits at times are heavily encrusted with these insects.

ADULTS: Scale insects are extremely variable in shape. Some are covered with a protective shell or scale of wax, usually hard and separate from the body, even though actually secreted by wax pores on the body surface. Such scales are often called armored scales. They remain stationary and pro-

duce their eggs under the scale. The eggs may overwinter
under the maternal scale. The so-called soft scales are naked
—that is, they are not covered by a scale—and most of them
can crawl about even though they are sluggish and may appear
to be stationary. Because their smooth, chitinous bodies
may conceal their small and rather poorly developed legs,
some soft scales might be mistaken for armored species.
Examination with a hand lens is usually sufficient to distinguish
them. Soft scales may lay a few eggs or a single egg
at a time or may amass a great number of eggs, perhaps a
thousand, underneath their bodies, which become lifeless,
protective covers for them. Mealybugs are soft scales with
oval, soft, distinctly segmented bodies that are covered with
a white, waxy secretion and with lateral fringes and sometimes
"tails" of the same material. The females have legs
with single-segmented tarsi on which they crawl slowly about.
Before dying, each female lays several hundred eggs in a waxy
thread-covered mass attached to the end of her body. Mealybugs
are found on leaves, under the leaf sheaths of grasses,
on twigs or fruits, and even on the roots of some plants. Male
scale insects are either 2-winged or wingless and die shortly
after mating. The winged forms are seldom seen, and it has
not been thought necessary to illustrate them. Some reproduce
parthenogenetically.

YOUNG: In this collection of oddities, the male insects exhibit
complex development. Female scale insects probably molt 2
to 5 times; males molt perhaps 3 times before maturity. Immature
mealybugs of both sexes look alike in the early stages.
The males finally form a cocoon in which they transform to
winged adults. The young of many scale insects, in the early
stages, are quite active and are called "crawlers."

IMPORTANCE: Heavy infestations of scales may kill branches or
entire trees or shrubs and dwarf or disfigure fruits. Mealybugs
transmit certain plant diseases and cause mechanical
damage by sucking the juices of plants and coating them with
honeydew, which nourishes a variety of sooty mold fungi. Ants
tend mealybugs to obtain their honeydew, and bees convert
this sweet into honey. Scales are parasitized by various minute
wasps, some of them effective controls, and are preyed upon
by syrphid fly, lacewing, and beetle larvae. According to

stomach examinations, scales are eaten by about 90 different birds, of which the brown creeper, titmice, and chickadees deserve special mention. Certain fungi are checks upon scale insects in the warmest and more humid parts of our region, especially in Florida, where scale control in citrus groves by this means has been tried with considerable success.

In fairness to scales we must add that in India, lac, a resinous substance from which commercial shellac is made, is the product of a scale insect, and that cochineal dyes are derived from the bodies of a cactus-infesting species which is cultured in Central and South America and elsewhere. Some other waxes and dyes come from scale insects in the Orient and Europe.

EXAMPLE 47a: Citrus Mealybug   *Pseudocóccus cítri*

One of the large group of soft scales known as mealybugs. It probably came to us from the Mediterranean region; now is cosmopolitan. It occurs in greenhouses on many kinds of plants, northward, and as an outdoor pest of citrus in Florida and California. The Argentine ant, which tends and protects this mealybug from its numerous enemies in order to maintain a rich source of honeydew, must be artificially controlled before insect parasites and predators can operate effectively.

EXAMPLE 47b: Cottony-cushion Scale   *Icèrya púrchasi*

This native of Australia once threatened the citrus industry of California but was brought under control by the importation of the Australian lady beetle, or vedalia (*Rodòlia cardinàlis*), one of its natural enemies. One of its more effective parasites in California is an Australian fly of the family Agromýzidae (*164*). It is a showy scale insect living upon the bark, leaves, and fruits of many different shrubs and trees in the southern United States and in greenhouses throughout our region.

EXAMPLE 47c: Oystershell Scale   *Lepidósaphes úlmi*

Another naturalized pest from southern Asia, one of the sedentary, hard or armored scales. It lives upon the bark of many different deciduous trees and evergreen broad-leaved trees throughout temperate North America and the world. Apple and pear are among the favored food plants.

MAYFLIES
Order Ephemeróptera

Those who have spent a summer on a river or fresh-water lake and witnessed a flight of Mayflies for themselves need not be told how numerous insects may become. The windrows of insects on the beaches, the soft, rotting piles, inches deep on sidewalks and streets under lights, are impressive evidence of the abundance of nature. The Mayfly order is not large in number of species, however. The adults are shining, elongate, soft-bodied insects of medium to large size with 2 or 3 conspicuous tail filaments (the outer 2 are true cerci while the middle one, when present, is the much-modified eleventh abdominal segment). The antennae are small and few-segmented. The transparent many-veined wings are held together vertically over the body when not in use. The hind pair is very much the smaller, or, in some species, may be vestigial or absent. The fore legs of the males often are greatly elongated to perform a special clasping function during the mating flights. Most Mayflies are nocturnal, but some are day flyers.

The aquatic nymphs are long-bodied, with 2 or 3 tail filaments which may be fringed and fern-like. There is a pair of external gills on some or all of the first 7 abdominal segments. They are chiefly herbivorous, consuming diatoms, algae, and bits of other vegetation, but some are known to eat other aquatic insects, at least occasionally. Nymphs choose a variety of habitats, some living in mud or muddy water, others in the riffles of clear streams, and still others on "wave-washed lake shores." Much remains to be discovered about the life histories of Mayflies, but it is known that some require 2 years or more to complete nymphal development. Metamorphosis is incomplete, but Mayflies are unique in having a "sub-adult" stage in their development. The mature nymphs crawl out of the water upon the stems or leaves of aquatic plants and attach themselves. Shortly thereafter, the skin splits down the back and the sub-adult emerges. This stage is winged and can fly, an exception to the rule that only fully developed insects have that power. The sub-adult stage lasts from a few minutes to several days, depending upon the species. It is a period of inactivity during which the legs and tail filaments elongate and the reproductive system matures. The entire skin of the sub-adult, including that over the wings, is shed by the adult insect, except in a few species that retain it. The eggs are laid in the water after a mating flight; soon afterward the adults die. During the entire adult life, which may consume a few hours or days, no food is taken; the mouth parts are degenerate.

48 Mayflies   *Family Ephemeridae*

ADULTS: There are 2 or 3 very long tail filaments, and hind wings are present. As with all Mayflies, the alimentary tract is filled with air. Inflation probably occurs just before the nymphs leave the water, at which time they have been seen to come to the surface and gulp air. The eggs are laid on the water surface or upon submerged stones.

YOUNG: As described for the order, except that there are always 3 tail filaments of equal length. The legs are fitted for digging in mud. The nymphs (naiads) of this family are found only in muddy waters, sometimes in the mud itself. Both gills and tail filaments are employed in swimming. First stage nymphs do not have gills but must take in oxygen directly through the skin.

IMPORTANCE: Swarming Mayfly adults are eaten by practically all insectivorous birds and by bats, dragonflies, and leaping fishes, especially bass; toads gorge on them. The nymphs are eaten by young stoneflies and dragonflies, by aquatic bugs, most fresh-water fishes, salamanders, turtles, and various wading birds. In the stomach of a godwit, 250 Mayfly nymphs once were found. Mayfly and stonefly nymphs together compose the greater part of the food of trout. In anglers' parlance, Mayfly adults are "drakes," as are the dry fly lures which imitate them. Numerous wet flies are patterned after the nymphs.

EXAMPLE: Mayfly   *Hexagènia bilineàta*

This is a common species, widespread east of the Rocky Mountains.

DAMSELFLIES AND DRAGONFLIES
Order Odonàta

The adults of this order are among our most beautiful as well as useful insects and have inspired poets in every land. They are all day flyers, with 2 pairs of long, narrow, almost equal, net-veined wings that are transparent and sometimes beautifully patterned with color, glistening black, or smoked with shades of brown or blue. The body is elongate, the thorax being very short in proportion to the abdomen. The cerci are 1-jointed and inconspicuous. The eyes almost cover the surface of the head, while the antennae are very short, mere bristles. Food is taken on the wing, and the legs, which are not fitted for walking, bear long hairs and are held so as to form a scoop or basket trap for catching insects and holding them while they are being eaten. The biting mouth parts are below the head. All of our species are large insects.

Two large natural groupings occur in this order: the damselflies (suborder Zygóptera) with 12 families, and the dragonflies (suborder Anisóptera) with 6. We have selected 2 important families from each suborder for illustration and discussion. Most readers probably will be satisfied with distinguishing dragonflies from damselflies without trying to recognize families. This is simple. Dragonflies are stronger flyers with larger bodies; they always hold their wings outstretched when resting. Their aquatic nymphs, or naiads, are robust monsters with gills concealed in a large chamber formed by an outpocketing of the rectum into the body cavity. Damselflies are weak flyers, delicately fashioned, with extremely slender abdomens; they hold their wings together over the back when at rest. Damselfly nymphs are slender and have 3 conspicious fin-like or leaf-like tracheal gills attached to their tails.

In good weather dragonflies are almost constantly on the wing. They have earned the name "mosquito hawks"; their nymphs consume mosquito larvae in quantity and are themselves important as food for fresh-water fishes. The larger nymphs are known to capture and eat small fishes. The adults will eat honeybees, sometimes endangering the existence of a hive. The adults of both suborders are preyed upon by birds of several species, especially martins, and by frogs. The nymphs are eaten by ducks, various wading birds, and magpies. To this day and for no known reason these insects are held in considerable respect by country boys as "snake doctors."

Most of us have seen adult dragonflies and damselflies flying about "in tandem," the males of the former holding the females by the back of the head with special clasping organs at the end of the body, the males of the latter holding their mates by the first thoracic segment. The reason for this is the unusual arrangement wherein the copulatory apparatus of the male is below the enlarged second abdominal segment, while the sperm duct openings are on the lower side of the ninth. Mating can occur only after the male has transferred a sperm capsule from his ninth to second segment. The female, while being towed through the air by the male, extends the tip of her abdomen underneath her body and makes contact with the male second segment.

Dragonflies lay their eggs on the water surface, on water plants, or insert them in plant tissues. Damselflies always place their eggs in the tissues of aquatic plants, sometimes below water level. The winter is passed as a nymph by all odonates. There may be from 10 to 15 nymphal stages, and in some species more than a year is required to reach maturity. A unique feature of the nymphs is the "lower lip," or labium, which is hinged and elongated so that it can be suddenly extended to seize a victim and draw it to the mouth. This remarkable organ, when not in use, fits over the rest of the mouth and a portion of the nymphal face like a bandit's mask.

49 Narrow-winged Damselflies *Family Coenagriónidae*

ADULTS: The adults of this family have wings narrower than those of other damselflies and, constricted basally so as to appear stalked. The protruding eyes of all damselflies also appear stalked, owing to a basal constriction.

YOUNG: More elongate and slender than dragonfly nymphs and differing from those of broad-winged damselflies in having flat rather than 3-sided tracheal gills.

IMPORTANCE: The adults feed largely on mosquitoes, midges, and other slow-flying insects. The nymphs are valuable as predators upon mosquito and other aquatic insect larvae and as food for fishes.

EXAMPLE: Common Bluet   *Enallágma èbrium*

A common species ranging from Nova Scotia and Maryland west to Washington. The greenish nymphs inhabit fresh-water lakes and ponds.

50 Broad-winged Damselflies   *Family Agriónidae*

ADULTS: Those of the genus *Ágrion* are dark-winged and slow-flying, with metallic green or blue bodies. The only other genus, *Hetaerìna,* is represented by our example, which is one of only 2 North American species.

YOUNG: The long-legged nymphs prefer rather rapid shallows in brooks. The 2 lateral tracheal gills are triangular in cross section.

IMPORTANCE: Probably no more nor less than that of other damselflies.

EXAMPLE: Ruby Spot   *Hetaerìna americàna*

A familiar species of clear streams almost everywhere in North America. The adults are present in late summer and fall, never very far from water. The female is not colored as the illustrated male, but is green-bodied and without the red patches on the wing bases.

51 Aeshnid Dragonflies   *Family Aèshnidae*

ADULTS: Large dragonflies, generally known as "darners" and "devil's darning needles" because it was once popularly believed that they sewed up the ears of truant schoolboys. (There are no authentic records of this ever having occurred.) Our example, the largest and best-known species in most of North America, is exceeded in size by *Ànax walsinghami* of California, which has a wingspread greater by about 1¼ inches and a red first abdominal segment. The enormous eyes of the aeshnids are united for some little distance above, distinguishing the family from the others of the suborder. The females have stout ovipositors with which they insert their eggs inside the stems of aquatic plants below the water surface or in floating plant debris.

Young: The nymphs are elongate, with a rather small "lower lip" and with gills concealed in a chamber off the rectum. They can propel themselves through the water with considerable speed and dexterity by forcefully ejecting the water from the gill chamber.

Importance: Voracious feeders as adults on mosquitoes and other flying insects. The chiefly pond-dwelling nymphs are predacious on practically any aquatic creature that they can catch and hold long enough to subdue. They are themselves eaten by the larger fresh-water fishes.

Example: Big Green Darner   *Ànax jùnius*

A high-flying species common throughout most of the United States and southern Canada, and occurring in Alaska. The pigeon hawk considers this species fair game.

52 Libellulid Dragonflies   *Family Libellùlidae*

Adults: Typically dull-colored, with bodies covered by a chalky "bloom" instead of being decorated with metallic greens and blues. These are the skimming dragonflies which fly low over the water of ponds and sloughs. Their wings are often spotted and partly clouded with white. The abdomen is usually triangular in cross section. The females lack well-developed ovipositors and simply shed the eggs over submerged plants during flights, dipping their tails into the water to wash off the eggs.

Young: The hairy nymphs have a large, spoon-like lower lip which, when retracted, covers the entire ventral and anterior surfaces of the head up to the antennae. They live in aquatic vegetation.

IMPORTANCE: Valuable predators, as are all dragonflies. While the adults are no more selective in their choice of food than nighthawks, the fact that they frequent water insures that a large proportion of their prey will consist of mosquitoes and midges.

EXAMPLE: Ten Spot *Libéllula pulchélla*

Common throughout the eastern half of the United States, often ranging far from water when hunting.

NERVE–WINGED INSECTS
Order Neuróptera

This order contains a moderate number of species but a very diverse, not to say bizarre, array of forms. With a few conspicuous exceptions, the neuropterons are a little-known group of insects. This is because the adults are active chiefly at dusk or night, and also because they are seldom abundant. The retiring habit well befits such insects, so many of them large, soft-bodied, clumsily flying creatures, which in daylight would be the easy prey of birds and other insect eaters. The 2 pairs of large, almost equal wings typically are membranous, transparent, and crisscrossed with innumerable fine veins. Both the adults and the young, which are called larvae, prey upon other insects, and some of the larvae are important enemies of agricultural pests. Development in this order is complex, there being a pupal stage between the larval and adult stages. We say, therefore, that these insects exhibit complete metamorphosis. All the orders which follow have the same kind of development. Since complexity, at least to mortals, seems to signify progress, we have come to regard these orders as the "higher" ones.

53 Dobsonflies and Alderflies   *Family Siálidae*

ADULTS: One of the largest and most striking of North American insects is the dobsonfly, the male of which has mandibles half as long as the body. These insects rest quietly during the day and probably do not eat during their brief existence. They lay eggs on plant foliage, stones, or other objects near water, in masses of several thousand, covered with a whitish, waxy secretion. The much smaller alderflies are active by day and differ from dobsonflies in lacking the long mandibles and ocelli and in having the fourth tarsal segments dilated into 2 large lobes instead of being simply cylindrical.

YOUNG: Newly hatched dobsonfly larvae, commonly called "hellgrammites," drop directly into the water or crawl to it from the egg mass. They live beneath stones in the shallow rapids of streams and rivers, feeding on all sorts of aquatic insects. Their mouth parts are of the simple, biting variety. They can swim but usually crawl. Tracheal gills, resembling tufts of hair, are at the bases of the unsegmented lateral appendages on the first 7 abdominal segments. Larvae leave the water to pupate in an earthen cell under a stone or log and emerge as adults 1 to 2 weeks later.

Alderfly larvae have 8 pairs of segmented, lateral abdominal appendages with gill filaments at their extremities and a long tail gill filament. Their way of life is much like that of the hellgrammite.

IMPORTANCE: Hellgrammites once were used extensively by fisherman as live bait for such fresh-water game fishes as trout, bass, and perch. All sialid larvae are voracious eaters but are generally not abundant enough to be of great importance as predators. Adult alderflies are imitated by fisherman in dry flies called "alders."

EXAMPLE: Dobsonfly   *Corýdalus cornùtus*

Occurs throughout eastern North America. Adult males reach a length of more than 5 inches. A western species, the California dobson, is less than half the length of this example. Our illustration shows a female, in which the mandibles are not greatly produced as they are in the male.

54 Brown Lacewings   *Family Hemerobìidae*

ADULTS: Very small, delicate insects, resembling those of the succeeding family, except that they are brown instead of green. All prey upon small insects, such as aphids and mealybugs. They are given to playing dead when violently disturbed. The long-oval eggs are glued on their sides to the surfaces of leaves or bark of trees, either singly or in small groups; apparently they are never stalked.

YOUNG: The larvae, called "aphidwolves," are rather important predators, with a pair of curved, hollow, tusk-like mandibles adapted for piercing and sucking out the contents of the thrips, mites, aphids, scale insects, and leafhopper nymphs, upon which they feed. They have smooth skins and, although hairy, do not camouflage themselves like some green lacewing larvae. After passing through 3 larval stages they pupate in crevices in bark or in rolled leaves, protected by elliptical, double-walled cocoons of coarsely woven silk spun from the anus. The pupa emerges from the cocoon and moves a short distance, then leaves the pupal skin as an adult.

IMPORTANCE: A useful family of predators. The adults are themselves the prey of bats, spiders, and birds, while the larvae are devoured by predacious beetles, fly larvae, and parasitic wasps.

EXAMPLE: Brown Lacewing   *Boriomyia fidèlis*

Widely distributed in eastern North America and occurring also in British Columbia.

The species of the small family Symprobìidae also are known as brown lacewings. The distinctions between these 2 groups of insects seem rather slight; the habits of all of them are similar, so far as known.

55 Green Lacewings   *Family Chrysópidae*

ADULTS: Beautiful insects with long hair-like antennae, green filmy wings, and iridescent red-gold eyes; familiar to almost everyone. There are about 50 species in our region. Green lacewings are nocturnal, slow-flying, attracted to lights and, on being handled, may emit an evil-smelling liquid from a pair of glands opening on each side of the first thoracic segment. Because of this last ability they are sometimes called "stink-flies." They live in trees or in low vegetation (some species in both situations) and prey upon small, soft-bodied insects, chiefly aphids. The oval, smooth, white or greenish eggs are attached by one end to a slender filament about ¼ inch long. Even with this protection the eggs are sometimes eaten by lacewing larvae and are parasitized by tiny trichogrammatid wasps (*131*). The adults of some species hibernate in protected sites.

YOUNG: Known as "aphidlions," the larvae are well named, for with their long, curved, hollowed "fangs" they impale countless aphids and suck their body juices until only an empty skin remains. Numerous species are covered with hairs, some hooked, upon which they build domes of aphid skins and debris of various sorts to form a protective and perhaps camouflaging armor. The skin along the sides of these trash carriers is raised into many conspicuous warts. Other chrysopid larvae are relatively smooth and do not carry trash. Usually the larva hibernates in a globular cocoon of silk spun from the anus and more or less hidden in a crevice under tree bark or attached to the underside of a fallen leaf. Special mandibles of the pupa snip the threads of the cocoon and release the insect through a hinged cap. The adults leave the pupal skin after emerging from the cocoon.

IMPORTANCE: They are considered valuable checks, especially as larvae, upon cabbage, woolly, pea, and cotton aphids, citrus mealybugs, cottony cushion scales, red spiders, thrips, and oriental fruit moth larvae. Aphidlions are eaten by some of the larger predacious bugs and are parasitized by certain wasps. The adults are the food of night birds and bats and are attacked by mites and by adult sand flies (*151*), which ride about on their wings, sucking blood from the wing veins.

EXAMPLE: Golden-eye Lacewing   *Chrysòpa oculàta*

A common species, distributed through most of our region. Quite a few different varieties of this insect have been described.

56 Antlions   *Family Myrmeleóntidae*

The antlions constitute the largest family in the order Neuróptera.

ADULTS: Large, normally nocturnal insects, which, because of their very long and rather narrow wings, are sometimes mistaken for damselflies. Unlike most neuropterons, these insects have short, often clubbed antennae. They are capable of feeding, but little is known of their diet, which possibly consists of smaller insects. The eggs are dropped upon the surface of the soil singly or in small groups.

YOUNG: The larvae, the real "antlions," make the familiar conical pits in dry sandy or powdery soil under rocky ledges and houses. The antlion is plump-bodied and hairy, with a small head but tremendous jaws, each one a food tube composed of a fused mandible and maxilla. It lies buried at the bottom of its pit with only head and jaws exposed. An ant, or other insect falling into the pit, is seized, rendered almost motionless by a paralyzing secretion, and sucked dry of body juices; then it is flipped out of the pit by an upward jerk of the long jaws. Many species do not make pits but simply bury themselves up to the head in the soil and wait for an insect to come within reach. The mature larva spins a globular, heavy silken cocoon, incorporating soil particles into its outer layers. The pupa cuts its way out of the cocoon, leaving a circular opening with a hinged lid. The winter is passed as a larva, either free in the soil or in the cocoon in which it will later pupate.

IMPORTANCE: Since antlions feed largely on ants, many of them useful predators in their own right, their value is difficult to appraise. Beyond a few hymenopterous parasites the young have few natural enemies. The adults fall prey to birds that hunt in the evening.

EXAMPLE: Antlion　　　　　*Myrmèleon immaculàtus*

The range of this species covers most of the United States and extends into southern Canada.

57 Snakeflies　　　　　*Family Raphidìidae*

ADULTS: Strange-looking insects of small or medium size which only those living in the western third of the continent may expect to see. They are rapid runners and slow flyers, preying upon aphids and other soft-bodied insects on the trunks and foliage of trees in shady forest depths. They place several eggs together in holes and crevices in tree bark.

YOUNG: Elongate, short-legged, with large flat heads and rather inconspicuous mouth parts, living under the bark of trees, where they feed upon wood-inhabiting insects and their larvae. After a developmental period which may last several years, the larva pupates in an unlined cell from which the pupa later cuts its way out through the bark and after a period of a day or two molts to the adult stage. The winter is passed in the larval or pupal stage.

IMPORTANCE: Raphidians are too few to be important as predators.

EXAMPLE: Common Raphidian *Agúlla adníxa*

A little-known species, generally distributed west of the Continental Divide in dense forests up to altitudes of 9000 feet or higher.

In this discussion of the nerve-winged insects, several of the less important families have been omitted. Mention will be made, however, of the rather rare "false-mantids" of the family Mantíspidae. In form and feeding habits, the adults of these insects do resemble tiny mantids, but the wings are typically neuropteran. The first thoracic segment is much elongated and the legs are stout, the first pair greatly modified as grasping organs; the antennae are quite short.

SCORPIONFLIES
Order Mecóptera

A small, rather primitive and ancient order represented by 4 families in our region. Scorpionflies are strange, long-faced creatures, usually with 2 pairs of long, slender wings. The antennae and legs are long and slender too. Little time has been given to life-history studies of these insects. The eggs are said to be laid in or upon the soil, and the larvae, which resemble caterpillars and have up to 9 pairs of abdominal sucker feet or prolegs, in addition to the true thoracic legs, feed in the soil on vegetable matter, are predacious, or scavenging. Pupation occurs in a cell in damp soil or rotting wood. One family, which includes some 10 North American species, is composed of very small, flightless, hopping, forest dwellers, which sometimes occur so abundantly on the surface of snow that they have earned the name of "snowfleas."

58 Snow Scorpionflies   *Family Borèidae*

ADULTS: These are the snowfleas, very small insects with only vestiges of wings. A pair of scale-like lobes, representing the fore wings, remains in the females, and the wings of the males are mere bristles, which in at least some species serve to clasp the female during copulation. The ovipositor of the female may be as long as her body. There are no ocelli. The legs are long and slender. Snow scorpionflies superficially resemble nymphal grasshoppers in general body shape. They can be found throughout the year beneath logs, stones, and forest litter, and, on warmer winter days as the name suggests, on snow surfaces, where they are more conspicuous. The bionomics of our species are largely a mystery at present. Most of them seem to prefer open woods, pasturelands, or field margins. They are probably predacious on springtails and may feed on dead vegetation. Boreids are good jumpers and are quite active during the winter months, which seems to be the season during which they are usually seen. One species, *Borèus boreàlis,* is known at present only on a tiny island in the Pribilofs, 300 miles off Alaska. They place their eggs in the soil.

YOUNG: The larvae of a European species, which has had some study, burrow through mosses or travel along the soil surface under moss plants, living on vegetable matter. The larvae and pupae of an American species have been found in cells constructed of earth among mosses at the bases of trees.

IMPORTANCE: None, economically.

EXAMPLE: Snow Scorpionfly   *Borèus brumàlis*

This is the smallest species of the genus. Recorded from Michigan and Massachusetts, south to Washington, D.C.

59 Scorpionflies   *Family Panórpidae*

ADULTS: These insects are more properly called scorpionflies than the other members of the order because in the males the abdomen is bulbous at the tip and curved upward and forward like that of a scorpion. Panorpids actually have been mistaken for scorpions by persons who did not know that true scorpions were wingless. They are weak flyers with long, narrow wings, usually mottled with brown. So far as is known, the food consists of disabled or dead insects, the juices of decaying fruit, pollen and nectar, and honeydew. The eggs are laid in large groups in the soil.

YOUNG: The food habits are like those of the adults. They attack disabled or dying insects and eat some dead animal and vegetable matter.

IMPORTANCE: Primarily scavengers. They are preyed upon by spiders, dragonflies, robberflies, and probably many other unrecorded predators.

EXAMPLE: Common Scorpionfly   *Panórpa nebulòsa*

A common species from Maine and Ontario to Ohio and South Carolina.

The 2 families of this order which we have not illustrated are the Bittácidae and the Merópidae. The members of the former resemble the scorpionflies of the family Panórpidae, but their longer legs differ in having single- rather than double-clawed tarsi, the fifth segment of which can be closed against the fourth to form a powerful grasping organ. They are active predators and are called "hanging flies" because of their habit of suspending themselves from vegetation by the front legs and grasping at passing flies and other insects with the other 4. This family contains a wingless form known only from central California. The Merópidae contains but a single rare species found in the eastern United States, an insect which differs from panorpids in having wide, almost oval wings with many more cross veins, and in lacking ocelli.

CADDISFLIES
Order Trichóptera

Adult caddisflies in general appearance resemble certain moths to which they are related closely but from which they differ in having longer antennae and a short, uncoiled proboscis. The 2 pairs of wings, held roof-like over the body, are usually hairy but may be almost naked or somewhat scaly. The wing venation is simple, the reduction in the number of cross veins distinguishing them from the nerve-winged insects and scorpion-flies. The thorax and abdomen are never scaled. Caddisflies are swift afoot but rather weak on the wing, never traveling far from the streams or lakes in which the larvae dwell. They are active only at night, often congregating at lights. Mating flights occur over water. They take liquid food principally and may live several months, the females laying from 300 to 1000 eggs enclosed in gelantinous ropes, blobs, or rings attached to submerged stones or to vegetation at the water's edge.

The aquatic young include the familiar case-making insects which cling to the undersides of stones in brooks. Some larvae lack any sort of protective case or may spin silken tubes and funnels attached to rocks or plants. Such fixed cases are often shielded at their upstream ends by nets which not only give protection against the current but catch food for the net makers. The inhabitants of portable cases use a variety of materials in their construction, but most commonly sand or bits of vegetable matter together with silk produced by very large glands with openings in the mouth. Caddisfly cases usually are distinctive for each species. Most larvae prefer slow to medium-fast currents in streams and rivers, but some live in ponds and lakes. They are generally omnivorous, eating microscopic plants and animals (plankton), insect larvae, and other small arthropods. Some genera are wholly predacious, others primarily herbivorous with cannabalistic tendencies, and still others are scavengers. There are from 4 to 6 larval stages. The winter is passed as a larva.

Pupation occurs within a cocoon inside the larval case. When the pupal period is completed, the pupa (really the adult within the pupal skin) cuts its way out of the cocoon, swims to the surface, and crawls out of the water upon some aquatic plant. After fastening itself firmly to leaf or stem the insect splits the pupal skin and emerges as an adult.

Fishes are probably the most important natural enemies of the aquatic stages; 30 per cent of the food of the eastern brook trout is caddisfly larvae; muskrats have been reported to eat large numbers of them. Several species of flies and wasps are recorded as parasites of the larvae in Europe. Adults are often snatched by leaping trout and are taken by bats and various birds. Caddisflies are called "duns" by anglers. Likenesses of the adults are used as dry flies and imitations of the larvae or "creepers" as wet flies.

60 Large Caddisflies   *Family Phryganèidae*

This is only 1 of 17 North American families of caddisflies; it contains the largest species of our region.

ADULTS: Typical of the order. There is usually one generation a year.

YOUNG: The larvae, which prefer the quiet water of swamps, make portable cylindrical cases of leaf fragments or twigs arranged in rings or a spiral pattern. They have strong mandibles, which are vestigial or absent in the adults. The head and thorax are the only exposed parts of the body, and they may be entirely withdrawn into the case when danger threatens. Oxygen is taken from the water by means of thread-like tracheal gills distributed in longitudinal rows along the sides of the abdomen. In certain other families, respiration occurs through the body surface itself or in blood gills. The legs are rather long and slender with a 1-segmented, single-clawed tarsus. At the end of the abdomen is a pair of hook-like prolegs which serve to hold the larvae in their cases.

IMPORTANCE: The larvae are useful as predators upon other aquatic insect larvae, as scavengers, and, most importantly, as food for fresh-water fishes.

EXAMPLE: Large Caddisfly   *Ptilóstomis semifasciàta*

Fairly common from Quebec to Illinois and eastward.

MOTHS AND BUTTERFLIES
Order Lepidóptera

The adults of this order have always been the most admired of insects. The ancients gave butterfly wings to Psyche, the beautiful maiden personifying the human soul. All of us, at least as children, have caught or tried to catch them, a few never giving up the chase. A king of Persia is said to have trained sparrows and starlings to hawk butterflies, just as falcons, in some countries, are trained to capture birds.

These insects are rather slow-flying, with large, often brightly colored wings covered with tiny scales that rub off like dust on the fingers. Colors in insects are pigmental, structural, or combinations of the 2 types. For example, butterfly scales are often beautiful not because of pigments, but because their surfaces are crossed by many minute, parallel ridges, which break up the light falling upon them into component colors. Iridescence may be due to the effect upon light of extremely thin, transparent films—an effect like that of the walls of a soap bubble. Structural colors, unlike many pigments, are not faded by sunlight and are quite permanent.

Butterfly antennae are filaments ending in knobs or thickenings; those of moths frequently are fern- or feather-like (doubly-combed) and may be simple, tapering filaments, but never are thickened or knobbed at the ends. Butterflies are day flyers; moths are usually nocturnal. The mouth parts, adapted for extracting nectar from the throats of flowers, have become a long tube called a proboscis or tongue, which, when not in use, is coiled beneath the head like a watch spring. The proboscis is formed of parts of the united maxillae; mandibles are absent or vestigial. Typically there are 2 pairs of palps, an upper pair, the maxillary, and a lower pair, the labial palps. The latter are usually the larger and may project forward or upward to look like a snout.

Moth eggs usually are laid in large clusters and often coated with scales or hairs from the mother's body or a frothy secretion which hardens to a protective crust. Butterfly eggs are laid in exposed situations, either singly or in small groups, without protective coverings.

The young, called caterpillars, are of variable shapes, sometimes grotesque. They may be hairy, naked, or adorned with spines which may be poisonous. The hairs may be barbed and irritating to the human skin. In addition to 3 pairs of thoracic legs, caterpillars typically have a pair of unjointed sucker-feet or prolegs on each of the third to sixth abdominal segments. These abdominal prolegs are provided with tiny hooks, the arrangement of which is important in the precise separation of genera and species in many families. There is still another pair of prolegs on the last abdominal segment, called anal prolegs or anal claspers. Metamorphosis is complete. The pupae of most lepidopterons differ from those of the preceding 3 orders in that the pupal appendages—legs, antennae, and wing pads—are fused with the body instead of being free. The mature larva of a moth may spin a silken cocoon in which to molt for the last time before becoming a pupa, but sometimes the cocoon consists of little more than the matted hairs of the larva. With the exception of the skipper butterflies (81), which in several respects are a compromise between butterflies and moths, butterfly pupae, sometimes called chrysalids, are not enclosed in a cocoon at all but are attached to the surface of a leaf or stem by a silken disk at the posterior end, and sometimes also by a narrow band of silk encircling their middles.

Only the larval stages of the Lepidóptera are destructive, and this is one of the most important of all orders from the economic standpoint. Most caterpillars feed upon living plant tissues, but some are scavengers or pests of vegetables or animal products and a few eat other insects. They are important items in the diets of birds, especially nestlings, and are the prey or hosts of countless predacious and parasitic insects. The adults of many species are valuable pollinators.

We have chosen to illustrate and describe 20 families of moths, less than a third of the total number generally recognized. Moths are divided into 2 major groups: the smaller and more primitive—the Jugátae—comprises 3 small, rather obscure families of moths having the fore and hind wings very similar in shape and venation, and at the base of the fore wing a small lobe (jugum) which rests upon the upper surface of the hind wing and serves as a coupling mechanism. Some have mouth parts fitted for chewing pollen rather than for siphoning liquid foods. None of the families in the Jugátae has been illustrated or described in this book. The other group, the Frenátae, comprises about 70 families of moths in which fore and hind wings differ both in shape and venation and are coupled in flight by one or more spines or by a specialized area at the base of the hind wing, which presses against the lower surface of the fore wing.

Among the primitive Frenátae, which for reasons of space we have not treated on a family basis, are some insects so well known to the general reader that an indication of their systematic position and brief mention of their remarkable behavior seem necessary here. These insects are the yucca moths of the family Incurvariidae. The female of *Tegetícula yuccasélla* has specialized mouth parts with which she gathers a ball of pollen from the stamens of yucca flowers, then goes to a new flower into whose ovary she inserts one or more eggs with her long ovipositor. This done, she clambers to the top of the pistil and packs her load of pollen into the depression there. The flower will now produce seeds, a percentage of which will be eaten by the moth larva. An individual flower of *Yúcca filamentòsa* opens for a single night and is said not to bear fruit unless visited by the little white moth as described.

61 Casebearer Moths   *Family Coleophóridae*

This and the families which follow, up to and including the bagworm moths (72), are commonly referred to by entomologists as microlepidopterons. The Microlepidóptera is a very large group of insects, rather difficult to separate even to families. We do not pretend adequately to have defined them here, but these brief characterizations, together with the illustrations of typical species, will acquaint the reader with the more important families in the group.

The more than 90 North American species of this family all are included in the single genus *Coleóphora*.

ADULTS: Brownish or grayish moths with slender, often pointed wings fringed along the hind margins and expanding less than ⅝ inch. Maxillary palps are lacking. The species are very difficult to distinguish. The collector is more likely to take the larvae or pupae in their cases than the moths themselves.

YOUNG: The larvae begin life as miners within leaf tissues, later leave their tunnels to construct portable, protecting cases of silk, which they bear about much as snails do their shells. In some species this case is quite hard and without camouflaging material—in others, bits of leaf or shreds of flower petal are attached to it. The case-bearing larvae are external feeders, skeletonizing the leaves of the food plants and feeding upon florets and seeds of flowers and the surfaces of fruits. The young larvae pass the winter inside their cases attached to the bark of the food plant. Pupation also takes place inside the cases.

IMPORTANCE: The 2 species of casebearer moths figured in this book are minor pests of some fruit trees, especially apple, pear, plum, cherry, and haw. The larvae that may be found on garden flowers after they have been cut and arranged in vases usually cause some consternation. The larch casebearer (*C. laricélla*), a European species, has become established in the northeastern United States and eastern Canada, where it is quite destructive. Casebearer larvae are attacked by many parasitic wasps and by a few flies.

EXAMPLE 61a: Pistol Casebearer

Coleóphora malivorélla

Found generally in the United States from Virginia and Kansas northward into Canada; especially abundant in apple-growing regions.

EXAMPLE 61b: Cigar Casebearer

Coleóphora fletcherélla

Distributed throughout the entire United States and southern Canada.

62 Clothes Moths and Allies   *Family Tinèidae*

ADULTS: Delicate moths with wing expanses of less than 1 inch. They do not feed. The better-known species are the "millers," which when seen flying about inside a house are always headed away from the light toward a darkened corner or closet. They lay minute, white eggs singly or in small groups on the food material of the young. Although only about ⅟₅₀ inch long, the eggs are often seen and recognized on black woolen goods by housewives.

YOUNG: The larvae feed upon dead and dried vegetable and animal substances. They are white, about ⅓ inch long when fully grown, and complete their development in from 6 weeks to several years, depending upon the species and conditions of existence. Infestations are recognized by the silken webs of the webbing clothes moth, by the presence of the larval cases of the casemaking clothes moth, or by fabric damage.

IMPORTANCE: The clothes moths are of great economic importance as destroyers of woolen fabrics, upholstered furniture, rugs, tapestries, and many kinds of stored animal products. They have been found in nature breeding in the nests of birds and wild bees and under the bark of dead trees.

EXAMPLE 62a: Casemaking Clothes Moth
Tínea pellionélla

Occurs in houses and other buildings throughout our region and the world. Probably not native to the New World.

EXAMPLE 62b: Webbing Clothes Moth
Tinèola bisselliélla

Also a cosmopolitan species of probable Old World origin.

63 Plutellid Moths   *Family Hyponomeùtidae*

ADULTS: Small, with narrow fore wings, pointed, fringed hind wings, and smooth hind tibiae. When resting the wings are tight-pressed against the sides of the slim body and the antennae are directed straight forward.

YOUNG: The larvae of our example are greenish with black heads and about ⅓ inch long when fully grown; they start life as leaf miners, later becoming surface feeders. They pupate in cocoons of very coarse lace on the undersides of cabbage leaves.

IMPORTANCE: Our example is a minor pest of cabbage, the larva being the smallest of the common "cabbageworms"; it is more injurious to other plants of the mustard family, especially ornamentals.

EXAMPLE: Diamond-backed Moth
Plutélla maculipénnis

Originally introduced from Europe, the cabbage plutella is now cosmopolitan, occurring wherever cabbage or its other cruciferous food plants grow. When the wings are closed, 3 light, diamond-shaped areas appear along the mid-line of the back.

64 Clear-wing Moths   *Family Aegeríidae*

A rather small, well-defined group comprising 113 species distributed among 26 genera in our region. This is about the only family of the Microlepidóptera that is popular with the average collector.

ADULTS: Day-flying moths averaging 1½ to 2 inches in wing-spread, with narrow, partially transparent (unscaled) wings. Numerous species are larger than some macrolepidopterons. The antennae are long, half to three fourths the length of the fore wings, and usually enlarged, although never knobbed, toward the tips, which may bear tufts of hair. Those of the male have a double row of teeth below; those of the female are smooth. A downward-directed fold along the rear edge of the fore wing fits over and locks with an upward-directed fold along the front edge of the hind wing—a unique family characteristic in the Lepidóptera. The abdomen, although scaled, appears smooth and shiny; in the male it bears a conspicuous terminal tuft of hairs. A most striking feature is the resemblance of the whole family to the wasps, both in general body shape and coloration and sometimes in flight habits. Males and females usually differ markedly in color and color pattern.

YOUNG: Whitish, cylindrical borers in the stems, bark, or roots of woody shrubs and trees and sometimes in herbaceous plants; a few bore in the galls of other insects. Pupation occurs in a cocoon, from which the adult partially extricates itself before leaving the pupal skin.

IMPORTANCE: More than 12 pests of economic importance are contained in this family, of which the most significant is our example. The larva of *Melíttia cucúrbitae,* the squash borer, which tunnels the vines of squash, pumpkin, cucumber, and related wild and cultivated plants, is a serious agricultural pest.

EXAMPLE: Peachtree Borer   *Sanninoìdea exitiòsa*

A native species, represented throughout the United States and southern Canada by one or more of its several varieties and geographical races. An example of a native insect which has practically forsaken its original hosts, wild plums and cherries, for the cultivated peach and other stone fruits. The larva burrows beneath the bark, often girdling and killing young trees, seriously weakening older ones.

65 Gelechiid Moths   *Family Gelechìidae*

ADULTS: Small, the wingspread of our largest species is less than an inch. Usually dull-colored, with narrow fore wings and a pair of long labial palps, upcurving and prominent, well separated at the pointed tips. In a good many species the front margin of the hind wing may project sharply, the outer margin being concave.

YOUNG: The naked, cylindrical, pinkish, or white larvae mine in leaves, stems, or tubers of the host plants or form galls; some are pests of stored cereals. Pupation occurs in a silken cocoon.

IMPORTANCE: The outstanding member of this family is the pink bollworm of cotton (*Pectinóphora gossypiélla*), a species probably of Indian origin. The larvae hatch from eggs laid at various places on the host plant and bore into the bud, where they soon pupate and emerge as adults or where they remain as larvae, passing the winter inside the boll. Pupation also occurs in the soil. Infested fields usually suffer a 20 to 50 per cent loss in yield. Federal quarantines and spot eradication efforts confine this insect very largely to that part of the

United States bordering on Mexico. An important pest of grains, both in the field and bin, is the Angoumois grain moth (*Sitótroga cerealélla*), one of the earliest immigrants from Europe, whose larva feeds and completes its development within a single kernel of corn or wheat.

EXAMPLE 65a: Potato Tuberworm
Gnorimoschèma operculélla

Widely distributed in the southern half of the United States. The younger larvae mine leaves or the surfaces of exposed potato tubers, then penetrate stems and tubers with silk-lined tunnels. Tobacco, eggplant, tomatoes, and weeds of the nightshade family (Solanàceae) also are attacked.

EXAMPLE 65b: Elliptical Goldenrod Gall Moth
Gnorimoschèma gallaesolidáginis

Widespread in our region. The presence of the larva in the stems of goldenrod causes a large swelling, or gall, which does not adversely affect the growth of the plant. The eggs overwinter. The larvae are often parasitized by an encyrtid wasp, *Copidosòma geléchiae,* which is polyembryonic (more than 1 embryo per egg). As many as 200 of these tiny parasites may issue from a single host larva.

66 Olethreutid Moths   *Family Olethreùtidae*

ADULTS: Small, dusk- and night-flying moths, with well-developed, forward-pointing labial palps. Mostly brown or gray, variously mottled or banded; sometimes with metallic-hued scales in localized areas on the fore wings. The minute eggs are laid singly, as a rule, on the larval food plants.

YOUNG: Smooth-skinned, pale-colored, feeding upon leaves and fruits of trees and vines and tunneling the branch tips of both deciduous and coniferous trees. Leaf-feeding species usually web leaves together or roll them.

IMPORTANCE: This family contains many important pests, the chief of which is the codling moth, one of the world's most destructive insects. In the absence of artificial control, almost no marketable apples are produced. The annual cost of codling moth control approaches $18,000,000. A major pest of peach is the oriental fruit moth (*Graphólitha molésta*), an

Asiatic species now occurring in most of our peach-growing districts. The pink or white larvae tunnel branch terminals, causing them to die back, and also enter the fruits. The braconid wasp, *Macrocéntrus ancylívorus*, (*126*), a native parasite, is being reared in large insectaries to combat this insect. The agitator inside the Mexican "jumping bean" of carnivals and novelty shops is the larva of an olethreutid moth, *Laspeyrèsia sáltitans*.

EXAMPLE 66a: Codling Moth   *Carpocápsa pomonélla*

A European species, now found everywhere that apple and related fruits are grown. The larva hibernates in a cocoon, usually on the bark of the host tree. There are 2 to 4 generations annually, depending upon latitude. The larvae of the first generation do some leaf feeding before penetrating the young fruits; the others hatch from eggs laid upon the fruit itself and so enter it directly. These insects also are serious pests of English walnuts, tunneling into green fruits to feed upon the kernels.

EXAMPLE 66b: Grape Berry Moth   *Polychròsis viteàna*

Distributed throughout our region. The larvae feed among the developing grapes in a cluster and, later in the season, inside the individual fruits. The pupa passes the winter in a silken cocoon inside a rolled-up flap of grape leaf.

67 Tortricid Moths   *Family Tortrícidae*

ADULTS: Wingspread seldom exceeds an inch. Night-flying moths, often attractively striped or spotted in browns or grays. They are sometimes called "bell moths" because many of the resting adults, viewed from above, are somewhat bell-shaped. The eggs, laid in masses upon the bark of the host tree, are oval, flat, overlapping like shingles, and are often covered with a waterproof, protective cement. The winter may be passed by the egg or by young larvae in cocoons under bark and in plant debris.

YOUNG: Usually greenish with scattered hairs springing from tiny raised areas and with the proleg hooklets arranged in a circle. They are mostly found in rolled leaves in which many of them finally pupate; some pupation occurs in crevices in the bark of trees. If disturbed, a larva may leave its protective leaf roll and drop toward the ground by a rope of silk which it ascends when danger has passed.

IMPORTANCE: Some very serious pests of fruit trees and both broad-leaved and coniferous forest and shade trees are included in this family, the examples chosen for illustration being the most important.

EXAMPLE 67a: Spruce Budworm   *Árchips fumiferàna*

A major forest pest, the larvae feeding on needles of fir, spruce, and to some extent on all conifers, often killing terminal shoots and the trees themselves. The first-stage larvae pass the winter in tiny cocoons attached to twigs of the host, emerging the following spring to feed on the buds and branch tips which they cover with webbing. The unprotected pupae hang head downward from the branches.

EXAMPLE 67b: Fruit Tree Leaf Roller
                              Árchips argyrospìla

Generally distributed in our region. Especially well known as an apple pest. The larvae roll leaves or tie 2 leaves together to form a nest and also web leaves to the fruits themselves and feed on the apple surfaces.

The carpenter moths of the family Cóssidae, a group of large insects of some economic importance, are situated, systematically, close to the tortricids. In general outline, carpenter moths strongly resemble sphinx moths (77), but differ, among other things, in lacking long, coiled, siphoning mouth parts. Cossid larvae are called carpenterworms; they are borers in the wood of many different kinds of deciduous trees and shrubs and may cause considerable damage locally. The larva of the best-known species, *Prionoxýstus robíniae,* requires 3 or 4 years to complete its development.

68 Pyraustid Moths   *Family Pyraùstidae*

ADULTS: Mostly small, dull-colored moths, about half the species with labial palps large and upcurving to form a conspicuous "snout." The maxillary palps are typically small and slender. Pyraustids are difficult to separate from the pyralid moths of the succeeding family without using differences in wing venation.

YOUNG: Usually naked, with scattered hairs, boring in stems and fruits or webbing over the foliage and stems of the food plants. Almost all the known pyraustids of one entire subfamily have aquatic larvae, some with tracheal gills, which live in cases either floating or attached to submerged objects, or under webs on rocks.

IMPORTANCE: In addition to the illustrated examples, this family contains the following serious pest species: the melonworm (*Diaphània hyalinàta*) and pickleworm (*D. nitidàlis*); the imported cabbage webworm (*Héllula undàlis*) of the South; the grape leaf folder (*Désmia funeràlis*), another European introduction, and the celery leaf tier (*Phlyctaènia rubigàlis*).

EXAMPLE 68a: European Corn Borer   *Pyraùsta nubilàlis*

Introduced from Europe, probably in broomcorn, and first found established near Boston; it has now spread over most of the northern half of our corn-growing area.

EXAMPLE 68b: Garden Webworm   *Loxóstege similàlis*

Generally distributed. The larvae feed upon many kinds of cultivated plants, especially alfalfa, clover, and other legumes, beets, and succulent weeds. They live in webs upon the foliage they are eating or in silk-lined tunnels in or on the soil below the food plants.

69 Pyralid Moths   *Family Pyralídidae*

ADULTS: Beautiful little insects, when closely examined, often called small snout moths because of their conspicuous labial and maxillary palps. Ocelli and proboscis are present. The meal moth, a species often seen in houses, has a very wide, light band across the middle of the dark brown wings and, at rest, holds the tip of the abdomen curved forward over the body.

YOUNG: Almost naked, with reddish-brown heads and gray or light brown bodies. They feed upon living and dead plant tissue, including stored grains and grain products. Pupation occurs in a thin-walled silken cocoon.

IMPORTANCE: The most destructive member of this family is the meal moth, *Pýralis farinàlis,* the larvae of which live in the surface layers of stored grains, webbing the kernels together. Like our example, it also occurs in damp haystacks.

EXAMPLE: Clover Hayworm   *Hypsopýgia costàlis*

A European species, now cosmopolitan and widely distributed in our region. The larvae are especially abundant in damp clover hay, where they feed upon the leaves.

70   Crambid Moths   *Family Crámbidae*

ADULTS: Small, silvery or brownish, long-legged moths, flying at night or at dusk. When flushed from their daytime roosts on grasses they take a short, zigzag flight and quickly alight. The labial palps form a long, forward-directed snout whose length is equal to that of the head and thorax combined. The fore wings are narrow. Ocelli usually are present.

YOUNG: The larvae vary in color from white to dark brown with low, dark, chitinized areas bearing hairs. Some are borers in stems or root bases of grasses and other monocotyledonous plants; others construct silken tunnels between the stems of grasses and feed upon the leaves.

IMPORTANCE: In our region this family is important for numerous grass webworms—pests of lawns and golf greens, and for borers in sugar cane, corn, and sorghums. In the Orient, a rice stem borer, *Chìlo símplex,* a very serious pest, is one of the major reasons for the rigid exclusion of rice straw from the United States.

EXAMPLE 70a: Vagabond Crambus
Crámbus vulgivagéllus

An abundant species throughout the eastern United States on various grasses, occasionally on corn.

EXAMPLE 70b: Sugarcane Borer   *Diatraèa saccharàlis*

Throughout the extreme southern United States, the larvae tunneling and stunting the young stalks of sugar cane, corn, sorghums, and rice. The annual losses sustained by these crops exceed $6,000,000.

71 Phycitid Moths
Family Phycítidae

ADULTS: Generally smaller than those of the preceding family, but, like them, are inconspicuously colored. The palps may curve upward but do not project forward as a "snout." A proboscis may or may not be present. The antennae are long and thread-like.

YOUNG: The larvae tunnel in stems, fruits, and seeds of their food plants, may construct silken tunnels among the florets of flowers, or may live in stored cereals and other foods. Some make elongate, tapering cases, crooked or straight, of silk coated with excrement. Unlike the casebearers of the family Coleophóridae (*61*), these larvae usually secrete themselves, cases and all, between 2 or more leaves webbed together.

IMPORTANCE: This family includes several major stored-product pests: the Mediterranean flour moth, chocolate moth, and raisin moth of the genus *Ephéstia;* several borers in beans in the pod (*Etiélla zinckenélla* and *Fundélla pellùcens*); the cactus moth (*Cactoblástis cactòrum*), a New World species which was exported to Australia and there used successfully to suppress the prickly-pear cactus. The sunflower moth (*Homoeosòma electéllum*), whose dark spotted, greenish caterpillars make silken tunnels among the florets of sunflower, coreopsis, and other composite plants and often tie the outer yellow petals over the "faces" of the flowers, is common throughout the southern two thirds of the United States.

EXAMPLE: Indian-meal Moth   *Plòdia interpunctélla*

One of the world's worst stored-product pests, originating in Europe, now found everywhere in stored grains, cereal products, dried fruits, roots, nuts, chocolate, and museum specimens. The larvae web together the kernels of grain in the surface layer in bins. They are attacked by a tiny wasp which frequently brings them under control.

72 Bagworm Moths
Family Psýchidae

ADULTS: The males lose most of their wing scales shortly after emergence and so usually have transparent wings. They are hairy-bodied with expanded, feathery antennae. Ocelli are absent, and the eyes are small and concealed. There is no proboscis, and the mouth parts are much reduced. The wingless female never leaves the larval case in which she pupated. However, she does perforate the lower end of the pendant cocoon in order to effect union with the male; she then lays a thousand or so flat, overwintering eggs in a mass inside the cocoon and dies.

YOUNG: The case-carrying larvae give this family its popular name. The young larvae weave about themselves an ever-enlarging band of silk to which they attach bits of leaves and leaf petioles. The larva clings to plants with its abdomen dangling, so the case is always in a suspended position. When molting, the larva fastens its case to a leaf or stem with a silken band. The growing insect forces its excrement out of a permanent opening at the bottom of its case. There are 5 larval stages.

IMPORTANCE: Not major pests. Some injury is done to citrus fruit, and young trees of various kinds are almost defoliated at times. Severe outbreaks among shade trees are usually quite localized. The bagworm would seem to be well protected by its sturdy case, but it is susceptible to the attack of many parasitic wasps and flies.

EXAMPLE: Bagworm   *Thyridópteryx ephemeraefórmis*

Generally distributed in the eastern half of our region on many different kinds of broad-leaved and coniferous trees and shrubs.

73 Arctiid Moths   *Family Arctìidae*

This and the remaining families of moths and butterflies are sometimes referred to collectively as the Macrolepidóptera. The "macros" average much larger than the "micros," but size difference alone will not always serve to distinguish them.

ADULTS: Medium to large insects with densely hairy bodies. Our better-known species are white, brown, or orange with darker spots or stripes. Ocelli and tibial spurs are present. The eggs are laid in large clusters on the food plants of the larvae and may be covered with a mat of hairs from the body of the parent.

YOUNG: Some of the larger caterpillars are the well-known "woolly bears" which are densely covered with tufts of hair and which roll up into a flat coil when disturbed. Other species have the webbing habit, the larvae living together in community webs on the foliage of deciduous trees. The winter is passed as a pupa in a light cocoon composed of the larval hairs and a little silk.

IMPORTANCE: The caterpillars of several arctiids feed upon a wide variety of field and garden crops, but their damage is usually minor. The tree-feeding species, particularly the fall webworm, one of our examples, is a great nuisance on broad-leaved shade trees and, if uncontrolled, a serious pest in cherry and pecan orchards.

EXAMPLE 73a: Salt-marsh Caterpillar   *Estigmène acrèa*

Found throughout our region, the larvae being destructive chiefly in the late summer, when they may be seen eating the leaves of almost every kind of field and garden plant.

EXAMPLE 73b: Fall Webworm   *Hyphántria cùnea*

Distributed throughout our region. The adults exhibit 2 distinct color phases, as shown in the illustrations, with much variation in the spotted forms. The pure-white phase predominates in the northern half of the range. The favorite food plant of the gregarious larvae is cherry. As the illustration shows, the web encloses the end of the branch, while the webs of the tent caterpillar, on the other hand, are always in the forks of branches or the crotches of young trees. Periodic outbreaks of fall webworms over very large areas are the rule. They are ordinarily controlled by a great many kinds of parasitic wasps and flies, of which one of the most important is the ichneumon wasp, *Hyposòter pilósulus* (*125b*). Cuckoos are notable feeders upon the larvae.

74 Phalaenid Moths   Family Phalaénidae

The largest family of moths, represented in our region by about 400 genera and more than 2000 species.

ADULTS: Medium to large moths, flying at dusk or at night, and among the most abundant of the insects attracted to lights. The fore wings are mostly somber gray or brown, variously striped, spotted, or mottled. The hind wings are typically paler and almost or entirely without pattern, notable exceptions being the underwing moths of the genus *Catocàla,* which have brightly colored hind wings. The heads are relatively small, with large eyes and long, slender antennae, the bodies stout and hairy, often tufted at the extremities. The almost globular eggs are deposited often in large masses on or near the food plants of the larvae.

YOUNG: Many phalaenid larvae are armyworms or cutworms, important agricultural pests. The former normally feed at night, but during severe outbreaks may migrate by day or night, feeding as they go. They are practically hairless and colored gray, brown, or blackish. A small group of species, represented among our examples by the cabbage looper, have 3 instead of 5 pairs of prolegs, and these are placed toward the posterior end of the body. This leaves the middle of the long, cylindrical body without legs and causes the insects to travel much like the true measuringworms of the family Geométridae (78) by arching their mid-sections, throwing the fore parts ahead, then racing the after legs to reconstruct the arch. They are called "semi-loopers." Cutworms, by day, are mostly in the soil, those that feed upon the aboveground parts of plants doing so at night. Some are completely subterranean, feeding upon roots or stems at or near the ground surface; still others tunnel in stems of wild and cultivated grasses. Larvae of underwing moths feed mostly upon the foliage of various deciduous forest trees.

IMPORTANCE: One of the most destructive groups of insects. Although numerous species feed upon wild grasses and other plants, too many feed upon cultivated ones. The habit of so many cutworm larvae of remaining below the soil surface during the hours of sunlight is a protection against many predators and parasites.

EXAMPLE 74a: Underwing Moth   *Catocàla irène*

A species of California and the intermountain area of the United States. At rest on a lichen-covered tree trunk, the wall of a cave mouth, or under a projecting rock ledge, these moths are almost invisible. The beautiful colors of the hind wings are flashed only during flight. Underwings are favorite prizes of many who go "sugaring" for moths on summer nights.

EXAMPLE 74b: Cabbage Looper   *Trichoplùsia nì*

A native species found throughout our region. The insect winters as a pupa in a loose cocoon attached to the food plant. An abundant, serious, and easily recognized pest of cabbage and related crucifers; occasionally attacking potato, tomato, and other plants.

EXAMPLE 74c: Black Cutworm   *Agròtis ýpsilon*

Generally distributed and cosmopolitan. One of the worst cutworm species, the larvae apparently delighting in toppling young plants. Field crops, including corn, are affected, especially in low-lying areas. Potato, tomato, and many different truck and garden plants are attacked. Under laboratory conditions, the average black cutworm larva has been found to consume about 65 square inches of corn foliage during its entire developmental period.

EXAMPLE 74d: Corn Earworm   *Heliòthis armígera*

One of the most serious of all pests of corn—the naked, brownish, pinkish, greenish, or almost black caterpillars which so often greet the eye of the housewife when she is removing the husks from ears of sweet corn. The illustration shows the corn earworm larva in typical pose. This species also attacks tomato, potato, cotton, and tobacco plants and goes by such names as tomato fruitworm, cotton bollworm, and tobacco budworm when discovered on those plants.

75 Prominents   *Family Notodóntidae*

ADULTS: Resembling phalaenids of medium size but with smaller hind wings and very much hairier bodies. There are also conspicuous tufts of hair on the rear margins of the wings which become prominent when the wings are folded over the back. The legs, especially the femora, are covered with long hairs. Their furry appearance is responsible for the common name of "puss moth," more widely used in Europe. At rest upon the bark of a tree, these grotesque insects are remarkably well camouflaged. They are night flyers, frequently coming to porch lights.

YOUNG: Gregarious, often brilliantly colored caterpillars, hump-backed, sometimes with spiny tubercles or sparsely scattered hairs. There are 4 pairs of prolegs at the middle of the body; the anal pair of prolegs is sometimes very much reduced and non-functional or is absent. Pupation occurs in a simple cell in the soil, or in a light cocoon among fallen leaves or other ground litter.

IMPORTANCE: Occasionally pests of orchard trees, especially apple, walnut, and plum. The larvae also feed upon the foliage of many kinds of broad-leaved forest and shade trees.

EXAMPLE: Yellow-necked Caterpillar *Datàna minístra*

Widespread in our region, particularly in the northern half of the United States and in Canada. The larvae prefer the leaves of oak, hickory, beech, and birch.

76 Tussock Moths and Allies *Family Lymantrìidae*

ADULTS: The females are hairy and may have wings too small for flight. The males are all fully winged and hairy, especially upon the legs. The antennae of the males are remarkably developed and may be described as being doubly combed on one side rather than feather-like. The eggs, in large masses, covered with matted hairs from the body of the female, are laid upon the cocoon from which the flightless insects have issued, or in other species, upon the foliage or bark of the host tree. The winter is passed in the egg stage by the tussock moths and by the young larvae of the brown-tail moth, another member of this family.

YOUNG: Hairy, some of the hairs being arranged in tufts. In the common genus *Hemerocámpa,* there is a dorsal row of erect "shaving brush" tufts, which are quite distinctive. The larvae of a few species in this family have barbed hairs connected with poison glands, and one must handle them with care to avoid a violent rash.

IMPORTANCE: This family includes the infamous gypsy moth (*Porthètria díspar*), which feeds very generally on deciduous and evergreen trees and shrubs, and the brown-tail moth (*Nŷgmia phaeorrhoèa*), a pest of deciduous shade and orchard trees. Both are European species, accidentally introduced into Massachusetts in the last century. The former first appeared in 1867 and did not become a serious pest for 20 years. Both are confined at present to New England by means of stringent quarantines and intensive control measures. The larvae of the fir tussock moth (*Hemerocámpa pseudotsugàta*) are serious pests of Douglas fir in several northwestern states.

EXAMPLE: White-marked Tussock Moth
Hemerocámpa leucostígma

A native species, present from British Columbia and Colorado eastward and southeastward to the Atlantic and Gulf coasts. The larvae feed on a wide variety of broad-leaved trees and are primarily shade-tree pests, but are occasionally a nuisance in orchards. The females are entirely wingless.

77 Sphinx Moths   *Family Sphíngidae*

ADULTS: Swift-flying, hairy-bodied moths with long, narrow, rather pointed fore wings, which may span 5 inches and are much longer than the hind, and stout bodies tapered fore and aft. The eyes are large and the proboscis is often remarkably long and fitted for extracting the nectar from the depths of tubular flowers such as petunias. They are excellent flyers, difficult to capture in a net, and said to be capable of 35 miles an hour. Some are day flyers, but most are active at dusk or after dark. Frequently they are mistaken for hummingbirds because of their large size and their habit of hovering before flowers with wings vibrating so rapidly as to be invisible. Some of the smaller "hawk moths," as they are sometimes called, have almost scaleless, transparent wings and so suggest the clear-wing moths of the family Aegerìidae (*64*), from which their heavier bodies, pointed fore wings, which do not form a tight union with the hind wings, and their inconspicuous legs will distinguish them.

YOUNG: The large, green larvae usually have a long, pointed horn or spur atop the eighth abdominal segment and so are called "hornworms." This horn is not poisonous and is quite harmless. The markings most often consist of a pattern of oblique white stripes on the sides. The fore part of the body is raised and held rigid when the insect is disturbed, the entire aspect becoming somewhat sphinx-like. Pupation takes place in a cell in the soil or in a light cocoon among leaves and rubbish on the ground surface. Some, but not all, sphinx moth pupae have the proboscis arched away from the body like the handle of a teacup.

IMPORTANCE: The moths are effective pollinators of plants, especially cultivated species. The larvae, sometimes rather general feeders, are more often restricted as to food plants. They are only minor pests of cultivated plants, tomato and tobacco being the most frequently attacked of garden and field crops; it is sometimes necessary to take control measures. The larvae are attacked by numerous parasitic wasps and flies.

EXAMPLE: Tomato Hornworm
Protopárce quinquemaculàta

Occurs throughout our region. *Apánteles congregàtus,* a braconid wasp, is the chief parasite and an effective one. The small white cocoons of this little wasp commonly are seen adhering by dozens to the skins of the dying larvae. Crows have been known to rid tomato patches of hornworms—but it is safer to hand-pick the insects than to attract birds to fruiting tomato plants.

78 Geometrid Moths   *Family Geométridae*

ADULTS: Rather small and delicate, slender-bodied moths, several species of which have wingless, or nearly wingless, robust females. They fly at dusk or night and often come to lights. The wing margins are sometimes angular or scalloped, and the patterns of these predominantly gray or brown moths consist of a simple or complex array of fine, zigzag, or wavy parallel lines. The eggs are quite variable in shape but are more frequently flattish and laid in large clusters of from 100 to 400 upon the bark, stems, or leaves of the food plants.

YOUNG: The true measuringworms, usually with only 2 pairs of prolegs (including the anal claspers) at the posterior end of the body. They travel with a looping movement much more pronounced than that of the semi-loopers of the family Phalaénidae. When frightened they may retain their grasp with

the prolegs and extend the fore part of the body rigidly outward at about a 45-degree angle from a branch and so resemble a twig, their colors aiding in the deception. Other
larvae when alarmed will drop from the leaf they have been
eating, at the end of a long silk thread spun from the mouth,
and, in ascending this thread after danger has passed, wind it
about the hind thoracic legs with the aid of mouth parts and
fore legs.

IMPORTANCE: The more important economic species are the
spring and fall cankerworms, which feed upon foliage and
fruit of orchard trees and the foliage of many broad-leaved
shade trees. Periodic increases in the number of cankerworms
sometimes result in the near defoliation of shade trees and
unsprayed orchards. There is considerable evidence to support the prevalent belief that the finding of a measuringworm
on one's person presages new raiment.

EXAMPLE 78a: Fall Cankerworm   *Alsóphila pometària*

Occurs throughout the northern United States and southern
Canada and in New Mexico and California, attacking the
fresh foliage of wild and cultivated fruit trees, elm, and
many other trees in May and June. Most of the moths emerge
in the fall and lay eggs which overwinter, but some hibernate
as pupae in thin, tough cocoons in the soil and emerge in the
spring with the adults of the true spring cankerworm
(*Paleácrita vernàta*).

EXAMPLE 78b: Raspberry Spanworm   *Synchlòra aeràta*

Distributed throughout the eastern United States. This is one
of the species whose larva attaches fragments of flowers or
foliage to its body. It feeds upon apple, willow, and yarrow
as well as raspberry.

79 Tent Caterpillars   *Family Lasiocámpidae*

ADULTS: Medium-sized, robust, very hairy moths, mostly reddish-brown, with simple wing patterns. The legs and even the
eyes are hairy. The antennae of both sexes are feathery. The
egg masses, which are laid on twigs of the trees whose foliage
will provide food for the caterpillars, are covered with a thick,

brown, foamy crust. The winter is passed as tiny larvae within the eggs.

YOUNG: Rather brightly colored, hairy, living gregariously inside large, many-layered webs in the forks of tree branches. The leaves of many different broad-leaved trees are eaten. The webs of tent caterpillars sometimes are confused with those of the fall webworm—the latter, however, are always at the branch tips, not at the forks. When fully grown the larvae wander about seeking protected places in which to spin their flimsy, silken cocoons.

IMPORTANCE: Tent caterpillars periodically build up huge populations over large areas. Their webs are unsightly, and trees may be almost or completely defoliated and young fruit destroyed. However, artificial control, either in forest, orchard, or dooryard, is not difficult. In fact, the presence of large webs on shade or fruit trees usually may be taken as a sign of laziness on the part of the owner, for it is so easy to destroy them. Tent caterpillars have many natural enemies. Many different parasitic wasps and flies and predacious beetles attack them. While hairy caterpillars usually are thought to be eschewed by birds, the yellow- and black-billed cuckoos are notoriously fond of tent caterpillars, and more than 40 other birds eat them too.

EXAMPLE: Eastern Tent Caterpillar
Malacosòma americàna

Throughout the United States and southern Canada east of the Rocky Mountains, and in scattered small areas in California. The egg mass of this species completely encircles the twig. The favorite food trees are wild cherry, apple, and plum.

80 Saturnid Moths   *Family Satúrnidae*

ADULTS: Very large insects with hairy bodies and wing bases. In many species each fore and hind wing has a small, transparent area or "window." The antennae are feather-like in the males, less so in the females. One of the very largest of all lepidopterons is a south Asian saturnid called the "Atlas moth," with a wingspread exceeding 10 inches. This family is often called the "giant silkworms" because in the Orient and even in South America certain species are more or less domesticated and the cocoons used to produce silk. Our species do not take nourishment, the mouth parts being much reduced.

YOUNG: Usually naked, sometimes with spiny tubercles of various lengths and shapes, and exceeding in size the largest hornworms (77). The cocoons, constructed of usable silk, are attached to twigs or leaves of the host plants, so that the pupae winter either on the tree or, more often, among the dead leaves on the ground.

IMPORTANCE: The larvae are seldom numerous enough to damage seriously the trees they feed upon. Indeed, it is almost necessary to protect them in towns and cities, where the conspicuous cocoons may be regularly pruned out of trees and shrubs by caretakers and boys. Leaders for fishing lines have been produced from the silk glands of the mature larvae of our examples. The larvae and pupae of the pandora moth (*Coloràdia pandòra*) are still dried and then stewed or roasted for food by Indians of the southwestern United States. This insect often defoliates large areas of ponderosa pine forests from the Rocky Mountains to the Pacific coast. The pupae are dug out of the soil and eaten by squirrels and other rodents. Night-flying saturnids are taken by screech owls; the others are attacked by a wide variety of birds.

This family is very closely related to the *Bombýcidae*, which contains the Chinese silkworm (*Bómbyx mòri*), an insect that after thousands of years of domestication exists nowhere in nature. Observations by the Italian biologist Bassi, in 1837, upon a malady of silkworms caused by the protozoön *Nosèma bómbycis* are believed to have been the basis for the germ theory of disease.

EXAMPLE 80a: Cecropia Moth   *Sàmia cecròpia*

Our largest moth, often called the "emperor," is common almost everywhere east of the Rocky Mountains. The larva feeds on maple, apple, elm, wild cherry, and many other broad-leaved trees and shrubs. The big, brown, somewhat spindle-shaped cocoon, attached by one side to a twig, is conspicuous in winter. Blue jays and some woodpeckers have beaks powerful enough to penetrate the tough cocoons and reach the tasty pupae. Phil Rau found that the males of this species fly to their mates during the space of an hour at dawn (3:30 to 4:40 A.M. at St. Louis), and that they are attracted, apparently, by the odor of the female. In experiments with marked males, which he liberated at various distances from caged females, the sex odor brought in moths 3 miles away.

EXAMPLE 80b: Luna Moth   *Tropaèa lùna*

Probably the people's choice for the most beautiful moth of our region. It occurs east of the Rocky Mountains, from southern Canada southward. The larvae prefer the foliage of walnut, birch, beech, willow, oak, and hickory. Their cocoons are attached to the leaves and so fall to the ground with the approach of cold weather.

The regal and imperial moths (*Citherònia regàlis* and *Èacles imperiàlis*) and a few close relatives are sometimes placed in the Satúrnidae, but more often are considered to constitute a separate family, the Citheronìidae, or the "royal moths." The species named are large, hairy-bodied moths, lacking transparent areas in the wings. The larvae always have a spine on the dorsal mid-line of the ninth abdominal segment never found in the larvae of saturnids.

81 Skippers   *Family Hesperìidae*

This, the first family of butterflies, has more features in common with moths than does any succeeding one. The chief distinctions between moths and butterflies have been pointed out in the description of the order Lepidóptera.

ADULTS: Mostly small butterflies, seldom reaching 1½ inches in wing expanse. The antennae, wider apart at the base than those of other butterflies, are filaments, thickened but never knobbed at the ends, with a short, hooked tip whose point is directed backward. Skippers are hairy on the body, on much of the wing surface, and over part of the eye. The hind tibiae are almost always spurred. At rest, the fore wings are usually held in a vertical position while the hind ones are partly spread.

The bodies are more robust than those of most butterflies. The flight is erratic, typically close to the ground, and well described as "skipping." The hemispherical eggs are laid singly on the food plants of the larvae.

YOUNG: The very large bulbous head of the larva is separated by a much-constricted neck from the naked body, which is thickest in the middle and tapered toward both ends. Easily distinguished from larvae of any other lepidopterous family. They frequently make "nests" by sewing together the edges of a leaf or 2 or more entire leaves with silk. Cultivated and wild grasses and legumes are the favored food plants. The overwintering pupa is suspended upside down in a light cocoon to which are attached leaves or other vegetable debris.

IMPORTANCE: As a group the family is unimportant economically, for skippers are seldom numerous enough to be pests. Our example, however, sometimes injures locust foliage rather severely.

EXAMPLE 81a: Silver-spotted Skipper   *Protèides clàrus*

Occurs quite generally from southern Canada southward in both forests and fields, but especially abundant about *Wistària* and black locust (*Robínia pseudocàcia*), on which the nocturnal larvae prefer to feed.

EXAMPLE 81b: Fawny-edged Skipper
Polìtes themístocles

Ranges from southern Canada southward, east of the Rocky Mountains. The larvae feed on grasses.

82 Swallowtails   *Family Papiliónidae*

These are our largest butterflies, and, except for South America, where the morpho and owl butterflies (*Calìgo*) exceed them, they are the largest in any other faunal region. Two species range north of the Arctic Circle in Alaska, and no part of our region is without its species.

ADULTS: All are large and brightly colored, with 2, 3, or no tail-like extensions on each hind wing. The head is rather large, with the antennae arising very close together. Swallowtails are day flyers like all butterflies and are visitors at flowers, being especially attracted to thistle and to butterfly weed (*Asclèpias tuberòsa*), the orange-flowered milkweed that so many butterflies prefer. They also gather at rotten fruit and seem to glory in ripe carcasses. One genus, *Parnássius*, is composed of mountaintop species, white, tailless butterflies with gray mottlings.

YOUNG: Large, smooth-skinned caterpillars, with the thoracic segments somewhat swollen, and in some species bearing eye-spots. A forked, malodorous retractile organ can be thrust out from an opening in the first thoracic segment just back of the head. The naked, angular pupa, the hibernating stage, which may have a conspicuous dorsal protuberance in the center of the third thoracic segment, is attached to its resting place by a silken plate at the end of the body and by a band of silk about its middle.

IMPORTANCE: Excepting the species which feed on citrus foliage and those which live on garden and field vegetables of the parsnip family (*Umbellíferae*), the caterpillars are seldom abundant enough to be of economic importance.

EXAMPLE: Zebra Swallowtail *Iphiclìdes marcéllus*

Found throughout eastern North America from early spring until late fall, there being 2 to 4 broods, according to latitude. The larvae feed on pawpaw foliage.

83 Pierid Butterflies *Family Piéridae*

ADULTS: Of about average butterfly size, orange, yellow, or white, often with dark wing margins, spots, or mottlings—our most familiar butterflies, frequenting the open fields and roadsides and characteristically gathering in dry weather on the exposed mud of ditches and streams. The fore and hind wings are more nearly the same size, and the latter are more nearly circular in outline than those of most other butterflies. The eyes are not hairy. Color differences between the sexes are many and often striking, and seasonal color variations between broods are the rule. The eggs are reticulate, elongate, and tapered at each end; they are laid singly or in small clusters or rows upon the larval food plants.

YOUNG: Mostly slender, naked-looking greenish or whitish caterpillars with longitudinal stripes, either darker or lighter than the ground color. Actually there are numerous small hairs (setae) and sometimes tubercles with hairs. The common species are present from early spring to late fall and may have from 2 to 5 annual generations. The pupae hibernate.

IMPORTANCE: The 2 examples are the most important economic species of the Piéridae in our region; together they destroy an estimated 20 per cent of the cabbage and cauliflower production of the United States. In Idaho and some other northwestern states, the pine butterfly (*Neophàsia menàpia*) periodically defoliates pine trees over extensive areas.

EXAMPLE 83a: Imported Cabbageworm   *Pìeris ràpae*

Apparently introduced from Europe into the neighborhood of Quebec in 1860; now established throughout our region. It is especially a pest of cabbage and cauliflower but feeds on other cultivated plants of the mustard family. The female of this species has 2 black dots on each fore wing, the male only 1. This "English sparrow" among butterflies is said largely to have displaced the native southern cabbageworm (*Pìeris protódice*) over much of its range. The males of certain butterflies, especially of this example, exhibit considerable aggressiveness toward both the males and females of other species, and by persistently annoying them drive them out of suitable breeding areas.

EXAMPLE 83b: Alfalfa Caterpillar
                                    Còlias philódice eurýtheme

One of the sulphur butterflies; found throughout North America. The larvae are serious pests of alfalfa, particularly in the West, but they also feed on clovers and some other legumes.

84 Milkweed Butterflies   *Family Danàidae*

ADULTS: This small family is represented by but 2 large and beautiful species in our region—the widespread monarch, our example, and the queen (*Dánaus berenìce*), which occurs in the southwestern United States. The monarch is remarkable for congregating in enormous numbers and migrating en masse to the extreme south of the United States and even on to the West Indies and Central and South America, where they hibernate. The following spring they straggle northward to lay their eggs on various species of milkweed (*Asclèpias*). What appears to be a dark swelling on a vein just below the center of each hind wing of the male butterfly is a patch of scent scales which emit an odor attractive to the opposite sex.

YOUNG: The smooth-skinned monarch caterpillars, found in small groups on milkweeds, are greenish-yellow, ringed with many narrow black bands. A pair of long, soft, fleshy filaments on top of the body near either end are lashed about when the caterpillars are disturbed. The pupa is naked, green with beautiful golden spots, and hangs from a leaf of the host plant by the prolonged tip of the abdomen, which is fastened to a plate of silk.

IMPORTANCE: None economically

EXAMPLE: Monarch Butterfly   *Dánaus plexíppus*

Breeds throughout our region on various kinds of milkweeds. They congregate in the fall and migrate southward, roosting at night in selected trees like flocks of birds. In winter quarters they are active but continue to stay in close company, congregating on cool, cloudy days and at night in chosen trees which, of course, in southern California and Florida are designated "butterfly trees." The viceroy butterfly (*Basilárchia archíppus*), a member of the family Nymphálidae (*86*), resembles the monarch so closely that it is thought by some to mimic it. The fact that the monarch is distasteful to birds might be a protection to the succulent viceroy if birds actually confuse them. However, it cannot be asserted with safety that the viceroy is a mimic; the similarity could be coincidental. This originally New World species has spread by ship to Hawaii, most of the islands of the Pacific, and to the coastal areas of western Europe.

85 Satyrs   *Family Satýridae*

ADULTS: The satyrs or wood-nymphs are a homogeneous group of about 60 species in our region, mostly about the size of the imported cabbageworm butterfly (*83a*). They are brownish or gray, with conspicuous eyespots near the outer margins of both fore and hind wings. The large veins of the fore wings have distinct swellings at their bases—this is a distinguishing character of the family. Some satyrs live at or above timber line on the highest mountain peaks and some occur above the Arctic Circle. They prefer shade, as their name suggests, and are found in open woods or along woods' borders. The females leave the shade at times to fly low over adjoining meadows and lay eggs upon grasses and sedges.

YOUNG: The greenish or brownish larvae are easily recognized by the combination of smooth skin with a "forked tail," the anal prolegs being long and divergent. Their heads may be deeply notched from above, horned, or plain. The only other caterpillars with bifurcated extremities belong to the genera *Chlorippe* and *Opsiphanes* of the family Nymphálidae (*86*) and are spiny on the skin behind the head as well as on the head itself. Satyr larvae are thickest at the middle and tapered toward either end. They feed on grasses and sedges and pupate suspended by the tail from the food plant or loosely among roots and debris at the bases of the plants.

IMPORTANCE: Our species are purely things of beauty, but in the Orient 2 members of this family are pests of bamboo, sugar cane, and other cereal grasses.

EXAMPLE: Grayling   *Minòis álope*

Distributed throughout our region. The species occurs in several varietal forms which sometimes have their own common names. The larva, a grass feeder, is green with 2 pale side stripes. The head is without horns.

86 Nymphalid Butterflies   *Family Nymphálidae*

This, numerically, is our largest butterfly family.

ADULTS: In both sexes, the fore legs are very much reduced and not fitted for walking—a distinguishing feature of the family. In the males, the fore legs may be brush-like, in the females comb-like. The names "brush-footed" and "4-footed" butterflies are sometimes applied to this family. The antennae are more distinctly knobbed than those of most other butterflies. The mourning cloak, painted lady, and buckeye are among the better-known species which have not been illustrated. Most nymphalids are of average butterfly size or larger, and a few are about as large as the monarch (*84*). There is tremendous variety in coloring, patterns, and wing outlines. The often-pictured dead leaf butterfly (*Doleschállia*) of India, which with wings closed does resemble a leaf, is a nymphalid. The eggs are scattered singly or in small clusters on the leaf surfaces of the larval food plants.

YOUNG: The larvae are most frequently spiny, but some are smooth-skinned; they never occur together in large numbers. The naked warty pupae, frequently with silver or gold markings, hang head downward, attached by the tail to the food plant.

IMPORTANCE: Not important economically. Butterflies, and moths as well, soon after leaving the pupal shell, void a large drop of liquid excrement; this may occur in the air, and the color of the drop in some species may be red. The marvelous "red rains" which are mentioned in both modern and ancient European writings, and which led variously to fear, repentance, and even massacre, probably were caused by nymphalid butterflies issuing simultaneously in great numbers.

EXAMPLE 86a: Red Admiral   *Vanéssa atalánta*

Abundant and generally distributed over our region and much of the world. The larvae feed on the leaves of hops and nettles. This species hibernates as an adult or a pupa.

EXAMPLE 86b: Regal Fritillary   *Speyèria idàlia*

A fairly common fritillary in the eastern United States, the adults prefering woods' borders. The orange-marked larvae have 6 longitudinal rows of thick spines. They feed by night on the foliage of ironweed, violet, goldenrod, and various other composites. The winter is passed as an egg or first-stage caterpillar.

EXAMPLE 86c: Question Mark   *Polygònia interrogatiònis*

This species, which is found throughout our region with the exception of the Pacific Coast, is the largest of a genus of nymphalids known as the angle-wings—characterized by the very irregular wing outlines. The angle-wings hibernate as adults in cavities in trees and other sheltered places.

EXAMPLE 86d: Pearl Crescent   *Phyciòdes thàros*

One of the crescent-spots, occurring everywhere in our region except on the California coast. The larvae feed in groups on asters and other composites. This species hibernates in the larval stage.

87 Blues, Coppers, and Hairstreaks *Family Lycaénidae*

ADULTS: Mostly small butterflies, with wingspreads ranging from ¾ inch to 1½ inches; brightly colored, sometimes with iridescent blue and green scales. The eyes are conspicuously bordered by white scales, and the antennae are ringed with alternating white and dark bands of scales. The hind wings of the species known collectively as the "hairstreaks" have 1 or 2 pairs of minute tails. These beautiful insects prefer open, sunny situations and dance through the air only a few inches above the ground. They may be approached quite closely when at rest or drinking on the mud or moist sand by a stream or pond. The eggs are laid singly on the larval food plants.

YOUNG: The larvae are almost oval in outline and resemble slugs. They may be smooth or covered with a velvety coating of short hairs. The legs are very short, and the small head can be greatly extended or retracted on the slender neck. Some lycaenid larvae are predacious upon aphids and scale insects (*46, 47*); others begin life as plant feeders and later are carried by ants into the nests, where they feed upon ant larvae, holding the favor of their hosts the while by secreting from a gland on top of the tenth body segment a sweet substance much relished by ants. The majority of larvae are plant feeders, preferring legumes, but at least one species feeds on pine. The winter is usually passed as a pupa.

IMPORTANCE: The hairstreak larvae which feed on cultivated legumes and cotton squares are rather minor pests. The species which feed upon aphids and scale insects might be considered beneficial, but their effect is probably small.

EXAMPLE 87a: Spring Azure *Lycaenópsis pseudargìolus*

One of the "blues"; generally distributed in our region and ranging into Alaska. Also occurring in much of the north temperate area of the world. This is one of the species which has been observed to attract ants by the secretion of a honey-like fluid from a gland on top of the tenth body segment.

(The function of 2 pairs of fleshy, bristly organs which can be protruded from tiny pockets near the honey gland is not understood.)

EXAMPLE 87b: American Copper *Lycaèna hypophlaèa*

Generally distributed north of the Gulf states. The larva feeds on sorrel (*Rùmex acetosélla*). The winter is passed as a pupa under rocks or ground litter.

EXAMPLE 87c: Great Purple Hairstreak *Átlides halèsus*

This largest of the hairstreaks occurs throughout the southern half of the United States, having spread northward from Central America and Mexico. The larvae eat mistletoe leaves.

EXAMPLE 87d: Cotton Square Borer *Strỳmon melìnus*

A hairstreak common throughout the United States; rare in Canada. The larva feeds on the flowers and green fruits of beans, hops, the young bolls (squares) of cotton and on numerous other plants. It is one of the few pest lycaenids. The extensible "neck" of the green, slug-like caterpillar permits it to feed upon a developing bean through a small hole in the pod that would not admit the entire insect.

BEETLES
Order Coleóptera

The adults of this order are easily identified by the hard, veinless fore wings, or elytra (singular—elytron), which meet in a straight line over the abdomen. The fore wings do not function directly as flight organs but serve as a protective covering for the membranous hind wings, which are folded below them. The mouth parts are for biting and chewing and usually are well developed. The compound eyes are prominent as a rule, and ocelli generally are wanting.

Beetles live in almost every conceivable kind of habitat. They are predacious on insects and other small invertebrates, feeders on carrion, dead vegetable matter, and dung; the most important species, economically, feed on living plants, stored food products, woods, or fabrics. Development is complex (complete metamorphosis), there being a pupal stage in all species. The larvae differ greatly in appearance and generally in habit from the adults; some of them have cerci. The pupal appendages usually are free from the body.

Some 23,000 species of beetles have been described from our region and more than 250,000 from the whole world, making the order Coleóptera easily the largest in number of species.

88 Tiger Beetles   *Family Cicindélidae*

ADULTS: Handsome, mostly swift-running beasts of prey, averaging about ½ inch long; frequenters of the shores of streams, lakes, or seas, barren ground, and woodland trails. The diurnal species are quick to take flight and rather difficult for the unpracticed to capture. The head with its large eyes is considerably broader than the neck-like first thoracic segment. The 11-segmented antennae are simple, thread-like, and arise just above the bases of the mandibles, which are large and powerful and move in the vertical plane. The legs are rather long, with 5-segmented tarsi and a large spur at the apical end of each tibia. These insects are often brilliantly colored with metallic greens and purples and attractively patterned, sometimes with the stripings which probably suggested the popular name of the family. Our commoner species are sun-loving, but some are nocturnal. The eggs are laid singly in the soil.

YOUNG: The larvae, locally called "doodlebugs," looking as though their powerfully jawed heads were on upside down, lie in wait for their insect prey with their great heads closing the burrow entrances like real pitfalls. These burrows may be several feet in depth, are usually in hard-packed earth, and are widely scattered or grouped in small "colonies," according to the species. On top of the fifth abdominal segment is a stout projection with hooks which assists the insect in moving up and down the cylindrical shaft and prevents its being dragged out by a struggling victim. The winter is passed in the second or third (final) larval stage, and 1 or 2 years may be required for a generation. The insect pupates in the burrow after closing the entrance hole.

IMPORTANCE: Predacious as larvae and adults on many different kinds of insects and other small invertebrates, but not numerous enough or sufficiently selective in choice of food to be important natural control factors for any particular kind of insect. Tiger beetles are not greatly troubled by natural enemies so far as we know.

EXAMPLE 88a: Six-spotted Tiger Beetle
Cicindèla sexguttàta

A woods-inhabiting form, hunting on paths and sand bars throughout our region. The ground color of this insect varies from brilliant green to blue. There may be from 0 to 5 white dots on each fore wing.

EXAMPLE 88b: Tiger Beetle *Amblycheìla cylindrifórmis*

This striking insect inhabits western Kansas and the plains of Colorado. The adults are nocturnal, slow-moving, and flightless, the fore wings being fused together and the hind wings atrophied. Before its nocturnal habits were known, this beetle was thought to be a great rarity and sold for $15 to $20 a specimen.

89 Ground Beetles   *Family Carábidae*

ADULTS: Elongate, flattened beetles with slender legs adapted for running rapidly over the ground and climbing over low vegetation or into trees. The head, which is narrower than the thorax, lies in the horizontal plane and bears generally large, powerful mandibles. The carabids are mostly predacious on other insects, earthworms, snails, or almost any small animal that they can hold and subdue with their jaws, but some are at least partially plant-feeding. Many ground beetles tear their prey apart and devour it piecemeal; others inject a powerful fluid into the body of the struggling victim which first paralyzes it and then commences to digest its tissues so they may be imbibed in liquid form. The eyes of carabids are relatively small, and those species which inhabit caves may lack them altogether. The antennae are thread-like and 11-segmented. These beetles feed mostly by night upon the ground, searching under rocks and debris or in the soil itself for food. Some species climb trees to seek out the caterpillars of moths, butterflies, and other beetles. In the species of the genus *Brachìnus* and in some others, a pungent, volatile liquid is explosively discharged from glands opening near the anus with a slight popping sound. The liquid quickly changes to a tiny cloud of ill-smelling and irritating vapor and may be a rather effective defense against some easily discouraged enemies. These insects are aptly called "bombardier beetles." In most species the adults hibernate. Adult carabids sometimes live for several years. The eggs usually are laid singly in shallow pits in the soil made with the ovipositor of the female, or in small cells of dried mud on foliage, rocks, or other objects aboveground.

YOUNG: Carabid larvae live on or in the ground and are almost exclusively predacious, but a few are known to be parasitic upon other insects. The large head usually bears 6 ocelli on each side and a pair of 4-segmented antennae. The tubular ninth abdominal segment bears a pair of cerci. Some of the larvae are well-armored above, the thick, chitinous plate which covers each segment extending some distance laterally like the eaves of a roof. Pupation usually takes place in a cell in the soil. There are 3 larval stages, and in most species only 1 year is required for development from egg to adult.

IMPORTANCE: Ground beetles probably are at least as important as lady beetles (*106*) as destroyers of noxious insects. In most instances the exact amount of pest control that can be attributed to the ground beetles has not been studied and is therefore unknown. A few species have been observed to feed on fruits and seeds and even leaf tissue, and others, in response to thirst, may be driven to feed on the juices of fruits, but they never are a serious problem as plant feeders. Carabid adults are eaten by larger ground-feeding birds, such as the crow, robin, and grackle, and insectivorous rodents; the odorous species do not seem to be eschewed by predators.

EXAMPLE 89a: Fiery Searcher   *Calosòma scrutàtor*

Occurring throughout most of our region. One of our largest and most beautiful beetles. Belonging to a genus of beetles known as the "caterpillar hunters," it destroys large numbers of hairy tent caterpillars. A European species, *C. sycophánta,* intentionally introduced into New England to combat the gypsy moth, feeds on all kinds of lepidopterous larvae and upon the larvae and pupae of sawflies. The larvae of this species also climb trees to eat gypsy moth caterpillars. The fiery searcher, if handled carelessly, will emit copious quantities of a blistering juice, which probably is the reason for the word "fiery" in its name.

EXAMPLE 89b: Ground Beetle   *Pasímachus depréssus*

Widely distributed in the United States east of the Rocky Mountains. You will find this impressive-looking beetle, black with blue-margined fore wings and thorax, under rocks or logs. It likewise is a caterpillar hunter, destroying many night-feeding armyworms and cutworms.

EXAMPLE 89c: Ground Beetle   *Lèbia grándis*

Occurs throughout the eastern United States and southern Canada under stones, logs, and trash. In appearance it very closely resembles the bombardier beetles mentioned previously.

EXAMPLE 89d: Ground Beetle   *Hárpalus caliginòsus*

Ranges almost everywhere in our region, being one of the commonest of the larger ground beetles. The larva builds a tunnel several inches long with a descending shaft and side passage and closes the opening with a mound of loose soil.

90 Predacious Diving Beetles   *Family Dytíscidae*

This is the largest family of aquatic beetles.

ADULTS: Somewhat oval, flattish, usually dark, shiny beetles which may be found suspended head downward in the water of a pond, with the posterior tip of the body, which bears 2 large breathing pores (spiracles), protruding above the surface film. A supply of air is carried under the hard fore wings when the insect dives. The hind legs, which are much the longest, have flat, short tibiae and 5-segmented tarsi bearing long hairs which aid in swimming. The antennae are comparatively long and thread-like; the eyes are large and usually round, placed at the outer margins of the head. These insects can emit a fluid from glands at the front and after ends of the body which is probably distasteful to fishes and other potential enemies. Dytiscids are good flyers and frequently come to lights at night, when they may be seeking another pond or stream in which to establish themselves. The eggs are usually inserted singly into the tissues of water plants. There is 1 generation a year, but adults may live more than a year, passing the winter buried in the mud.

YOUNG: Predacious and cannabalistic, aquatic insects, sometimes called "water-tigers." They feed differently from the adults, taking only liquid food, which they suck through a groove on the inner side of each long, curved mandible. Like many ground beetle larvae, these inject a digestive juice into their prey to make possible the ingestion of more body tissue in liquid form. Dytiscid larvae are crawlers on lake and stream

bottoms, but can swim. Long hairs on the last 2 abdominal
segments enable them to cling to the surface film while ob-
taining air. Most dytiscid larvae have no gills. Although adult
and larva are both aquatic, the pupal period is passed inside
a cell in the soil or in an earthen cell under a stone or log,
away from the water. The larvae can partially regenerate
severed appendages with succeeding molts and can do a complete job of replacement at pupation.

IMPORTANCE: Principally feeders on other aquatic insects, but
attacking all sorts of other animals, including snails, mussels,
salamanders, tadpoles, and small fishes. Losses in fish hatch-
eries are sometimes severe. In the Orient, certain of the
adults are used as human food and medicine. Dytiscid eggs
are parasitized by at least 4 species of tiny wasps which enter
the water to find them. Several species of thread worms
parasitize the larvae. The adults are attacked by mites and
eaten by ducks, such as the teals, the wood duck, mallard,
and pintail, and by fishes, frogs, salamanders, and turtles.

EXAMPLE: Predacious Diving Beetle *Dytíscus marginàlis*
Widespread in our region; also in England.

91 Whirligig Beetles *Family Gyrínidae*

ADULTS: Black, oval, aquatic beetles, more flattened, especially
at the margins, than the adults of the preceding family. They
cruise about in circular courses on fresh-water surfaces in
groups of a few or even hundreds of individuals and, when
sufficiently alarmed, may cease their excited gyrations and
dive to the bottom to hide. Most species prefer quiet water,
some choose running water; all prefer the shade on bright
days and occasionally crawl out of the water to rest on sticks
and rocks. One of their most distinctive structural features
is the possession of what appear to be 2 pairs of compound
eyes. Actually, each eye is divided by the lateral margin of
the head into a dorsal portion and a ventral, submerged
portion. The antennae are quite short and thick. The slender,
grasping fore legs are much the longest; the short, wide
middle and hind legs, the ones used in swimming, are scarcely
visible from above. Adult gyrinids can give off a milky fluid,
probably protective in function, which is usually described as

having an odor of ripe apples. They are chiefly scavengers, feeding on the bodies of insects which fall into the water. The eggs are laid end to end in rows upon submerged vegetation. There is but 1 generation a year. The winter is passed as an adult.

Young: Aquatic, each abdominal segment bearing a pair of tracheal gills. They feed upon fly larvae, the nymphs of damselflies and Mayflies, and other animals, leaving the water to pupate in thin, spindle-shaped cocoons attached to rocks or vegetation.

Importance: Like practically all other aquatic insects, these figure in the diets of fishes and water birds.

Example: Whirligig Beetle   *Dineùtes americànus*

This is one of the species having an apple odor. It is generally distributed in our region.

92 Water Scavenger Beetles and Allies
Family Hydrophílidae

Adults: Aquatic or terrestrial, mostly black or brown, oval beetles, shaped much as the dytiscids and gyrinids, but generally more convex above. The antennae are very short, clubbed, and may not be as long as the prominent maxillary palps. All hydrophilids are good flyers. The middle and hind legs of aquatic species bear long hairy fringes used in swimming; air is carried under the fore wings and on the under surface of the body. The aquatic forms feed largely upon decaying animal and vegetable matter, but some are at least partially predacious upon other insects. Those living in damp soil and dung also are predacious to some extent, the latter devouring the fly larvae which may be abundant. The eggs in aquatic species are laid in a silken case or cocoon which is carried under the abdomen of the mother, attached to water plants or simply released to float on the water surface. The adults hibernate.

Young: Slender, crawling, small-headed, aquatic forms with a pair of gill-like structures on each of the first 7 abdominal segments and usually a pair of cerci in a terminal breathing pocket. Unlike the adults, they are almost entirely predacious on insects and other small animals. They pupate in cells above water level, in or on the soil, or attached to plants and other objects.

IMPORTANCE: Our species are useful as scavengers and predators, even though some of the larvae may attack small fishes. At least one oriental species, a land form, has been utilized in the biological control of beetle larvae boring in stems of sugar cane and banana in Hawaii and Jamaica, respectively. In parts of China certain hydrophilid adults are used as food.

EXAMPLE 92a: Water Scavenger Beetle
Hydróphilus trianguláris

Widely distributed in our region. Frequently seen at lights.

EXAMPLE 92b: Hydrophilid Beetle
Sphaerídium scarabaeoìdes

This is an introduced European species; now rather generally distributed in the eastern United States. The larvae live in dung and feed on fly larvae.

93 Carrion Beetles   *Family Sílphidae*

ADULTS: Extremely variable, but our commoner species are of medium size, moderately or strongly flattened, frequently with shortened fore wings which do not completely cover the abdomen; they are good flyers. The mouth usually is at the front of the head; the antennae are short and clubbed. The eyes are typically large, but some cave-dwelling species are eyeless. The legs are developed for digging, the tibiae being broad and armed with stout spines at their extremities. Silphids are scavengers to a large extent but also are predators, eating the insect larvae present in or under dead animals. Some species eat living plant tissue, some feed on decaying fungi, and others live in ant colonies. Usually the adults hibernate.

YOUNG: Oval in outline and usually covered with heavy chitinous plates. The antennae have 3 (sometimes 4) segments, and there are 6 ocelli on each side of the head. The body ends in 2 cercus-like extensions. The feeding habits are similar to those of the adults. Larval development often is quite rapid and may be completed in no more than a week.

IMPORTANCE: Useful as scavengers; some bury the whole carcasses of small birds and mice in a few hours of tireless labor. The fact that part of the diet of some species living in carrion consists of scavenging fly larvae does not make them less useful, for they are not numerous enough in a single cadaver to reduce seriously the maggot population. *Blitóphaga opàca,* a European species whose larvae feed on beet foliage, has become established in the United States but is not yet a serious pest.

EXAMPLE 93a: Sexton Beetle   *Nicróphorus marginàtus*

Widely distributed. A pair of sexton beetles will fly to a dead mouse and, by digging away the soil from below, bury it completely. The female then lays her eggs in a short tunnel leading to the buried treasure. Adults and young live on the ripening carrion, the former feeding the first-stage larvae and newly molted individuals in the later stages from their own mouths.

EXAMPLE 93b: Carrion Beetle   *Sílpha noveboracénsis*

Generally distributed in our region. A feeder on carrion and the fly larvae therein; also occurring in dung and decaying fungi.

94 Rove Beetles   *Family Staphylínidae*

A vast group of primarily predacious insects. About 20,000 species are known for the entire world.

ADULTS: Rather flattish, elongated insects with the head as broad as the thorax and abdomen and bearing stout mandibles. Mostly small or very small insects with the fore wings characteristically much shortened, leaving 7 or 8 abdominal segments exposed, but covering a pair of hind wings capable of strong flight. Occasionally, however, the hind wings may not be developed for flight or may be absent. In some species the alarmed insect runs about with the tip of the abdomen held above its back and directed forward toward an enemy; a pair of glands at the apex of the abdomen, which can emit a fine, ill-smelling mist, are thus brought to bear upon an attacker. Sometimes a drop of odorous liquid from the tip of the abdomen is smeared on an adversary. This flexible manipulation of the body is common in the family. The absence of terminal forceps distinguishes rove beetles from earwigs (*14*), which they rather resemble. Some 300 species dwell in close association with ants, either as harmless "guests" or as predators; a few are parasitic upon fly pupae inside the host puparia. A very few rove beetles feed upon carrion and decaying vegetable matter and an occasional species upon living plant tissues—foliage, fruit, and pollen; most appear to be predacious upon other insects and mites.

YOUNG: The larvae, but for the absence of wings, resemble the adults quite closely, and their food habits are almost indentical. There are 3 to 4 larval stages, and it has been reported that the pupae are sometimes enclosed in a case of fine threads or other larval exudate.

IMPORTANCE: Difficult to evaluate, but since they are almost wholly predacious, they are probably beneficial to man. Some live on plant-eating mites; others are known to consume the eggs and larvae of bark beetles. They certainly consume beneficial scavenging species, especially fly larvae. Some Central and South American species are external parasites of small mammals.

EXAMPLE 94a: Hairy Rove Beetle *Creóphilus maxillòsus*

Occurs from Newfoundland and Labrador to Florida and west and south to southern California. This is one of the species found about carrion, feeding upon scavenging insects of various species.

EXAMPLE 94b: Rove Beetle   *Paèderus littoràrius*

Occurs throughout much of the eastern United States.

A rather small family (about 300 species in our region) of minute or very small hairy insects which were formerly grouped with the rove beetles is the Pseláphidae, or ant-loving beetles. They seldom exceed ⅛ inch in length, averaging much smaller, and are mostly predacious upon mites and tiny insects in leaf mold, although some live in the galleries of ants and termites. Unlike rove beetles, pselaphids have relatively inflexible abdomens with only 5 or 6 exposed segments.

95 Hister Beetles *Family Histéridae*

ADULTS: Small and very small, hard-bodied, usually dark and shining insects, commonly found in pastures in or under cow dung, in dead animals and decaying fungi. The remarkably flattened forms, one of which is illustrated, are found under the bark of dead trees or branches. The first thoracic segment is very large and the fore wings do not cover the last 2 abdominal segments. Most species are good flyers. The short, flattened legs are fitted for digging. The head is very small and scarcely visible from above. This is the first of the beetle families considered so far which has elbowed antennae.

YOUNG: The soft-bodied larvae are mostly cylindrical, warty, or spiny, and may have a pair of cerci. Their food habits, so far as known, are like those of the adults.

IMPORTANCE: Not well understood. The histerids are largely predacious upon scavenging insects and so may not be beneficial from the human standpoint. Some prey upon plant-feeding insects such as caterpillars of moths and butterflies, and some live with ants. Those living under the bark of trees feed upon fly larvae, immature stages of bark beetles, and long-horned beetles. Several species have been found in stored grains, feeding upon other insects.

EXAMPLE 95a: Hister Beetle *Platysòma lecóntei*

Widely distributed in our region; especially abundant under the dead bark of oak and elm.

EXAMPLE 95b: Hister Beetle *Híster abbreviàtus*

Rather generally distributed in the central and southeastern United States. This species is representative of the more or less hemispherically shaped histerids that live in carrion and feed primarily upon fly larvae.

96 Net-winged Beetles *Family Lýcidae*

ADULTS: Very small- to medium-sized insects, resembling adults of the next family, the fireflies, and formerly classified with them. However, they are not luminescent, are active by day, and the fore wings in most species are strongly reticulate, as the name implies. Only a few lycids, such as our example,

have the fore wings dilated to give a wedge-shaped outline
to the body.

YOUNG: The larvae are found under bark and about decaying
vegetation, but their food habits are not known.

IMPORTANCE: So little is certainly known of the biologies of
these insects that no definite statement about their importance can be made. Some of the adults and larvae have been
reported to be predacious on other insects, but well-authenti-
cated observations do not seem to have been published.

EXAMPLE: Net-winged Beetle   *Calópteron reticulàtum*

A common species, occurring throughout the eastern United
States.

97 Fireflies   *Family Lampýridae*

ADULTS: The appearance of these insects at night scarcely
needs description. The last several abdominal segments of
the male are luminous with a cold, greenish-yellow light,
which alternately brightens and dims as the "lightningbug"
wings slowly and silently about in the dewy night. Children
imprison them in glass jars to use as lanterns. The practically
heatless light of these insects is due to a most efficient
chemical reaction in which a cell product called luciferin is
burned in the presence of an enzyme, luciferase. The females
also have light organs, but they may be confined to a single
abdominal segment, usually the sixth. The flashing lights of
these nocturnally active insects serve to bring the opposite
sexes together for mating and, in at least one common species
(*Photùris pennsylvánica*), may also serve as a lure to bring
the males of certain other species of fireflies to the jaws of
the carnivorous females. In a European species, the ability
of the female to emit light has been observed to disappear
shortly after mating. The flashing of fireflies is rhythmic;
flashes are single or double, according to species, and are
more frequent at higher temperatures. Rarely, outside the
tropics, the flashes of thousands of individuals have been observed to synchronize.

Fireflies are elongate, flattish, with soft black or brown fore
wings, often margined with a lighter color and usually cov-

ering the abdomen completely. The head, in our species, typically is covered by the broadly extended first thoracic segment. The antennae are usually slender, but in some kinds may be developed into comb-like organs. The eyes are large, those of the males usually being the larger. The wingless females of some species might be mistaken for larval fireflies, which they strongly resemble. Other females may have much-shortened fore wings and also be unable to fly. Most adult fireflies apparently do not feed at all. The eggs are placed in or upon the ground, among mosses or at the bases of moisture-loving plants.

YOUNG: The strongly flattened larvae have small, narrow heads which can be retracted into the thorax, and stout, curved mandibles. They may have a pair of luminous organs on the eighth abdominal segment and may emit light even before hatching from the egg. The larvae are entirely predacious. Snails are the chief food of many species and, as would be expected, firefly larvae are found most abundantly in the damp situations suitable for their prey. Earthworms and cutworms also figure in their diet. "Glowworms," as these insects are often called (along with adult females of larval shape), inject a paralyzing fluid into their prey which may greatly exceed them in size. The larva requires 1 or 2 years to complete development, passing the winter in a cell in the soil. Pupation takes place in the soil or in an earthen cell constructed on top of the ground, beneath a rock or in debris.

IMPORTANCE: Fireflies are important controls on snails and slugs, which sometimes are damaging to cultivated plants. In the Orient, where certain aquatic snails are serious crop pests or the intermediate hosts for certain worms parasitic in man or domesticated animals, the aquatic or nearly aquatic larvae of several fireflies are quite beneficial. Surprisingly little is known of the habits of these very common and interesting insects.

EXAMPLE 97a: Firefly   *Photìnus pyràlis*

This species is abundant east of the Rocky Mountains. Both sexes are long-winged in the adult stage, but the female flies only a little.

EXAMPLE 97b: Firefly   *Photìnus scíntillans*

A species common in Pennsylvania and neighboring states. The male, which has normally developed wings, flies only in the early twilight; the female, which is illustrated, is short-winged and flightless. The narrow head of the larva, which also has been figured, can be greatly extended from under the large plate covering the first thoracic segment. It is believed that the adults take no food.

98 Soldier Beetles   *Family Cantháridae*

ADULTS: Soldier beetles bear a superficial resemblance to fire-flies and once, like the net-winged beetles, were grouped with them. These insects have no light-producing organs, and their heads, instead of being covered by the first thoracic segments, are freely attached to them by a rather long neck. The leathery fore wings are narrower than those of the fireflies. Look for soldier beetles on large showy flower clusters, such as those of goldenrod and elderberry, where they feed on pollen and nectar. They feed upon aphids, mealybugs, and other small insects for the most part, and upon plant tissues to a lesser extent. The clusters of eggs are placed in the soil or in protecting crevices. There are 1 or 2 generations a year.

YOUNG: Soldier beetle larvae, as a rule, are predacious upon other insects, especially the eggs and young, which they hunt upon the ground, upon plants, and under the bark of trees. They pass the winter in a late stage of development and pupate in cells in the soil.

IMPORTANCE: Probably a useful family as predators and deserving of more study.

EXAMPLE: Common Soldier Beetle

Chauliógnathus pennsylvánicus

Our commonest soldier beetle; widely distributed east of the Rocky Mountains.

99 Checkered Beetles   *Family Cléridae*

ADULTS: Clerids are usually elongate, almost cylindrical, and covered with a dense coat of short hairs. The first thoracic segment is rather long and much constricted at the rear. The antennae are somewhat club-like, with 3 enlarged terminal segments. The patterns of often bright contrasting colors on the fore wings may be checkered—hence the popular name for the group. Adult clerids frequent flowers, gather where sap is flowing, and search for insects on plants and in the soil. The eggs are laid near the food supply of the young. There may be 1 to several generations a year, the life cycle corresponding with that of the prey species.

YOUNG: These are the ferrets of the insect world, preying upon the larvae of bark beetles and other wood-boring beetles, moths, wasps, and bees. Although usually found in the tunnels of its victims, clerid larvae are able to cut their own way through dead wood. They are flat or cylindrical, hairy, often reddish or yellow, and usually with 2 horny, hook-like projections, which may be united basally, on top of the ninth abdominal segment. The tenth segment has become an organ of locomotion and is actually below the ninth. The tarsi and claws are fused together rather than jointed.

IMPORTANCE: Clerids are among the most important natural checks on the populations of many different wood-boring beetles. Occasionally they are pests in beehives, where the larvae may devour young bees.

EXAMPLE: Checkered Beetle   *Enoclèrus sphègeus*

Occurs from British Columbia and Colorado southward through California and New Mexico. The larvae prey upon the eggs, larvae, and pupae of the Black Hills beetle (*Dendróctonus ponderòsae*) and other bark beetles, migrating at maturity to the soil at the base of the tree and pupating in an earthen cell lined with a secretion from the mouth. The adult is a more general predator, feeding on numerous small insects in addition to bark beetle adults.

100 Click Beetles   *Family Elatéridae*

There are about 700 species of click beetles in our region. The larvae, popularly known as "wireworms," live in the soil and are serious crop pests as well as useful predators.

ADULTS: Click beetles may be recognized at once because of the long extension of the first thoracic segment which fits into a socket on the underside of the second thoracic segment. When these beetles are placed on their backs they regain their feet by arching themselves, then snapping this process back into its socket so suddenly that they flip into the air; this maneuver is accompanied by a characteristic clicking sound. Elongate, flattened, short-legged insects, ranging in size from very small to large. They are dull-colored in browns, grays, and black. The head, with large compound eyes, is sunken into a notch in the first thoracic segment, the posterior angles of which are prolonged as spine-like processes. Both the adults and larvae of certain tropical species are luminous. The females of the species whose larvae are injurious to crop plants lay their eggs in the soil, about the roots of grasses and other plants. The adult often passes the winter in the pupal cell in the soil, emerging the following spring.

YOUNG: Wireworms are elongate, cylindrical, usually hard-bodied, with a smooth, shining integument usually brown or yellowish in color. The head is darker and bears short, 3-segmented antennae. The ninth segment of the abdomen often is flattened and divided into 2 horny processes which are edged with teeth, but in some species the terminal segment is entire, as in our illustrated example. Wireworms are most easily distinguished from "false wireworms," the larvae of darkling beetles (*109*), which they superficially resemble, by the legs, those of the former being relatively much smaller (compare illustrations). Practically all of our wireworms are found in the soil, where they feed on the underground portions of living plants or are predacious on other insect larvae; a few species live in rotten wood aboveground, feeding upon insects. They pupate in a cell in the soil. Several years usually are required for development from egg to adult. Under laboratory conditions wireworms have been induced to molt and grow larger and to molt and grow smaller, according to the amount of food supplied. The number of larval stages also can be varied by manipulating the food supply.

IMPORTANCE: The value of wireworms as predators cannot be estimated from the small amount of information that has been published on the subject. White grubs and many other injurious insect larvae are eaten, perhaps indiscriminately. Some species are very destructive to potatoes, boring into them and rendering them unfit for sale. Corn and other cereal and wild grasses, many garden vegetables and flowers, and some leguminous field crops are susceptible to severe injury by wireworms. The adults, although vegetarian, are of negligible economic importance.

EXAMPLE: Wheat Wireworm   *Agriòtes máncus*

A widespread North American species. The larvae are very injurious to sprouting wheat, destroying the grains, roots, and shoots.

101 Metallic Wood-borers   *Family Bupréstidae*

ADULTS: Very hard-bodied flat or cylindrical insects, mostly of medium or small size, with striking metallic coloring, especially iridescent blues and bronzes, which may be most brilliant on the underside of the body. Many common species bear a superficial resemblance to the click beetles of the preceding family. The thick fore wings are corrugated, and the head is deeply inserted into the first thoracic segment and so appears quite short, with little more than the large, dorsally situated eyes exposed. The antennae are short, usually sawtoothed, and 11-segmented. Many buprestids are forest dwellers, and while they may be found visiting flowers to feed on pollen and nectar, it is more likely that they will be seen resting on the sunny sides of tree trunks; other species infest herbaceous plants and inhabit open country. Some adults eat plant foliage. The eggs are laid in cavities excavated in the bark of the food plants, which usually are weakened, or dying trees and shrubs.

YOUNG: The legless larva is elongate, soft, white or yellowish, with a small head and a very broad, flat thorax. Evidencing some confusion as to just what constitutes a "head," the popular name for the buprestid larva is "flatheaded borer." The long, tapering abdomen is somewhat flattened too. The broad, shallow, sawdust-packed tunnels of these insects are exposed when dead bark is removed from tree trunks and branches. The tunnels may extend into the sapwood, in which case they are loosely filled with wood fibers suggesting excelsior. The larvae take their nourishment from the wood itself and winter in the sapwood. Before pupating, they chew out a chamber just under the bark, so that the adults will have only a thin wall to penetrate in order to escape. The larvae of some species live in the stems and roots of shrubs and herbaceous plants, and some mine leaves, pupating in cells in the leaves; still others make galls on the stems of their host plants.

IMPORTANCE: Most of the injury done by buprestids is to unhealthy trees, but some of the most serious pest species attack sound ones of both coniferous and broad-leaved species.

EXAMPLE: Flatheaded Apple Tree Borer
Chrysobóthris femoráta

This is an important pest of apple and most other deciduous trees and shrubs throughout the United States and much of Canada, being one of the species that attacks sound plant tissue. The presence of larvae in young trees often is indicated by extensive areas of dead bark and exuding sap. Sometimes the tree is completely girdled and killed.

102 Carpet Beetles and Allies *Family Derméstidae*

ADULTS: The adults of this little family are mostly very small insects, oval or long-oval in outline, and typically rather convex. They are generally rather dull-colored, with scaly or hairy fore wings concealing all the abdominal segments and the well-developed hind wings. The legs are relatively short. The head is small, with large compound eyes and short, usually clubbed, antennae. Dermestids are mostly feeders on dead, dry animal and plant substances and upon the pollen of flowers.

YOUNG: Densely hairy, the longer hairs so arranged that they give the body a ringed appearance. Often there are conspicuous tufts of hair at the end of the body.

IMPORTANCE: *Derméstes maculàtus* larvae sometimes are used by museum workers to clear the dried flesh from the delicate skeletons of small animals; other species, also, are useful as scavengers. Some commonly occur in bird and rodent nests, and in the nests and webs of certain insects and spiders, feeding upon offal and dead individuals. The family is best known, however, for those species which feed on cured meats, stored hides, cheese, cereals, and museum specimens, and on the wool of carpets and upholstery. Only the larvae of carpet beetles are injurious, the adults feeding harmlessly upon flower pollen.

EXAMPLE: Hide Beetle   *Derméstes maculàtus*

Cosmopolitan. One of the destructive species, doing much damage throughout the world to stored hides. It is said that London merchants once offered a prize of £20,000 for a practical plan of control for this insect, whose damage has sometimes resulted in the condemnation of entire shiploads of hides.

103 Dried-fruit Beetles and Allies *Family Nitidùlidae*

ADULTS: Very small, active insects. They are flattish, with fore wings too short to conceal the last 2 or 3 abdominal segments. The head is rather large, with conspicuous eyes and 11-segmented, clubbed antennae. The legs are short and stout. These beetles feed upon fungi, pollen, dried or rotten fruits, and other plant materials.

YOUNG: The larvae have the food habits of the adults; they also are quite active. They are not hairy; the body sometimes ends in a pair of cerci.

IMPORTANCE: A few species are serious pests of stored, dried fruits and cereals or cereal products, but in the main they are scavengers of fallen and broken fruits and other decaying vegetable matter. Some species cause the souring of figs by spreading yeasts; others live in ant nests and in the tunnels of wood-boring insects. A species which in nature has been found on the carcasses of birds and reptiles sometimes infests stored hides.

EXAMPLE: Dried-fruit Beetle   *Carpóphilus hemípterus*

Occurs throughout the temperate and warmer parts of North America and the world. One of the more important pests of stored foods.

104 Cucujid Beetles   *Family Cucùjidae*

ADULTS: Very flat, elongate, mostly small insects with mouth parts at the front of the head. The eyes are small and the antennae rather heavy and bead-like. Many of our common species live under the dead bark of trees, a habitat for which their almost paper-thin bodies are admirably adapted, feeding upon bark beetle larvae and other insects. In addition to the predatory species, there are some that feed on stored cereals, cereal products, and molds, and some that are at least partially scavenging.

YOUNG: Either flat or cylindrical with a pair of tail appendages (cerci). They live in the same situations as the adults and have similar food habits.

IMPORTANCE: Our first example is probably the most abundant and important species. It and several other cucujids are pests of stored grains and cereal products. The predatory species, which probably outnumber the rest, are beneficial, for they feed upon many wood-destroying insects.

EXAMPLE 104a: Saw-toothed Grain Beetle
Oryzaèphilus surinaménsis
A prime pest of stored grains and cereal products throughout the world.

EXAMPLE 104b: Flat Bark Beetle   *Cùcujus clávipes*
A widely distributed species in our region. This rather attractive cucujid is a predator on other insects under the bark of trees.

105 Languriid Beetles   *Family Langurìidae*

ADULTS: Small, narrow, parallel-sided, elongate insects, almost cylindrical in cross section. They are hard-bodied and shining. This family is rather poorly represented in our region— the majority of species living in the tropics. There are 5 tarsal segments, but the fourth is so small that there appear to be only 4. The 11-segmented antennae are club-shaped, with 5 or 6 segments in the gradually expanded terminal portion.

YOUNG: Elongate, with a pair of upward-curving, hook-like processes on top of the ninth abdominal segment; borers in the stems and roots of plants.

IMPORTANCE: With the exception of our example, the languriids are relatively unimportant economically in our region.

EXAMPLE: Clover Stem Borer   *Langùria mozárdi*
A borer in the stems of clovers, lettuce, celery, and some other crop plants. Widespread in our region, but particularly injurious in the western and southwestern United States.

The languriids were once included in the family Erotýlidae
—the so-called "pleasing fungus beetles." Erotylids are robust, more or less oblong, readily distinguished by their different body shape and by the smaller number of segments
(3 or 4) in the expanded portion of the antennae. They are
often brightly colored. The larvae live in fungi.

106 Lady Beetles   *Family Coccinéllidae*

ADULTS: Very small insects, typically hemispherical in shape,
the underside quite flat and the fore wings completely covering the body. The small head, with its large eyes and short,
clubbed, 11-segmented antennae, is sunken into and almost
hidden under the first thoracic segment. "Ladybirds," as they
are often called, are sometimes confused with the leaf beetles
(*118*), especially those species known as tortoise beetles, some
of which they resemble superficially. However, the short
legs of lady beetles have apparently 3-jointed tarsi (actually
there are 4, but the third is very small and concealed), while
the tarsi of the leaf beetles appear to be 4-segmented. These
insects all winter as adults, often assembling in large numbers
in the fall before going into hibernation under rocks and
forest litter and inside hollow trees. Our commonest and
best-known species are voracious feeders on aphids, mealybugs, whiteflies, and scale insects. Other insects and their eggs
also may be consumed. Except for extreme variations in color
pattern, one lady beetle is very like another, so when one
has become well acquainted with one he will be able to
recognize practically all the others. There are a few destructive, plant-feeding species. The typically spindle-shaped
eggs may be attached by one end, singly or in small clusters,
to the plants upon which the larvae or their prey will feed.
Sometimes the eggs are laid horizontally upon a plant surface,
or may be placed upon or under a stationary or slow-moving
host, such as certain scale insects.

YOUNG: Rather flattened, long-oval in body outline, with slender legs and often a black-and-yellow checkered or solid
yellow or orange coloration. They may be almost naked,
somewhat hairy, thickly beset with branched spines, or covered
with woolly-looking wax secretions and resembling large

mealybugs. There are 4 larval stages; pupation occurs on the plant surface upon which the larva was feeding. The mature larva glues down the end of the abdomen, then transforms into a pupa. The old larval skin may be shed and slipped down around the attached end of the pupa, or it may simply split down the back and remain as a partial envelope for the pupa. The larvae have the same food habits as their parents, but much bigger appetites.

IMPORTANCE: Lady beetles are among the most useful of all insects. Two Australian species have been imported into the United States and into various other parts of the world to effect control of the citrus mealybug and cottony-cushion scale (*47a-b*). In California, where the original introductions of these foreign predators were made, some of the native species are collected at their fall swarmings, which often take place high up in the mountains, and are liberated the following spring on farms and in orchards to control various aphids and mealybugs. The Mexican bean beetle (*Epiláchna variéstis*) is the most important of the plant-feeding species. For a great many years it was confined to the southwestern part of the United States but has now spread over most of the country and into southern Canada. Adults and larvae skeletonize the foliage and also feed on the flowers and pods of lima and snap beans, some other garden and field legumes, and such related weeds as the begger-tick.

EXAMPLE: Two-spotted Lady Beetle   *Adàlia bipunctàta*

Widespread throughout our region and much of the world. One of the many beneficial species, living largely on aphids. In its natural position, the pupa hangs head downward, usually from the underside of a leaf, with the end of its abdomen concealed by the crumpled skin of the last larval stage.

107 Tumbling Flower Beetles   *Family Mordéllidae*

ADULTS: Very small insects, strongly compressed from side to side. The back typically is high-humped and the head almost underneath the large first thoracic segment. The body tapers strongly to the rear and ends, almost always, in a pointed abdominal segment not covered by the fore wings. The entire body is covered with short, silky hairs which make the insect rather slippery and difficult to hold between the fingers. The antennae are relatively short and thread-like. The legs, especially the hind ones, are quite long. These insects frequent flowers, particularly those with large, disk-like heads, such as sunflowers. When frightened, they loose their hold and jump and tumble to the ground or take flight before completing their fall.

YOUNG: Elongate, pale, with prominent humps on top of the abdominal segments. They are borers in the pith of annual weeds and in dead wood and are miners in leaves. Some are said to be predacious upon other insect larvae. In general we know very little about their life histories.

IMPORTANCE: Small, economically.

EXAMPLE: Tumbling Flower Beetle   *Mordellistèna árida*

Widely distributed in the eastern half of the United States. So far, 193 species in 15 genera have been described from our region.

108 Blister Beetles   *Family Meloìdae*

ADULTS: Elongate, usually cylindrical, soft-bodied insects of small or medium size, frequently exceeding ½ inch in length. The large head with its short, thread-like antennae is well set off from the thorax. The legs are long and slender; the fore and middle tarsi have 5 segments, the hind tarsi 4. The leathery fore wings may or may not completely cover the abdomen. The wings in some species are absent and in many others they are not fitted for flight. If an adult is accidentally crushed against the skin, a painful blister may result. All blister beetle adults are plant feeders, several species being important pests of garden and field crops. The larvae of blister beetles are predacious or parasitic, chiefly upon the eggs of grasshoppers and soil-inhabiting bees, so many of the eggs are laid in masses in pits in the soil excavated and later filled up by the females.

YOUNG: There are 6 larval stages in the species whose life histories are known. The tiny insect that hatches from the egg is called a "triungulin." It has a large head armed with large jaws, rather long, slender, grasping legs, and, at the end of the body, usually some elongate spines and an adhesive pad. This sticky pad permits the larva to stand on its tail and grasp for the leg or body hairs of a bee. Of course the bee will eventually visit its nest, whereupon the triungulin will detach itself and seek an egg or young larva or perhaps the food supply intended for the host larva. Usually more than one bee egg or larva is consumed by an individual triungulin, and in these instances we call it a predator rather than a parasite. (By a widely accepted definition, a parasite requires no more than one individual of a single host species in or upon which to complete its development.) The first-stage larvae of the species feeding on grasshopper eggs, find their way directly through the soil to an egg cluster. Each larval stage is quite different from the one preceding. The last 4 stages are rather sluggish, and the legs may be little developed or absent. Sometimes the last-stage larva is enveloped by the unshed skins of the preceding 2 or 3 stages. Metamorphosis in the blister beetles is not only "complete," —the process more properly is called "hypermetamorphosis." The winter is passed as an egg or, more frequently, perhaps, as a late-stage larva. There is usually one generation a year, but some species have more and some require as many as 3 years to complete development.

IMPORTANCE: Several species of blister beetles are important pests of potatoes, tomatoes, beans, cotton, and many other crop plants and flowers. Before effective insecticides were as available as they are now, children used to drive blister beetles or "old-fashioned potato beetles" by beating on pans and threshing the ground and plants with leafy branches. When the insects had been herded into the grass at the fence row, a fire was set to destroy them. The blistering ingredient of the adult insect is called cantharidin. For centuries it has been used in so-called love potions. Its internal use is highly dangerous; as an external application it is employed as a counterirritant. The larvae, which are destroyers of grasshopper eggs, are probably abundant enough at times to be control factors of some importance. Adult beetles are eaten by magpies and about 50 other birds, none of which seems to be adversely affected.

EXAMPLE: Margined Blister Beetle   *Epicaùta solàni*

A widely distributed species. A pest on many cultivated plants, especially members of the potato or nightshade family.

There is a small family of beetles somewhat resembling the mordellids (*107*) but closely related to the blister beetles, which we have not figured because they are not often collected. This is the Rhipiphóridae. Unlike tumbling flower beetles, these insects have doubly-combed or saw-toothed antennae instead of thread-like ones, and the tip of the abdomen is not pointed. So although the general body outlines are similar, and although they both may be found in the same situations, still they can be separated easily by these characters. Rhipiphorids are unique beetles in that part of the larval period is spent as an internal parasite in the bodies of certain wasp larvae.

109 Darkling Beetles and Allies *Family Tenebriónidae*

ADULTS: Variable in size and body shape. The species one finds outdoors under rocks or the bark of dead trees are mostly the larger, smooth, black, slow-moving, long-legged forms with elongate, cylindrical, or short, almost globular bodies. These are the insects usually called darkling beetles; they are mostly nocturnal and are feeders on dead plants and fungi and on a wide range of living green plants. Several species have been observed to assemble about anthills, gleaning the grass and weed seeds dropped by the inhabitants. Some darkling beetles have the habit of standing almost on their heads when alarmed. The members of this family have 5 tarsal segments on the first and second pairs of legs and only 4 on the third pair. Darkling beetles are mostly unable to fly, the hind wings being poorly developed or absent; the fore wings cover the abdomen completely. Some tenebrionids are small, flatter-bodied insects which live entirely in such products as flour and are major economic pests. All are ill-smelling.

YOUNG: The larvae of the larger species, especially those found in soil or humus, are called "false wireworms" because of their strong resemblance to the larvae of click beetles (*100*). The conspicuous legs of the tenebrionid larva distinguish it from the true wireworm, whose legs are very short and hardly visible when viewed from above. These larvae are also more distinctly segmented. The body often ends in a pair of hooks.

IMPORTANCE: This family contains a number of serious pests of stored cereals and cereal products. One of these, the meal-worm (*Tenébrio mólitor*), is so easily bred in quantity that the larvae are sold commercially as food for birds, fishes, and other insectivorous pets. The plant-feeding species are seldom of economic importance in our region. Many species are fungus eaters and some are predacious upon other insects.

EXAMPLE 109a: Darkling Beetle *Alobàtes pennsylvánica*

Widely distributed. The adults congregate under loose bark to hibernate. One of the predacious species, both as adult and larva.

EXAMPLE 109b: Confused Flour Beetle
Tribòlium confùsum

In stored cereals and cereal products everywhere. Originally introduced, probably from Europe. This little insect, because of the ease with which it may be reared in captivity, has become, like houseflies and roaches, an important "laboratory animal." It has figured in numerous scientific studies of population growth and of the effect of fumigants.

110 Powder Post Beetles   *Family Lýctidae*

ADULTS: Mostly very small, about ¼ inch long. Reddish-brown, elongated beetles with the head free of the thorax. The short, club-like antennae have 2-segmented heads. The slender legs have 5-segmented tarsi. The first abdominal segment, seen from below, is longer than the rest. In the family which follows, this segment is about equal to the others. The adults bore out of the hardwood board, hoe handle, or table leg in which they may have spent their larval lives, mate, and seek suitable egg-laying sites. The seasoned sapwood of deciduous trees is preferred, but heartwood and pine and other softwoods are attacked by some species. The minute eggs are laid in the pores of the wood.

YOUNG: The white larvae, which may reach ⅓ inch in length, are bowed and have relatively large heads. They bore about, leaving their tunnels filled with very fine sawdust. Infested flooring may exhibit small cones of sawdust pushed out through pin-point openings.

IMPORTANCE: Beams and flooring may be reduced to powder with a mere shell of firmer wood enclosing it before the damage is discovered. Roofs and floors in old buildings are sometimes weakened to the point where they must be condemned and either razed or partially rebuilt. Painted or varnished furniture made of infested wood may be ruined by the exit holes of the emerging adults. The annual monetary loss occasioned by lyctids probably approaches $20,000,000.

EXAMPLE: Powder Post Beetle   *Lýctus opáculus*

Widespread in the eastern United States. Tunnels in the dead branches of oak and some other deciduous trees.

111 Bostrichid Beetles   *Family Bostríchidae*

ADULTS: Our species are small- or medium-sized insects. Their bodies are cylindrical and dull-colored, varying from brown or gray to almost black. The head, which bears the mouth parts on its lower side, is almost or entirely hidden below the very much enlarged first thoracic segment; this segment is separated from the other thoracic segments by a wide constriction. The short, clubbed antennae have 3 enlarged segments at the tips. The first abdominal segment is not longer than the others. The fore wings slope abruptly at their ends and may terminate in a circle of stout teeth. The legs are short, slender, and hairy, with 5-segmented tarsi. Most species lay their eggs in pores and crevices in fallen timber.

YOUNG: The robust larvae are distinctly curved in outline, with a very small head and greatly enlarged thorax bearing well-developed legs. The antennae are 2- or 3-segmented. The larval tunnels are tightly packed with sawdust and excrement. There is frequently one generation a year, but often, in the same species, some larvae take an extra year or 2 to mature.

IMPORTANCE: Like the preceding family, this one is important economically for those members which bore in hardwood lumber in storage, in boxes and crates, wine barrels, corks in wine bottles, and in flooring, beams, and furniture. Several species are pests of stored grains and grain products. In California, a small bostrichid is called the "lead cable borer" and "short-circuit beetle" because of the frequency with which it penetrates telephone cables. Some species tunnel in the wood of living trees.

EXAMPLE: Apple Twig Borer   *Amphícerus hamàtus*

Distributed widely in North America east of the Rocky Mountains. The larvae tunnel in dead or dying branch tips or shoots of apple, pear, and peach trees, various shrubs, forest and shade trees, and grapevines. The adults cause real damage by tunneling into new terminal growth.

112 Anobiid Beetles   *Family Anobìidae*

ADULTS: Very small, cylindrical insects with mouth parts below the head, which is mostly concealed under the first thoracic segment. The short antennae are variable in shape but arise at the side of the head very near the front margin of the eye. The antennal bases are much farther apart than they are in the family which follows (Ptìnidae). The anobiids are best known for those species which live in the hardwood timbers of buildings. These tiny insects, during the spring and early summer, pound their bodies against the walls of their galleries to produce a faint rapping noise audible in a quiet house, especially at night. The superstitious once believed that what was actually a serenade was a portent of death— hence the old name of "death watch" for these insects. Numerous anobiids are pests of stored products, such as tobacco, drugs, herbs and spices, dried fruits, meats, and cereal products in general. The eggs are laid in galleries in wood or loosely in whatever material the adults may be feeding in.

YOUNG: The tiny, curved, robust larvae, with well-developed heads and short legs, have the feeding habits of the adults.

IMPORTANCE: The wood-inhabiting species have done inestimable damage to wooden construction. Because of them much of the supporting timber in the ancient buildings of Europe has been gradually supplanted by chemically treated wood or by steel. The cigarette beetle (*Lasiodérma serricórne*) ruins cigarettes and cigars by boring through the papers and wrapping leaves and is a very general feeder in dried animal and plant products. The drugstore beetle (*Stegòbium paníceum*) consumes herbs and drugs and can thrive on a steady diet of red pepper.

EXAMPLE: Anobiid Beetle   *Catoràma punctàtum*

Widespread in the southern half of the United States.

113 Spider Beetles and Allies   *Family Ptìnidae*

ADULTS: Minute and very small insects, dark-colored, with head and first thoracic segment much narrower than the rest of the body, which may be cylindrical but more often is broadly oval. The combination of an oval, almost globular body with very long, slender legs results in a somewhat spidery outline. The long antennae arise very close together at the front of the head; they are thread-like or bead-like and often somewhat clubbed. All species feed on dead animal and plant material.

YOUNG: Small, curved, short-legged. Some of them make cocoons in which to pupate. The food habits are similar to those of the adults.

IMPORTANCE: Our native species are mostly scavengers, but some are fairly important pests of a great variety of stored products. A few live in the nests of wasps, ants, and bees.

EXAMPLE: White-marked Spider Beetle   *Ptìnus fúr*

Introduced from Europe; now cosmopolitan. Often abundant in granaries and warehouses, occasionally attacking the bindings of books. They have been found in the nests of honey bees and wild bees, feeding on pollen.

114 Scarab Beetles   *Family Scarabaèidae*

This is a large family of easily recognized insects with more than 30,000 named species in the entire world and many more yet to be discovered. It contains numerous insects of medium and some of large size.

ADULTS: Mostly oval, some almost circular in outline. Scarabs are compact, robust, with stout, often spiny legs, which may be fitted for digging. The most distinctive characteristic of the family is the short, usually elbowed antennae, the clubs of which consist of several broad, thin plates or "leaves" which can be closely pressed together like the pages of a book. The first thoracic segment is quite large. The fore wings are very hard, often polished and beautifully colored; the hind wings are usually well developed. Scarab beetles have diverse feeding habits. Some eat plant foliage and fungi, some eat dung, and a lesser number feed on carrion, especially skin and sinew. The eggs are laid in or on the material in which the larvae will feed.

YOUNG: The larvae are plump, whitish, mostly C-shaped, and usually called "grubs." Thoracic legs are well developed. The end of the body is blunt and smooth. Practically all live in the soil and feed either on plant roots or on dung supplied by the parent. Pupation occurs in the soil in a simple cell or in hardened balls of dung.

IMPORTANCE: Those scarabs which are scavengers are, of course, beneficial. The sacred scarab of Egypt has figured importantly in art and religion for thousands of years. It was taken as the symbol of immortality because it was observed to enter the soil and later reappear as though resurrected. Its periodic recurrence in tremendous numbers upon the surface of Nile mud also seemed to support the old belief in spontaneous generation. The plant-feeding scarabs are quite important economically. The larvae of the May beetles, known as white grubs, are especially destructive to the roots of crops planted in freshly broken sodlands. The adults of some scarabs damage the foliage, flowers, and fruits of many different kinds of plants.

EXAMPLE 114a: Dung Beetle   *Cánthon pilulàrius*

Widely distributed in our region. Probably the commonest of the dung rollers or "tumblebugs." The adults, singly or in pairs, may be seen rolling balls of fresh cattle dung, which they bury and devour. The female places a single large egg inside a pear-shaped dung ball which she has previously buried. The larva completes its development and transforms to an adult inside the hard-walled ball.

EXAMPLE 114b: Dung Beetle   *Phanaèus víndex*

Probably our most striking dung beetle. Not uncommon in the United States east of the Rocky Mountains. It is a "tumblebug," like the preceding. The female does not have the horn on her head.

EXAMPLE 114c: Small Dung Beetle *Aphòdius fimetàrius*

A European species which now occurs throughout our region. Very common in cow dung.

EXAMPLE 114d: Dung Beetle   *Geotrùpes spléndidus*

Occurs throughout the eastern United States. It burys and feeds on cattle dung but does not roll it.

EXAMPLE 114e: Skin Beetle   *Tróx unistriàtus*

One of a group of rather repulsive-looking scarabs which feed on dried skin, sinew, and other of the more durable portions of well-decayed animal carcasses. This species occurs throughout eastern North America.

EXAMPLE 114f: May Beetle   *Phyllóphaga fúsca*

A widely distributed species, especially abundant in the northeastern quarter of the United States and adjacent parts of Canada. The adults, called May beetles and June beetles, feed by night on the foliage of deciduous trees, such as oak, elm, willow, and poplar, and hide in the soil of pastures or other grasslands during the day. They are strongly attracted to lights. The larvae are white grubs, feeders on the roots of grasses under natural conditions, and attacking the roots of almost any plant grown on newly turned sod. They are frequently injurious to the roots of coniferous trees.

EXAMPLE 114g: Rose Chafer *Macrodáctylus subspinòsus*

A widely distributed insect, the adults feeding on roses and other garden flowers, and the leaves and flowers of grape. When eaten in large quantities, these beetles may be fatally poisonous to young chickens.

EXAMPLE 114h: Japanese Beetle   *Popíllia japónica*

This accidental and unfortunate importation from the Orient was discovered at Riverton, New Jersey, in 1916. The grubs feed on the roots of a variety of plants, being especially injurious to the grasses of lawns and golf courses. The adults feed on the foliage, flowers, and fleshy fruits of a great variety of trees, shrubs, and herbaceous plants. The damaging populations are still confined to the North Atlantic states, but insects penetrating the quarantine lines have started isolated infestations as far west as Iowa and south to Florida. A combination of natural enemies—parasitic wasps and flies, some of them imported from Japan, milky disease of the grubs, caused by a bacterium, and parasitic nematodes of the genus *Neoaplectàna*—shows promise of holding beetle populations within reasonable bounds, even in the absence of chemical control.

EXAMPLE 114i: Rhinoceros Beetle   *Dynástes títyus*

This, the largest of the beetles in our region, occurs from Arizona eastward throughout the southern United States. The large grub lives in rotting wood, especially in tree roots, and sometimes invades healthy tissues. The adult female has no horns on the thorax and only a suggestion of one on the head.

EXAMPLE 114j: Fig-eater   *Cótinis nítida*

This beautiful beetle, common in the southeastern quarter of the United States, feeds upon the leaves and young fruits of the peach tree, the foliage of numerous other trees, the ears of corn, and leaves and fruits of a variety of orchard trees and garden vegetables. The larvae are sometimes very destructive to grass roots and to tobacco plants in seed beds. The fig-eater represents a number of common flat-backed scarabs, all rather similar in general body outline and commonly called "flower beetles."

115 Bessybugs (Horned Beetles)   *Family Passálidae*

ADULTS: There is only one representative of this small family in our region, and the illustration makes a detailed description unnecessary. These large, shiny beetles are found inside well-rotted logs; when picked up they make a high-pitched, angry, but faint grating noise by scraping the abdomen against the underside of the hard fore wings. The larvae are able to make a similar sound with their legs, and it may be that parents and offspring are thus enabled to communicate. The adults bestow great care upon the young, even chewing the wood which the latter eat.

YOUNG: The larvae live in close contact with the adults, which guard them throughout their development. They consume decaying wood and the fungi in it, but can subsist on wood alone. Unlike termites, these insects do not need protozoa in their alimentary tracts to assist in the digestion of cellulose. Their sounds are made by scraping the poorly developed hind legs against the coxae of the middle legs.

IMPORTANCE: These wood borers are not destructive from our standpoint, for they are found only in wood so rotten that it could have no use as timber. The larvae of tropical species, the adults of which range up to 3 inches in length, are used as food by certain natives.

 EXAMPLE: Bessybug   *Popílius disjúnctus*

Widespread east of the Rocky Mountains in deciduous woodlands. Oak wood is preferred by this insect.

116   Stag Beetles   *Family Lucánidae*

ADULTS: This family has acquired its popular name from the fact that in some of the larger species the mandibles of the males are so very long, with great, coarse teeth, that they resemble antlers. Pugnacity is well developed in this sex, and duels over the possession of mates are frequent and deadly serious. The better-known stag beetles are a polished brown or black; the fore wings are very hard, completely protecting the abdomen. The head is very large in both sexes. The 11-segmented antennae are elbowed and club-like, with the enlarged joints of the "head" somewhat separated to give the appearance of a comb. The family contains some small and inconspicuous insects with roughened rather than smooth fore wings and bodies. Lucanids are woods dwellers, but many species are attracted to the lights of towns at night.

YOUNG: The whitish larvae, which resemble those of scarabs (*115*), live in the damp, decaying wood of logs or the trunks and branches of trees.

IMPORTANCE: The wood attacked by the larvae is too rotten to have commercial value.

 EXAMPLE: Stag Beetle   *Pseudolucànus capreòlus*

Common in the eastern half of the United States. This

species is commonly called the "pinchingbug." On summer
nights, battling males are frequently found on porches and
sidewalks under lights.

117 Long-horned Beetles   *Family Cerambýcidae*

ADULTS: Very small to large, elongate insects, usually somewhat
cylindrical, with long thread-like but heavy antennae which
may greatly exceed the body in length. The antennae usually
arise from prominences on the front of the head; in many
species their bases are partly enclosed by the C-shaped eyes.
The mandibles are strongly developed and are situated at the
front or at the lower corners of the head. The legs have 5-
segmented tarsi. Almost all cerambycids can fly, but in general
they are rather sluggish. The fore wings and all the body surfaces are sometimes sparsely hairy or scaly. They feed on the
foliage or bark of plants, chiefly trees and shrubs, and visit
flowers for pollen, feed on fungi, or may not feed at all. The
eggs are laid in cavities in the bark of the host plant, cut with
the mandibles of the female.

YOUNG: Wood borers with small heads and long, almost cylindrical bodies. The thorax is enlarged and the last abdominal
segment is usually the longest. They are legless or with legs
much reduced in size. These insects are found in living or
dead wood, chiefly just under the bark, but often penetrating
to the heartwood. The life cycle requires from 1 to 4 years,
the winter being passed as a larva. Pupation occurs in an
especially constructed chamber in the wood.

IMPORTANCE: The long-horned beetles are an economically important group. The larvae ruin or blemish wood by tunneling
in it. Almost every part of the woody tissues of trees and
shrubs is subject to attack. It is a common occurrence for
cerambycid adults to emerge from furniture, particularly
porch or lawn furniture of the rustic variety, or from cellar
woodpiles, to the accompaniment of rather loud gnawing
sounds and considerable production of sawdust. The adults
of some species girdle the twigs or branches in which the eggs
have been laid, causing them to die and break off. The tunneling of the larvae, especially in young trees, may result in the
girdling of the cambium and death of the tree. North American Indians used the larger larvae as food.

EXAMPLE: Roundheaded Apple Tree Borer
Sapérda cándida

Occurs throughout the United States and Canada east of the
Rocky Mountains. A very serious pest of apple, pear, quince,
and some related native trees. The larva bores in the wood at
the base of the tree, sometimes girdling and killing it. Ac-
cumulations of sawdust and dark discoloration of the bark
at the foot of the tree are indications of the borer's presence.
Development from egg to adult requires either 2 or 3 years.

118 Leaf Beetles   *Family Chrysomélidae*

This is one of the largest insect families and one of the most
important from the economic standpoint.

ADULTS: Mostly very small and quite variable in shape, some
being almost circular or oval in outline, others elongate and
slender, and a few somewhat wedge-shaped. The surface of
the fore wings is usually smooth but may be coarsely pitted,
ridged, and even reticulate. The head is rather small and
sometimes is concealed beneath the forward-projecting first
thoracic segment. The mouth parts are on the underside of
the head. The 11-segmented antennae are short and thread-
like or slightly broadened at the tips. The legs are short, and
in some species the hind femora are much thickened and
fitted with muscles for jumping (the flea beetles). Although
the tarsi have 5 segments, the fourth one is so small that they
appear 4-segmented. All species are leaf feeders, except a
few which live with ants or termites and are probably
scavenging, and some which feed on dead vegetable matter
on the surface of the ground. The eggs may be laid in or on
the food plants or in the debris or soil under them. A few
species feed on aquatic plants, their larvae tunneling in the
submerged stems.

YOUNG: Variously shaped, mostly active, with well-developed
legs. They may feed on leaf surfaces, mine leaves, tunnel in
stems or roots, or feed externally upon the latter. The larvae
pupate in a cell in the soil, upon the food plant or in its
tissues; some, including those that live in aquatic plant tissues,
make cocoons.

IMPORTANCE: Many economically important species are found in this family. Two of the most destructive—the Colorado potato beetle and the twelve-spotted cucumber beetle—are among our examples. Certain flea beetles, in addition to riddling foliage, feeding upon roots, or tunneling tubers, are spreaders of fungus and bacterial diseases of cultivated plants. Probably the worst pest of tobacco, wherever cultivated in our region, is a flea beetle, *Epítrix hirtipénnis,* the adult of which eats holes in the leaves at every stage of the plant's development while its larvae attack the roots and sometimes the underground portions of the stem.

EXAMPLE 118a: Asparagus Beetle   *Criócerus aspáragi*

One of the long-bodied chrysomelids. It was originally introduced from Europe and is now widely distributed and abundant in our region. The adults hibernate in surface litter. The several generations of larvae feed upon the foliage of asparagus.

EXAMPLE 118b: Twelve-spotted Cucumber Beetle
Diabrótica undecimpunctàta howárdi

The adults of this subspecies, which is generally distributed in the eastern half of our region, feed upon many kinds of blossoms and upon the foliage of cucumbers, melons, beans, and numerous other cultivated plants. They, and the adults of a related species, the striped cucumber beetle (*D. vittàta*), transmit a bacterial wilt disease of cucurbits. The larvae, even more destructive, are called "southern corn rootworms"; they bore into seedling corn plants an inch or 2 below the soil surface and excavate within the stem, killing or stunting them so that ears are not produced. Pupation occurs in the soil. The adults hibernate in rubble.

EXAMPLE 118c: Colorado Potato Beetle
Leptinotársa decemlineàta

This insect was an innocuous feeder on native plants of the nightshade or potato family along the Missouri River until the middle of the last century, when it exhibited a strong preference for the Irish or white potato which was becoming increasingly available in the garden patches of emigrants to the Northwest. It has now spread to all potato-growing sections in our region, except those in California, and since 1922 has established itself in Europe.

EXAMPLE 118d: Grape Flea Beetle   *Áltica chalybèa*

A common feeder on the buds and foliage of grape throughout the eastern two thirds of the United States. Both the adults and the larvae, which are tan with many black dots, feed on the leaves. There are 2 generations a year, the adults of the summer generation hibernating. Hind femora much enlarged for jumping.

EXAMPLE 118e: Golden Tortoise Beetle *Metrìòna bìcolor*

Widely distributed on sweet potato, bindweed, and other plants of the morning-glory family. The larvae, which feed externally on the foliage, have a long fork at the end of the body on which they gather the molted skins, excrement, and other debris to form a large camouflaging mass over themselves; pupation occurs under this same canopy. The adult can quickly change the color of its "carapace" from a dull reddish-brown to a glorious, glittering gold. Upon the death of the insect, unfortunately, the more beautiful color phase is lost forever.

119 Seed Weevils   *Family Brúchidae*

ADULTS: Minute or very small, oval insects, mostly less than ⅛ inch in length. The fore wings, which do not quite cover the abdomen, are hairy or scaly like the rest of the body. They are blackish, grayish, or brownish, sometimes mottled with white. The head bears relatively large and prominent eyes and straight, sometimes clubbed antennae. The mouth parts are ventral. The tarsi are 5-segmented, the first segment being very long and the fourth small and concealed. Our species are mostly feeders on the seeds of leguminous plants—including cultivated beans and peas. The adults of some single-brooded species may hibernate. In those many-generationed species which live in stored seeds, any and all stages are present at a given time if the temperature does not fall too low. The tiny eggs are laid singly on the seeds or seed pods.

YOUNG: The first-stage larva resembles a young ground beetle —usually with well-developed legs and the necessary armament (a spined or toothed plate on the first thoracic segment) for penetrating the hard, smooth coats of the seeds it will feed on. The other larval stages usually are apparently legless, C-shaped, and robust. The larvae pupate in their burrows in seeds.

IMPORTANCE: Bruchids are very destructive to legumes everywhere. Most of the economic species have become cosmopolitan through commerce. Tiny wasps of the family Eurytómidae (*130*) search deep down among the beans in a bin to parasitize the larvae in the seeds.

EXAMPLE: Cowpea Weevil   *Callosobrùchus maculàtus*

A cosmopolitan species quite injurious to stored cowpeas.

120 Snout Beetles   *Family Curculiónidae*

This is the largest family of insects in any order.

ADULTS: The mouth parts are situated at the end of a beak, or snout, of varying length which usually curves downward. The antennae are usually elbowed, with a very long first segment and the remaining joints short, the last 3 forming a club. Comparatively few of the species in our region exceed ½ inch in length. They are mostly dull-colored—gray, brown, or black—and hard-bodied. The hind wings may be well developed, vestigial, or absent. The fore wings cover the abdomen or may expose the extreme tip. The eggs usually are laid singly in punctures made by the beak of the female, but may be placed in the soil and at the bases of plants. Some species in various genera are parthenogenetic; that is, the females produce eggs which hatch without having been fertilized. In many such species the male does not occur at all. Almost all of these insects are feeders upon or in living plants; a few feed on stored cereals and cereal products.

YOUNG: Legless, C-shaped, usually white with a large brown head. They feed in or on the roots and other underground parts of plants, in stems, fruits, on foliage, and mine leaves. Pupation usually takes place inside plant tissue or in the soil; they may be naked or in light cocoons of silk or plant fibers. The life cycle usually requires a year for completion, but sometimes 2 or more years are necessary. It sometimes happens that in the same species some larvae take 1 year to mature while others take 2 or 3.

IMPORTANCE: Very important pests of all kinds of cultivated plants. The boll weevil alone is responsible for an estimated $200,000,000 annual loss to cotton growers, taking 1 bale of every 7 produced. The granary and rice weevils (*Sitóphilus granàrius* and *S. orỳza*) cause tremendous yearly losses to stored cereals. The sweet potato weevil and white-fringed beetles are introduced insects, like the boll weevil, and are the reasons for the existence of federal and state quarantines on the movements of products likely to disseminate the pests, and for expensive federal and state programs of inspection, crop protection, and pest eradication.

EXAMPLE 120a: White-fringed Beetle
Graphógnathus leucolòma

Several species and races of the genus *Graphógnathus* have been introduced into the United States at various points in the Southeast from temperate South America. The larva feeds on the underground parts of almost every kind of plant grown in garden or field and pupates in a cell in the soil. The freshly emerged adult has a pair of tooth-like processes attached to its mandibles with which it cuts its way out of the soil; these accessories are soon lost. The light band edging the fore wing of the adult gives these beetles their common names. No males are known in the genus *Graphógnathus*.

EXAMPLE 120b: Sweet Potato Weevil
Cỳlas formicàrius elegántulus

This beautiful insect appears to have been introduced from the Old World; in the United States it is at present largely confined to the Gulf region. The larvae tunnel in the vines and roots and may destroy up to 75 per cent of a crop. They are also active in stored sweet potatoes. It has been eradicated from entire counties by clean cultural practices and methodical destruction of the wild host plants, which are members of the morning-glory family.

EXAMPLE 120c: Low-tide Billbug   *Caléndra sètiger*

The beetles of the genus *Caléndra*, popularly known as billbugs, are primarily pests of corn and other cereal and pasture grasses. The eggs are laid in cavities, usually cut in the stem bases of the food plants. The larvae tunnel in the stems, down into the roots, and may consume much of the root system. The adults that feed on corn frequently puncture the tender growing tip of the plant so that when the leaves fully unroll there is displayed one or more rows of evenly spaced, elongated holes. Our example breeds in salt reed grass (*Spartìna cynosuroìdes*) in Atlantic tidal lands. All stages of the insect may be submerged in salt water twice daily. In the laboratory, A. F. Satterthwait reared this species through 2 generations in cornstalks—indicating that it might prove dangerously adaptable in its food habits.

121 Brentid Beetles   *Family Bréntidae*

ADULTS: These insects resemble the snout beetles of the preceding family in possessing a well-developed beak, but this beak is not curved downward. Furthermore, the brentid antennae are straight rather than elbowed, and the entire body is much narrower. The beak of the female is relatively longer than that of the male, while the male is usually larger than the female and has heavier mandibles. Ordinarily, of course, the female of an insect species is the larger. It is the long-beaked female which drills a hole through the bark and into the wood of a dead or dying tree in which to lay a single egg. Observers report that the male assumes her defense while she is excavating and that he assists her to extricate her beak from the pit by pressing down upon the end of her abdomen with his body.

YOUNG: Borers in dead or dying wood.

IMPORTANCE: Of little economic importance. Some species are said to be predacious upon other wood-inhabiting insects.

EXAMPLE: Oak Timberworm   *Arrhenòdes minùta*

Occurs throughout eastern North America. The larvae tunnel in oak, beech, elm, and other deciduous trees.

122 Bark Beetles and Allies   *Family Scolýtidae*

ADULTS: Mostly minute, ⅛ inch or less in length, although a few attain a length of about ⅜ inch. Cylindrical, usually brownish or black, with a small head and very large first thoracic segment. The mouth parts are small and inconspicuous and may be at the front of the head or below it. The apical 3 or 4 segments of the short antennae are expanded into a club. Bark beetles have well-developed wings but are weak flyers, seldom traveling more than a mile or 2 by their own efforts. The female of a typical species burrows through the bark of trees or shrubs and constructs a vertical tunnel or broad chamber with many niches on each side. In every niche she lays an egg. The tunnels usually are partly in the sapwood and partly in the bark. In this position they sever the cambium layer, the all-important growing tissue of the tree. Some bark beetles are polygamous. Tree bark may be peppered with hundreds of tiny, round exit holes cut by emerging adults, which on that account are often called "shot-hole borers." Healthy, weakened, or dead standing trees and fallen timber may be attacked, according to the species of beetle.

A group of scolytids, popularly known as ambrosia beetles, make tunnels or "pinholes" that penetrate the sapwood and even heartwood of dead trees and unseasoned lumber. They feed upon the spores of various species of "ambrosia" fungi, which grow in practically pure culture upon the walls of their tunnels, staining the wood. These insects carry quantities of fungus spores on their bodies and in their alimentary tracts, so that when they migrate to a new tree they are certain to take along with them the particular fungus upon which they depend for food. Some other scolytids bore in the pith of twigs and the cones of coniferous trees.

Young: Bark beetle larvae tunnel outward from the egg niches of the brood chamber, feeding upon the cambium. When bark is removed from infested tree trunks or branches, the rather complicated groovings of the wood by bark beetles may form patterns that are quite pleasing to the eye. The size and shape of the brood chamber and the radiating larval tunnels are characteristic for the various species. The larvae pupate in chambers at the ends of their tunnels, which may be in the bark. Ambrosia beetle larvae feed wholly upon the spores of the fungus and are said to be fed to some extent, at least, by the adults.

IMPORTANCE: Highly destructive to our best timber trees. Practically all deciduous and coniferous trees are subject to attack by one or more of the 545 species (contained in 71 genera) in our region. In addition to killing trees or parts of trees by "girdling" or destroying the cambium layer, some of these insects do far greater harm by transmitting pathogenic organisms from diseased to healthy trees. The spread of the Dutch elm disease, caused by the fungus *Ceratostomélla úlmi,* is due very largely to the breeding of several bark beetle species, notably the smaller European elm bark beetle (*Scólytus multistriàtus*), an introduced insect.

Bark beetles are hosts to more than 75 different kinds of parasitic wasps and to numerous fungus diseases and nematodes. The more important insect predators of bark beetles are the adults and larvae of rove, cucujid, clerid, histerid, and click beetles, several kinds of fly and snakefly larvae and ants. Most woodpeckers feed upon bark beetles to some extent but do not figure importantly in their control.

The dark-stained pinhole borings of the ambrosia beetles greatly lessen the value of woods for cabinetwork.

EXAMPLE: Native Elm Bark Beetle *Hylurgopìnus rùfipes*

Widely distributed in our region; one of the vectors of Dutch elm disease fungus.

In the following plates:

The names in large, light-face capitals are those of insect orders.

The names in bold face, preceded by numbers, are those of insect families, or, in some instances, of large groups of species of less than family rank.

The bold-face family numbers on the plates correspond with those in the text, the table of contents, and the index.

and, to repeat:

        ♂ —male

        ♀ —female

|——| —actual length of an insect's body, exclusive of antennae and tail appendages, or its actual wing expanse

    x—a number following a times sign indicates the amount of magnification or reduction, if any, in an illustration. For example, **x1** means natural size, **x½** means half natural size, **x10** means 10 times natural size.

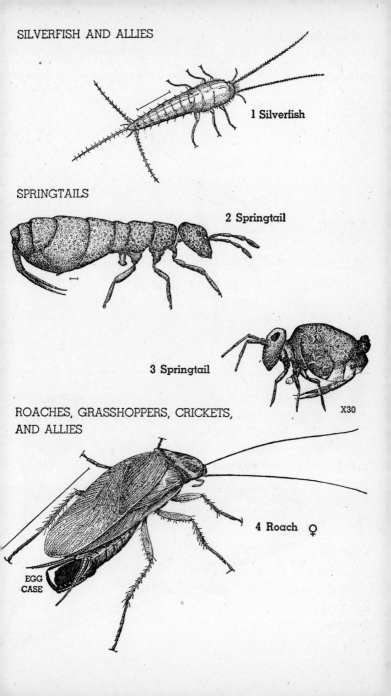

SILVERFISH AND ALLIES

1 Silverfish

SPRINGTAILS

2 Springtail

3 Springtail

X30

ROACHES, GRASSHOPPERS, CRICKETS, AND ALLIES

4 Roach ♀

EGG CASE

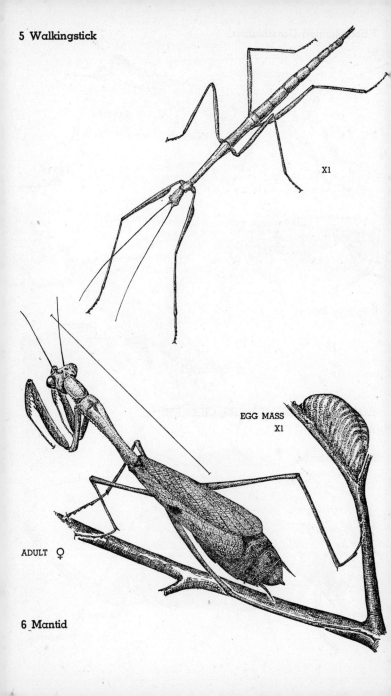

5 Walkingstick

X1

EGG MASS
X1

ADULT ♀

6 Mantid

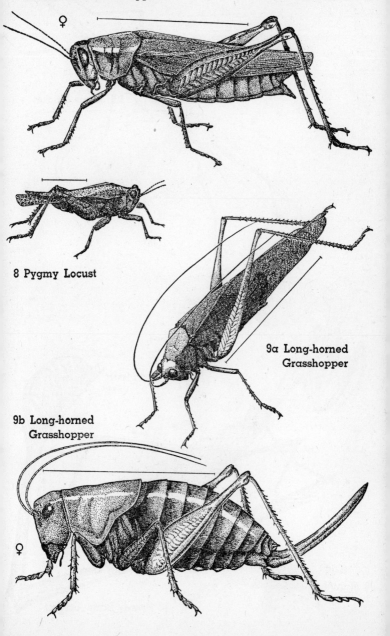

7 Short-horned Grasshopper

♀

8 Pygmy Locust

9a Long-horned Grasshopper

9b Long-horned Grasshopper

♀

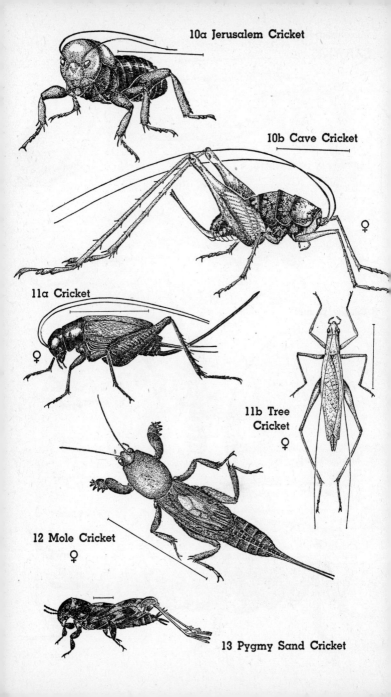

10a Jerusalem Cricket

10b Cave Cricket ♀

11a Cricket ♀

11b Tree Cricket ♀

12 Mole Cricket ♀

13 Pygmy Sand Cricket

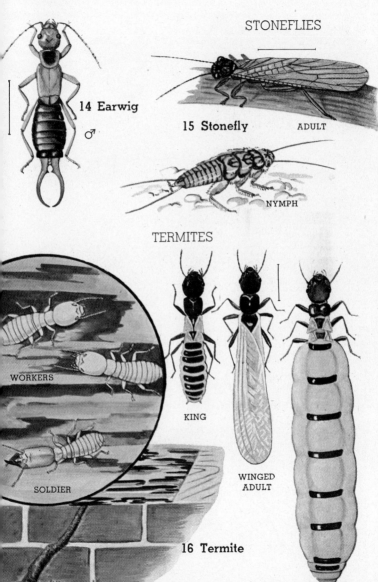

EARWIGS

14 Earwig ♂

STONEFLIES

15 Stonefly ADULT

NYMPH

TERMITES

WORKERS

SOLDIER

KING

WINGED ADULT

16 Termite

QUEEN

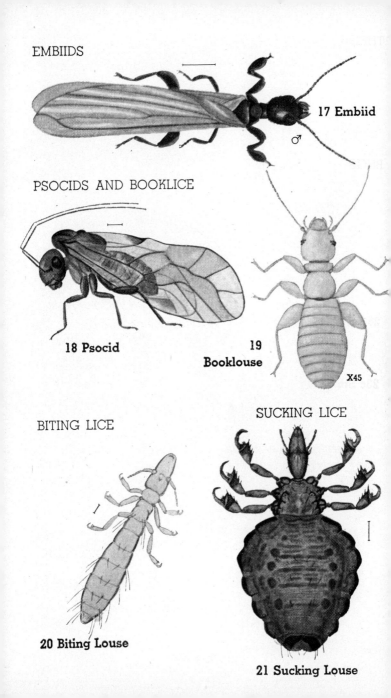

EMBIIDS

17 Embiid ♂

PSOCIDS AND BOOKLICE

18 Psocid

19 Booklouse

X45

BITING LICE

20 Biting Louse

SUCKING LICE

21 Sucking Louse

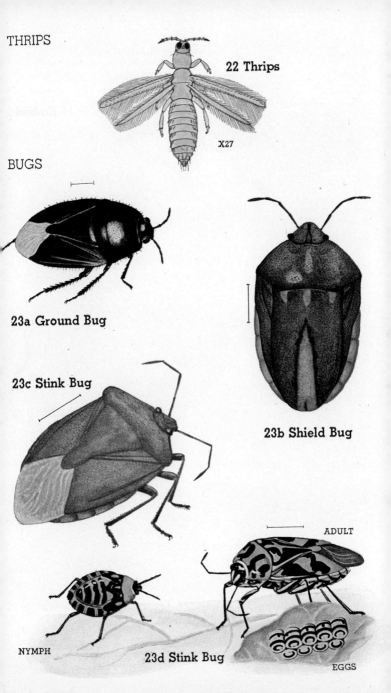

THRIPS

22 Thrips

X27

BUGS

23a Ground Bug

23b Shield Bug

23c Stink Bug

23d Stink Bug

NYMPH

ADULT

EGGS

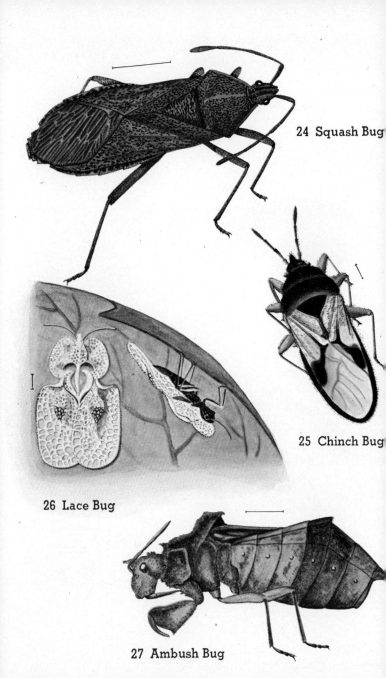

24 Squash Bug

25 Chinch Bug

26 Lace Bug

27 Ambush Bug

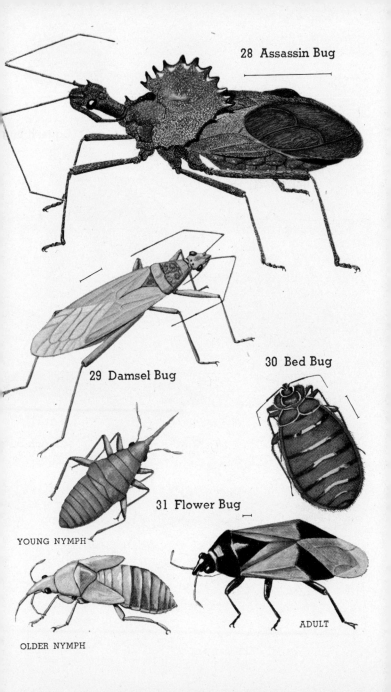

28 Assassin Bug

29 Damsel Bug

30 Bed Bug

31 Flower Bug

YOUNG NYMPH

OLDER NYMPH

ADULT

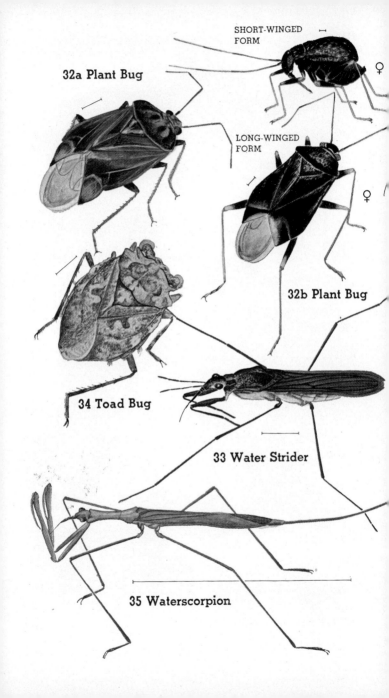

SHORT-WINGED FORM

♀

32a Plant Bug

LONG-WINGED FORM

♀

32b Plant Bug

34 Toad Bug

33 Water Strider

35 Waterscorpion

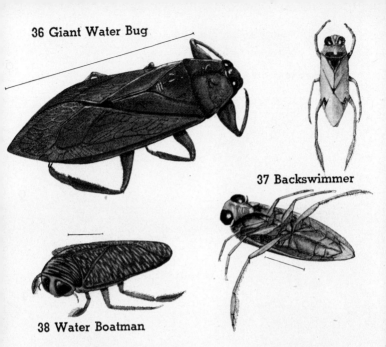

36 Giant Water Bug

37 Backswimmer

38 Water Boatman

LEAFHOPPERS, APHIDS, SCALES, AND ALLIES

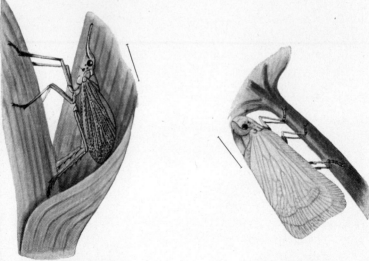

39a Planthopper

39b Planthopper

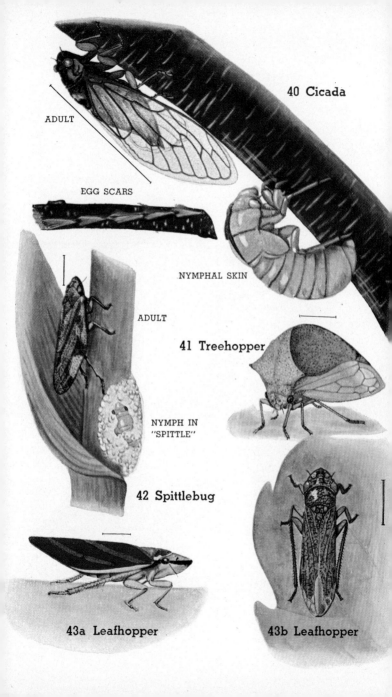

40 Cicada

ADULT

EGG SCARS

NYMPHAL SKIN

ADULT

41 Treehopper

NYMPH IN "SPITTLE"

42 Spittlebug

43a Leafhopper

43b Leafhopper

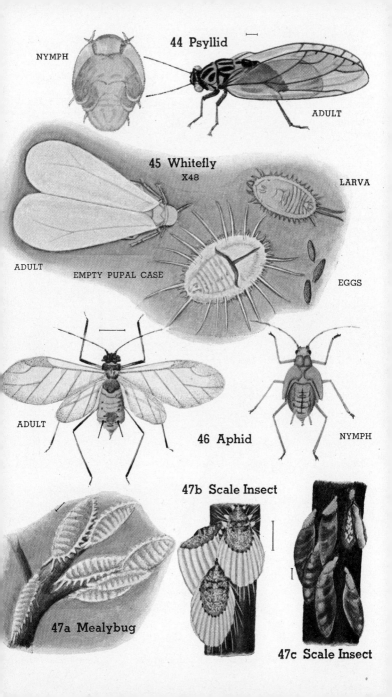

NYMPH

44 Psyllid

ADULT

45 Whitefly
X48

LARVA

ADULT

EMPTY PUPAL CASE

EGGS

ADULT

46 Aphid

NYMPH

47b Scale Insect

47a Mealybug

47c Scale Insect

MAYFLIES

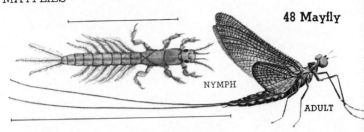

NYMPH

48 Mayfly

ADULT

DAMSELFLIES AND DRAGON FLIES

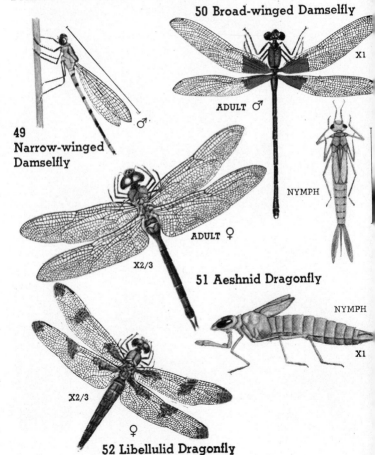

50 Broad-winged Damselfly

ADULT ♂

X1

49 Narrow-winged Damselfly

♂

NYMPH

ADULT ♀

X2/3

51 Aeshnid Dragonfly

NYMPH

X1

X2/3

♀

52 Libellulid Dragonfly

NERVE-WINGED INSECTS

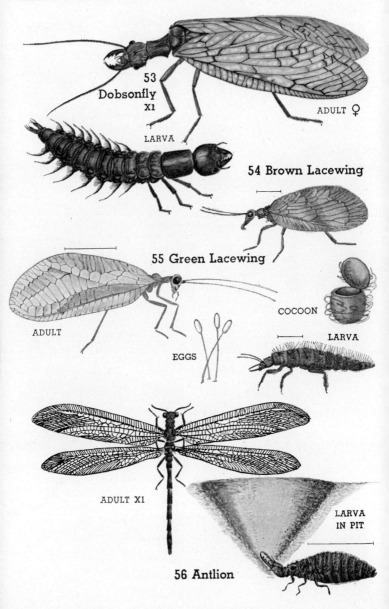

53 Dobsonfly X1

ADULT ♀

LARVA

54 Brown Lacewing

55 Green Lacewing

ADULT

EGGS

COCOON

LARVA

ADULT X1

LARVA IN PIT

56 Antlion

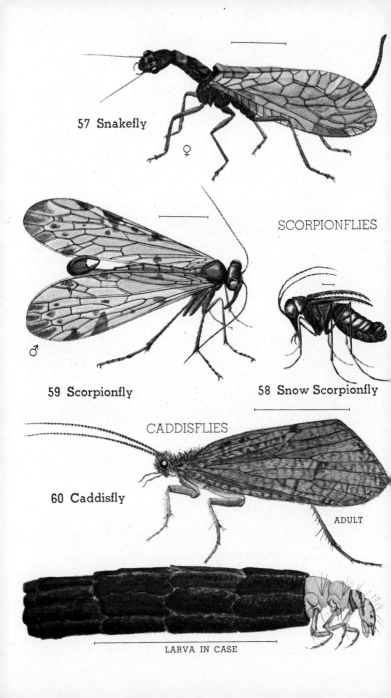

57 Snakefly ♀

SCORPIONFLIES

♂

59 Scorpionfly

58 Snow Scorpionfly

CADDISFLIES

60 Caddisfly

ADULT

LARVA IN CASE

MOTHS AND BUTTERFLIES

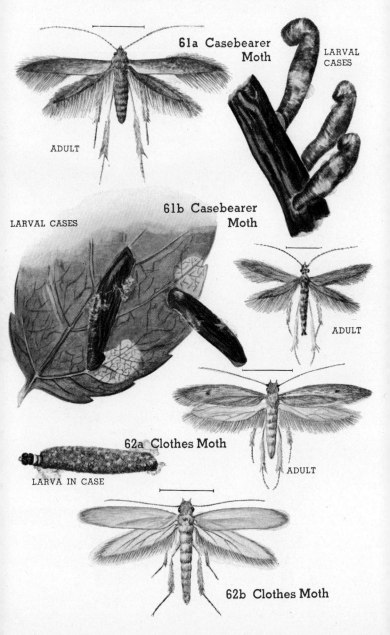

61a Casebearer Moth

LARVAL CASES

ADULT

61b Casebearer Moth

LARVAL CASES

ADULT

62a Clothes Moth

LARVA IN CASE

ADULT

62b Clothes Moth

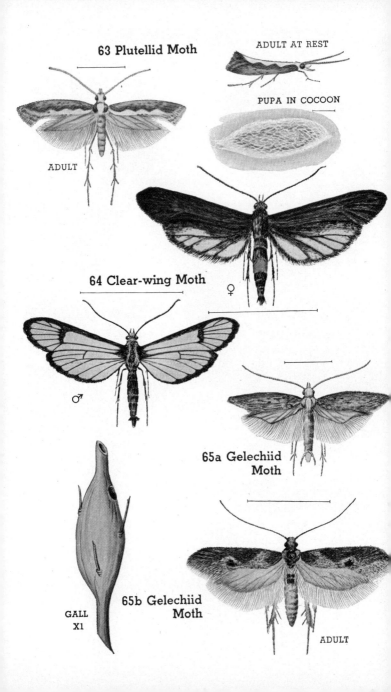

63 Plutellid Moth

ADULT AT REST

PUPA IN COCOON

ADULT

♀

64 Clear-wing Moth

♂

65a Gelechiid Moth

GALL
X1

65b Gelechiid Moth

ADULT

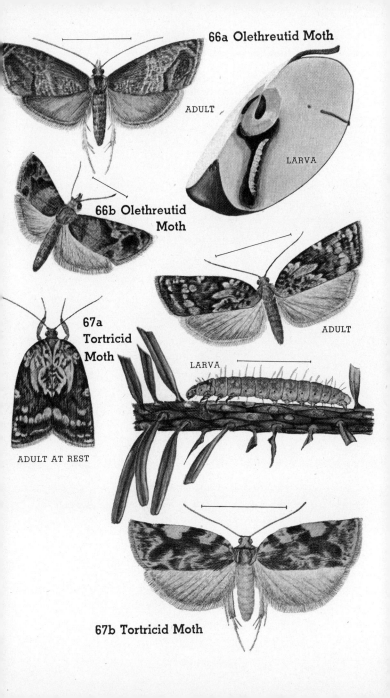

66a Olethreutid Moth

ADULT

LARVA

66b Olethreutid Moth

ADULT

67a Tortricid Moth

LARVA

ADULT AT REST

67b Tortricid Moth

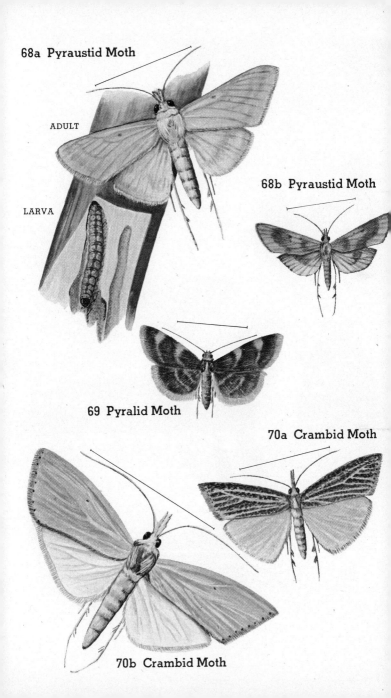

68a Pyraustid Moth

ADULT

LARVA

68b Pyraustid Moth

69 Pyralid Moth

70a Crambid Moth

70b Crambid Moth

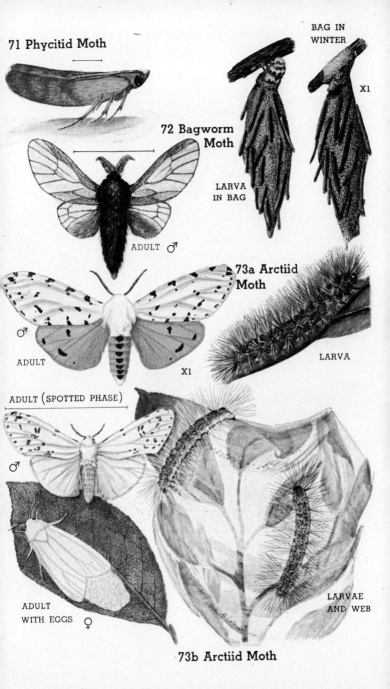

71 Phycitid Moth

72 Bagworm Moth

BAG IN
WINTER

X1

LARVA
IN BAG

ADULT ♂

73a Arctiid Moth

♂

ADULT

X1

LARVA

ADULT (SPOTTED PHASE)

♂

ADULT
WITH EGGS ♀

LARVAE
AND WEB

73b Arctiid Moth

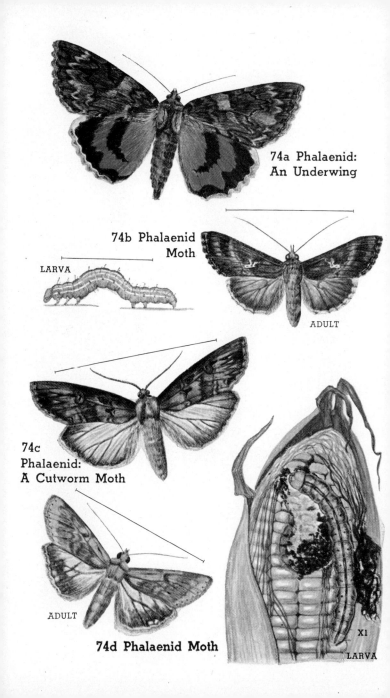

74a Phalaenid: An Underwing

74b Phalaenid Moth

LARVA

ADULT

74c Phalaenid: A Cutworm Moth

ADULT

74d Phalaenid Moth

X1

LARVA

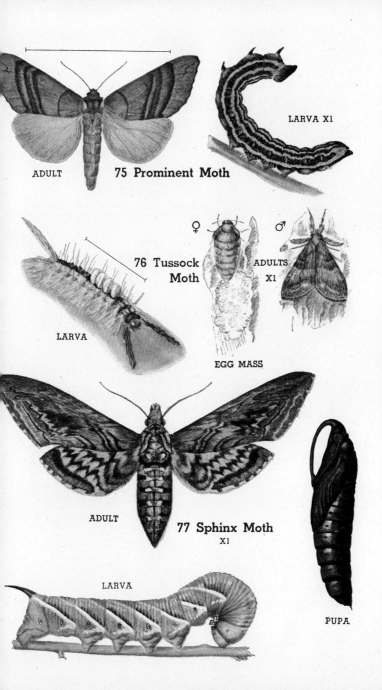

ADULT

LARVA X1

75 Prominent Moth

♀ ♂

76 Tussock Moth

ADULTS X1

LARVA

EGG MASS

ADULT

77 Sphinx Moth X1

LARVA

PUPA

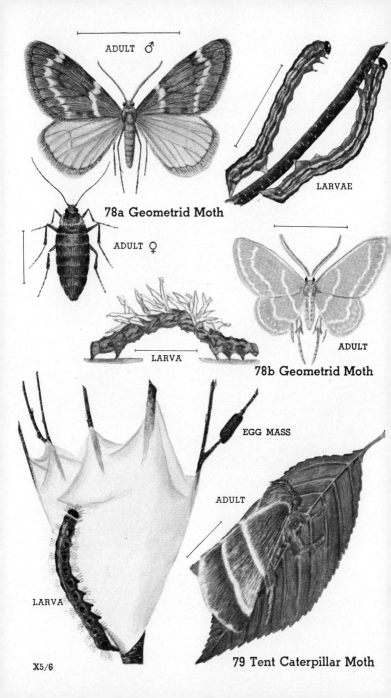

ADULT ♂

LARVAE

78a Geometrid Moth

ADULT ♀

LARVA

ADULT

78b Geometrid Moth

EGG MASS

ADULT

LARVA

79 Tent Caterpillar Moth

X5/6

80a Saturnid Moth

♂

80b Saturnid Moth

♀

X2/3

ADULTS

81a Skipper Butterfly

X1

LARVA

81b Skipper Butterfly

ADULT
X 4/5

PUPA

82 Swallowtail Butterfly

LARVA

X1

83a Pierid:
A White

83b Pierid:
A Sulphur

84 Milkweed
Butterfly

ADULT

LARVA

X1

85 Satyr Butterfly

86a
Nymphalid
Butterfly

86b
Nymphalid:
A Fritillary

86c Nymphalid:
An Angle-wing

86d Nymphalid:
A Crescent-spot

X3/4

87a
Lycaenid:
A Blue

87b
Lycaenid:
A Copper

87c Lycaenid:
A Hairstreak

87d Lycaenid:
A Hairstreak

X1

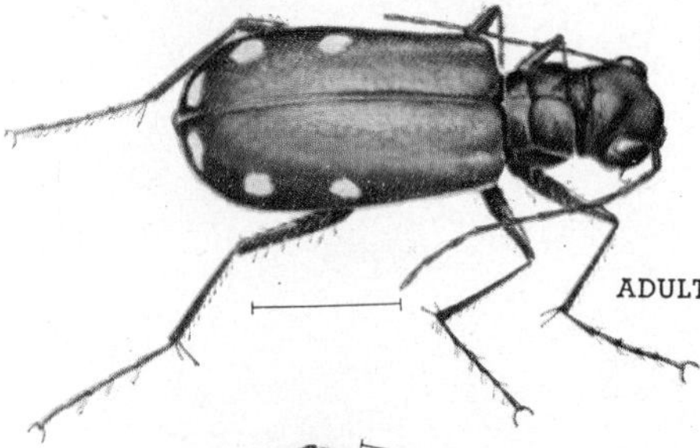

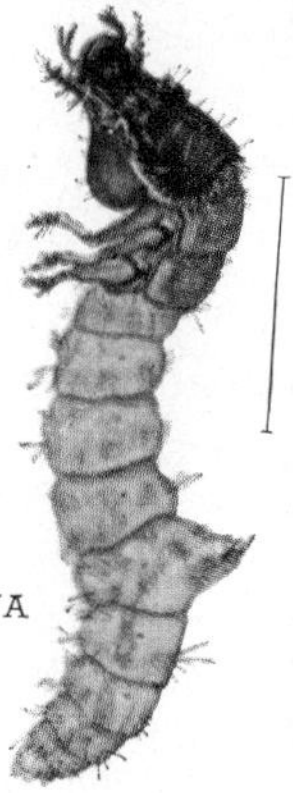

BEETLES

88a Tiger Beetle

ADULT

LARVA

88b Tiger Beetle

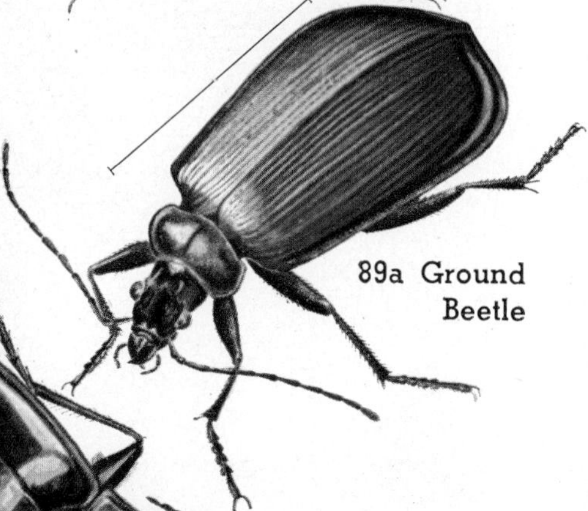

89a Ground Beetle

89b Ground Beetle

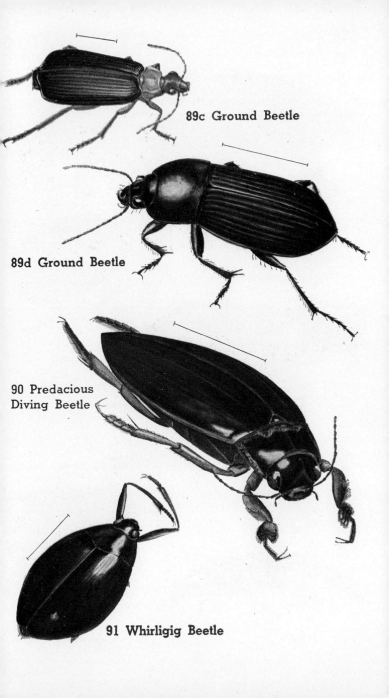

89c Ground Beetle

89d Ground Beetle

90 Predacious
Diving Beetle

91 Whirligig Beetle

92a Water Scavenger Beetle

92b Hydrophilid Beetle

93a Carrion Beetle

93b Carrion Beetle

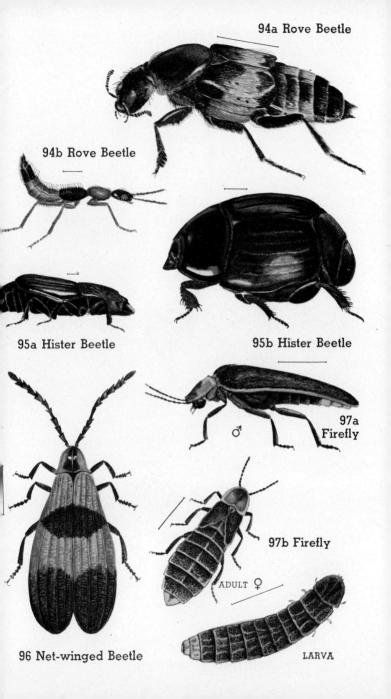

94a Rove Beetle

94b Rove Beetle

95a Hister Beetle

95b Hister Beetle

96 Net-winged Beetle

97a Firefly

♂

97b Firefly

ADULT ♀

LARVA

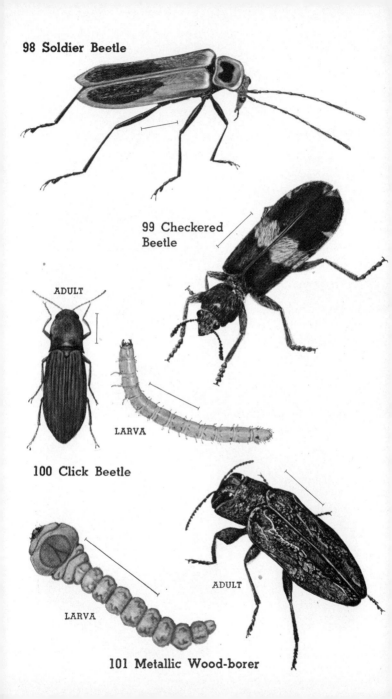

98 Soldier Beetle

99 Checkered Beetle

ADULT

LARVA

100 Click Beetle

LARVA

ADULT

101 Metallic Wood-borer

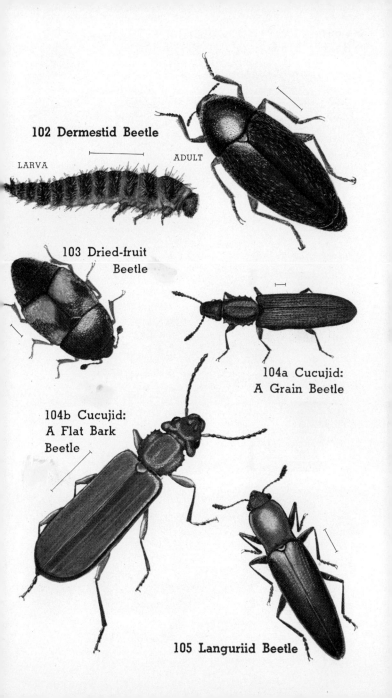

102 Dermestid Beetle

LARVA   ADULT

103 Dried-fruit Beetle

104a Cucujid: A Grain Beetle

104b Cucujid: A Flat Bark Beetle

105 Languriid Beetle

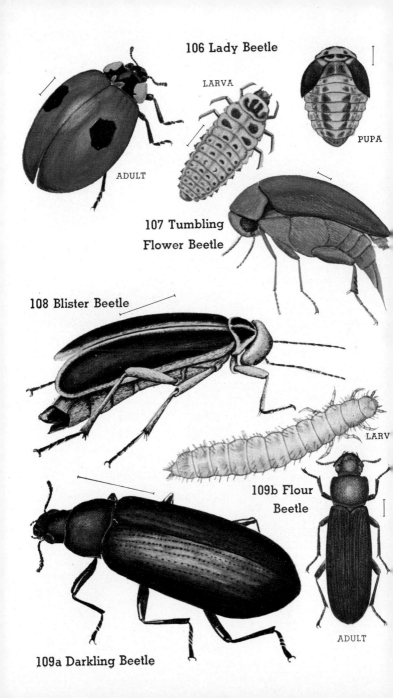

106 Lady Beetle

LARVA

ADULT

PUPA

107 Tumbling Flower Beetle

108 Blister Beetle

LARV

109b Flour Beetle

ADULT

109a Darkling Beetle

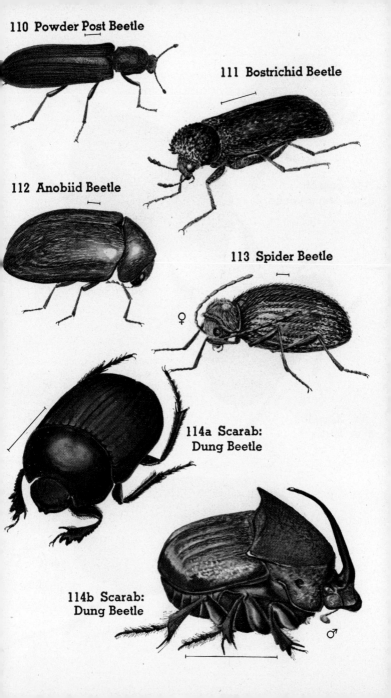

110 Powder Post Beetle

111 Bostrichid Beetle

112 Anobiid Beetle

113 Spider Beetle

♀

114a Scarab:
Dung Beetle

114b Scarab:
Dung Beetle

♂

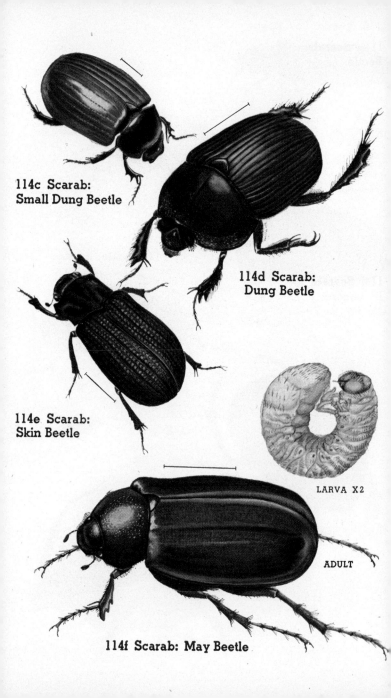

114c Scarab:
Small Dung Beetle

114d Scarab:
Dung Beetle

114e Scarab:
Skin Beetle

LARVA X2

ADULT

114f Scarab: May Beetle

114g Scarab Beetle

114h Scarab Beetle

114i Scarab: Rhinoceros Beetle

114j Scarab Beetle

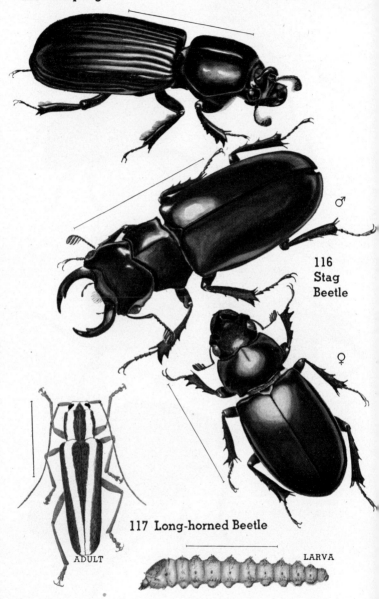

115 Bessybug

116 Stag Beetle

♂

♀

117 Long-horned Beetle

ADULT

LARVA

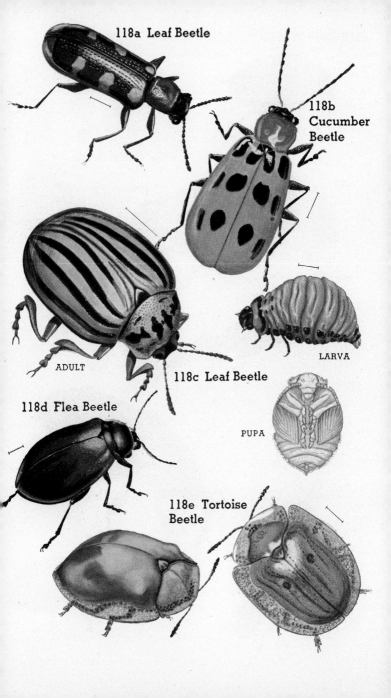

118a Leaf Beetle

118b Cucumber Beetle

ADULT

LARVA

118c Leaf Beetle

PUPA

118d Flea Beetle

118e Tortoise Beetle

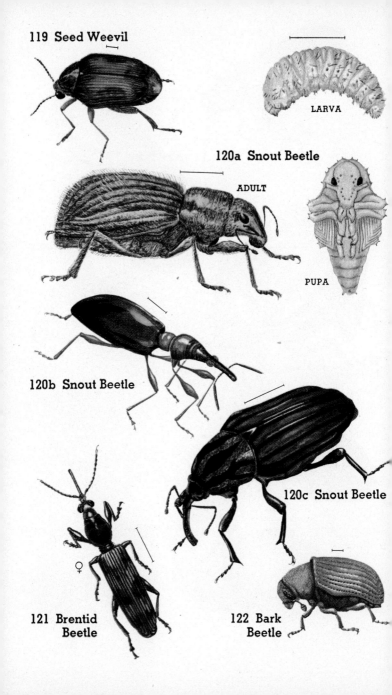

119 Seed Weevil

LARVA

120a Snout Beetle

ADULT

PUPA

120b Snout Beetle

120c Snout Beetle

♀

121 Brentid Beetle

122 Bark Beetle

WASPS, ANTS, BEES, AND ALLIES

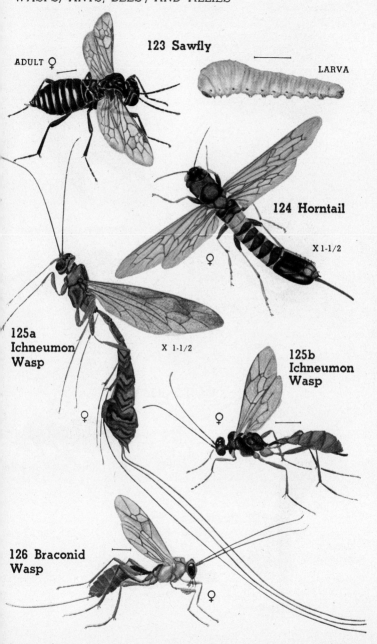

123 Sawfly

ADULT ♀

LARVA

124 Horntail

X 1-1/2

♀

125a Ichneumon Wasp

X 1-1/2

♀

125b Ichneumon Wasp

♀

126 Braconid Wasp

♀

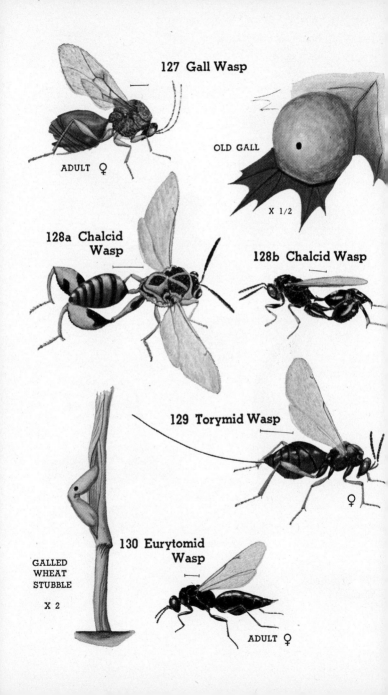

127 Gall Wasp

ADULT ♀

OLD GALL

X 1/2

128a Chalcid Wasp

128b Chalcid Wasp

129 Torymid Wasp

♀

GALLED WHEAT STUBBLE

X 2

130 Eurytomid Wasp

ADULT ♀

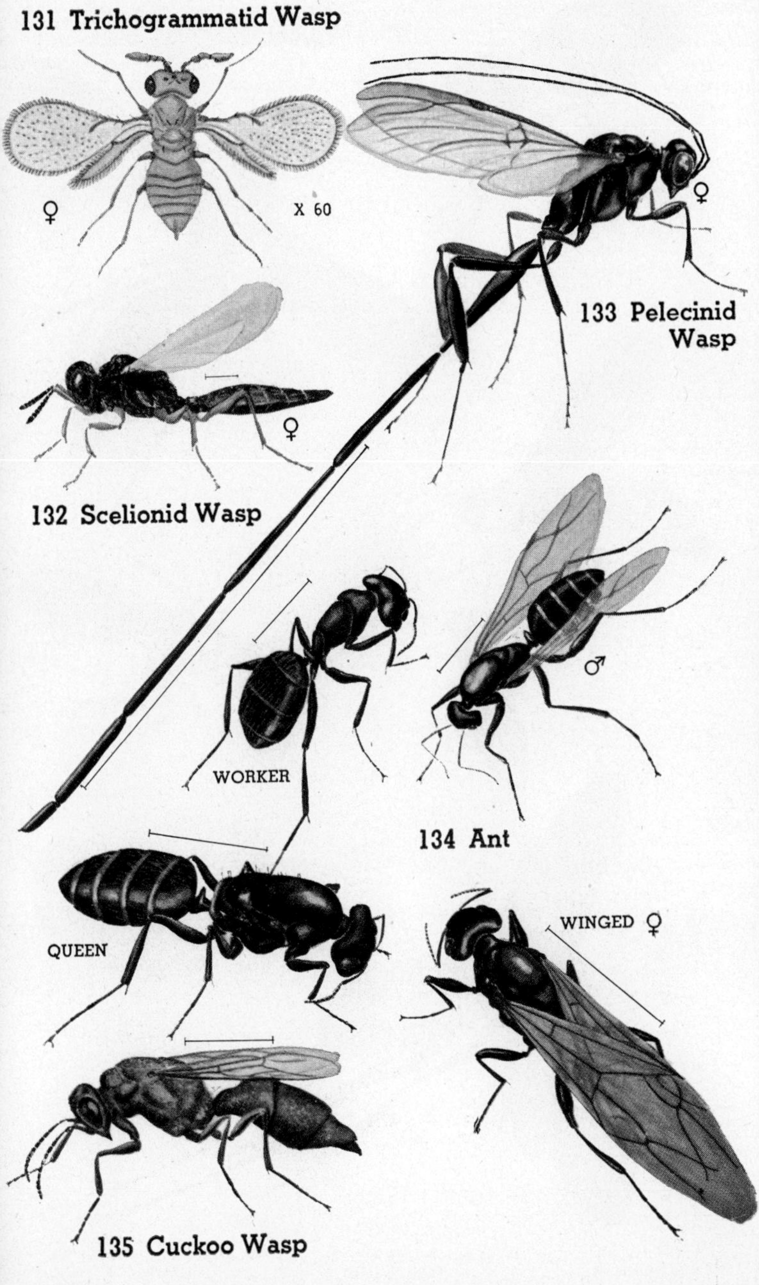

131 Trichogrammatid Wasp

♀   X 60

133 Pelecinid Wasp

♀

132 Scelionid Wasp

♀

WORKER

134 Ant

♂

QUEEN

WINGED ♀

135 Cuckoo Wasp

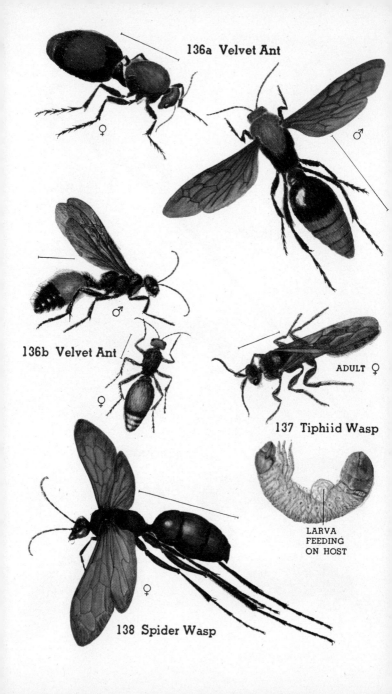

136a Velvet Ant

♀

♂

136b Velvet Ant

♂

♀

137 Tiphiid Wasp

ADULT ♀

LARVA
FEEDING
ON HOST

138 Spider Wasp

♀

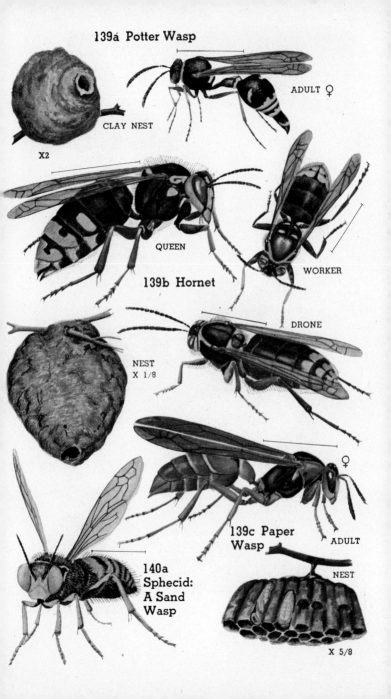

139a Potter Wasp

CLAY NEST

X2

ADULT ♀

QUEEN

WORKER

139b Hornet

DRONE

NEST
X 1/8

139c Paper Wasp

ADULT ♀

NEST

140a Sphecid: A Sand Wasp

X 5/8

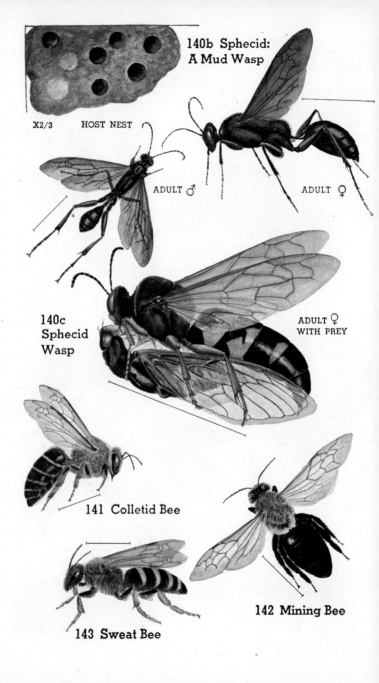

140b Sphecid: A Mud Wasp

X2/3   HOST NEST

ADULT ♂

ADULT ♀

140c Sphecid Wasp

ADULT ♀ WITH PREY

141 Colletid Bee

142 Mining Bee

143 Sweat Bee

144 Leafcutting Bee

145a Hairy Flower Bee

145b Carpenter Bee

DRONE

WORKER

145c Bumble Bee

QUEEN

WORKER

145d Honey Bee

QUEEN

DRONE

X2

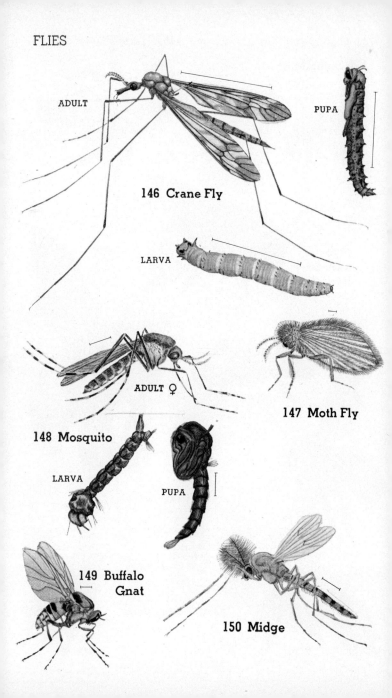

FLIES

ADULT

146 Crane Fly

PUPA

LARVA

ADULT ♀

147 Moth Fly

148 Mosquito

LARVA

PUPA

149 Buffalo Gnat

150 Midge

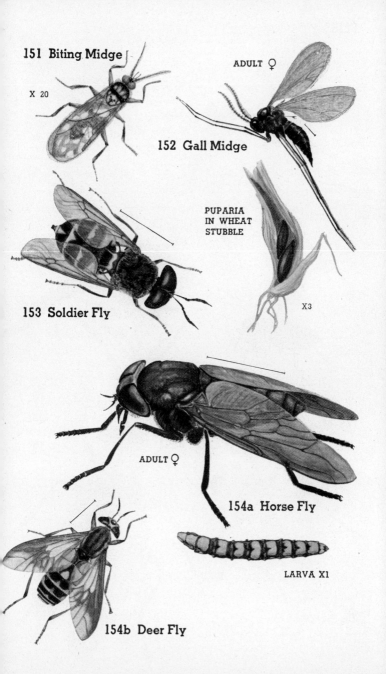

151 Biting Midge

X 20

ADULT ♀

152 Gall Midge

153 Soldier Fly

PUPARIA
IN WHEAT
STUBBLE

X3

ADULT ♀

154a Horse Fly

LARVA X1

154b Deer Fly

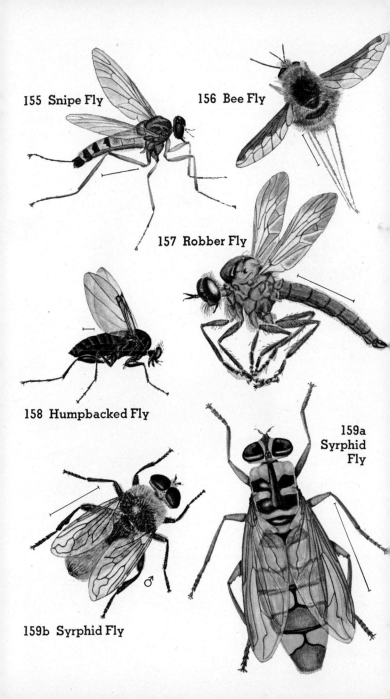

155 Snipe Fly

156 Bee Fly

157 Robber Fly

158 Humpbacked Fly

159a Syrphid Fly

159b Syrphid Fly

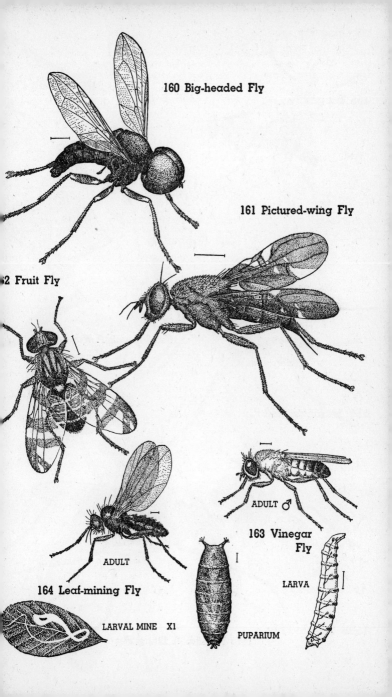

160 Big-headed Fly

161 Pictured-wing Fly

2 Fruit Fly

163 Vinegar
Fly

ADULT ♂

164 Leaf-mining Fly

ADULT

LARVA

LARVAL MINE X1

PUPARIUM

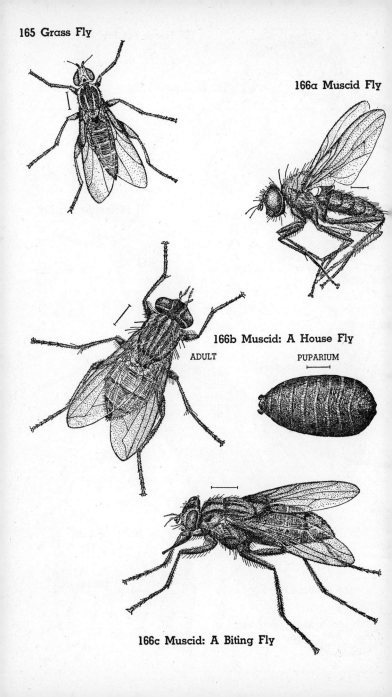

165 Grass Fly

166a Muscid Fly

166b Muscid: A House Fly

ADULT

PUPARIUM

166c Muscid: A Biting Fly

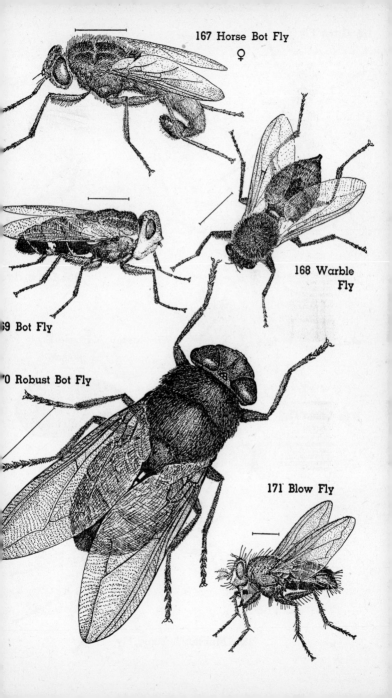

167 Horse Bot Fly
♀

168 Warble
Fly

69 Bot Fly

0 Robust Bot Fly

171 Blow Fly

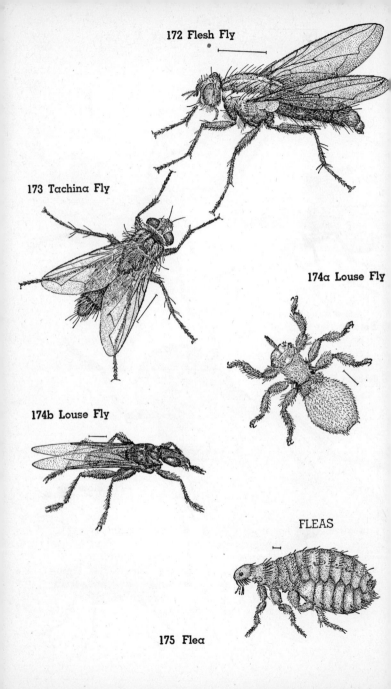

172 Flesh Fly

173 Tachina Fly

174a Louse Fly

174b Louse Fly

FLEAS

175 Flea

STREPSIPTERONS
Order Strepsíptera

These remarkable insects, mostly minute in size, are omitted from the picture guide only because so few persons ever see them or are aware of their existence. The adult female, in many species, is a wingless, legless parasite whose body, enclosed in the last larval skin, lies in the abdomen of a bug, leafhopper, wasp, bee, or some other insect, with only the head and thorax protruding between the segments of the host. The male adult is

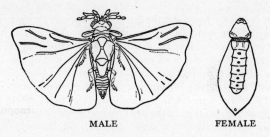

MALE   FEMALE

free-living and has 2 pairs of wings, the fore pair reduced to mere scales, the hind pair enormously developed and folded lengthwise when at rest, giving rise to the common name of "twisted-winged insects." Three of the 6 families are represented in our region. Above are figured a male and female adult of *Stỳlops mediónitans,* a parasite of mining bees in western North America (redrawn from Essig, 1942).

WASPS, ANTS, BEES, AND ALLIES
Order Hymenóptera

All of the truly social insects, except the termites, of the order Isóptera belong to this large and important order, distinguished for the many beneficial species it contains—the parasites of noxious insects, the efficient plant pollinators, and the only honey producers. The comparatively few pest species are usually either ants or sawflies. About 90,000 species have been described so far from the entire world. Hymenopterons have 2 pairs of simply veined, transparent, membranous wings, the hind pair being somewhat smaller and held to the fore wings by a row of tiny hooks on the front margins, which catch in a fold of the fore wings. They are often strong flyers, though the wings are not very large in proportion to the size of the body; the females of some species are wingless. The mouth parts are of the biting type but are variously modified, often with a "tongue" or proboscis for lapping or sucking liquid foods. The first abdominal segment is fused to the last thoracic segment, but the second (except in the sawflies and their close relatives) is much constricted into a stem (pedicel) for the rest of the abdomen, so that 3 distinct body regions result. Development is complex. The larvae are usually legless, with small, unpigmented but distinct heads. The appendages of the pupa are free of the body, and the pupa itself is sometimes enclosed in a silken cocoon.

This order is the only one containing insects which have a genuine "stinger." The sting of certain wasps, bees, and ants is the modified ovipositor of the female; no male insects, therefore, can sting. In spite of the fact that many of its members can inflict painful wounds, the order Hymenóptera is not immune to the attacks of birds and insect-eating mammals; indeed, it furnishes a third, perhaps more, of the food of our flycatchers.

123 Sawflies *Family Tenthredínidae*

The members of this and of the following family (Sirícidae), together with a few other families not considered in this book, constitute 1 of 2 suborders of the Hymenóptera. This group of insects differs from the others—the wasps, ants, and bees— in having no constriction of the second abdominal segment into a stem, or pedicel.

ADULTS: Mostly small, a few of medium size. Robust-appearing, although usually somewhat flattened in the abdominal region. The color is generally black, sometimes with yellow or brown markings. The ovipositors of sawflies consist of 2 short outer plates, which serve as guides, and 2 saw-toothed blades. These 2 little "saws" are moved in opposite directions when the female is slitting a leaf or stem preparatory to inserting an egg. The wings are rather broad. The fore tibiae of sawflies have 2 spurs at their extremities, differing in this respect from the horntails, which have only 1.

YOUNG: The smooth, spiny, or hairy larvae are cylindrical, with distinct heads. Most of them eat plant foliage, but some tunnel in stems or leaves, or live in plant galls caused by their own presence or by a substance injected into the plant by the adult sawfly at time of oviposition. Sawfly larvae are frequently mistaken for the caterpillars of Lepidóptera, or for slugs. There are 3 pairs of well-developed thoracic legs, and from 6 to 8 pairs of abdominal prolegs, which differ from those of caterpillars in lacking hooks (crochets). Remember that the larvae of moths and butterflies never have more than 5 pairs of prolegs, one pair always at the end of the body. The larvae of many sawflies are gregarious. They are often conspicuous for their bright colors, which may be green or yellow with many small black spots, and for the peculiar positions they assume—the end of the abdomen curled and held aloft, to one side, or wrapped about the stem of the leaf they are feeding on. Pupation occurs in a usually broadly oval, papery cocoon either in surface litter or in the ground.

IMPORTANCE: The larch sawfly (*Pristíphora erichsònii*), the outstanding sawfly pest of coniferous trees, periodically defoliates larch, tamarack, and some other trees in Canada and the northern United States. The imported currantworm (*Némathus ribèsii*) is one of the best-known and most widely distributed sawflies, occurring on currant and gooseberry wherever grown in our region. Sawflies of various species attack a wide range of trees and shrubs and even grasses. In all cases the larvae devour the foliage, but those of a species infesting rose, enter the pithy stems at maturity to hollow out a pupal chamber.

At least 30 species of birds eat sawfly larvae. From 50 to 100 larvae have been dissected from single stomachs of mockingbirds. Adult sawflies appear to derive no benefit from their resemblance to stinging members of the Hymenóptera.

EXAMPLE: Pear-slug   *Calíroa cérasi*

Introduced into New England from Europe during the days of settlement, now found wherever its food plants—pear, cherry, and plum—are cultivated. The eggs are laid singly under the epidermis of the leaves of the host plants. The larvae, which resemble slugs in being coated with a brownish slime, feed on the upper epidermis of the leaves. There are 5 larval stages. Pupation occurs in a cocoon several inches below the soil surface. The illustration shows a large larva with the slime removed.

124 Horntails   *Family Sirícidae*

ADULTS: The horntails are closely related to the sawflies and, with them, are set apart from the other Hymenóptera by their lack of a "waist," the second abdominal segment having no constriction. The abdomen is tipped with a spine in both sexes and the ovipositor of the female is stout and long. The eggs are laid in the wood or bark of trees. Quite frequently the females have difficulty in removing their ovipositors from a tree and may die in unsuccessful efforts to do so.

YOUNG: The cylindrical, large-headed larvae, like the adults, have a short, sharp, horn-like extension at the end of the body; they may appear S-shaped when removed from their burrows. Thoracic legs are present but are very small. They bore in the wood of coniferous and broad-leaved trees and in felled timber. The larva pupates in a thin papery cocoon in its burrow.

IMPORTANCE: Rather minor pests of forest trees; seldom abundant.

EXAMPLE: Pigeon Tremex   *Trèmex colúmba*

One geographical race or another is found everywhere in the United States from Arizona and Utah eastward and in much of eastern Canada. The ichneumon wasp (*Megarhýssa macrùrus*) is an important parasite of the larvae, which bore in the heartwood of maple, elm, and beech trees.

125 Ichneumon Wasps   *Family Ichneumónidae*

ADULTS: Mostly small or medium-sized insects, but some of our larger hymenopterons are included in this exclusively parasitic family. Slender insects with an elongate abdomen which in about half the species is somewhat sickle-shaped and much flattened from side to side, and in the others is cylindrical. The many-segmented antennae are very long and thread-like. The 3 ocelli are in a triangle on top of the head midway between the large eyes. The wings of most ichneumons are comparatively large, but the females of a few species are wingless. The eggs are laid near, on, or in the body of the host, which may be the larva or pupa of a moth or butterfly, or more rarely another hymenopteron, beetle, or fly. The ovipositors are of various lengths, some being much longer than the body. The host may be paralyzed or even killed by stinging before oviposition occurs. A few ichneumons are attracted to the nectar of flowers and to lights at night.

YOUNG: The larvae pass through 4 or 5 stages with accompanying changes in shape that vary according to the nature of the relationship with the host. They are mostly primary parasites and may feed either externally or internally upon the host. Those which hatch inside the body of the host or bore into it soon after hatching may spin their cocoons inside or outside it. If the host was a larva at the time it was parasitized, it frequently pupates before being killed by the parasite.

IMPORTANCE: Ichneumons are among the most important natural controls upon the populations of numerous agricultural pests. They also parasitize spiders.

EXAMPLE 125a: Ichneumon Wasp
Megarhýssa macrùrus

Widely distributed. The female drills through the bark of trees to reach the tunnels of horntail larvae (*124*) and oviposits probably upon the insects themselves.

EXAMPLE 125b: Ichneumon Wasp *Hyposòter pilósulus*

An important parasite of the fall webworm (*73b*) wherever the latter occurs. The parasite larva spins a cocoon inside the distended skin of the host larva, which remains hanging rather conspicuously in the webbing. This species hibernates as an adult.

126 Braconid Wasps   *Family Bracónidae*

ADULTS: Another important group of parasites, averaging very much smaller than the ichneumon wasps, few attaining $\frac{1}{2}$ inch in length, and differing further in having a relatively shorter abdomen, which is more or less cylindrical rather than laterally compressed. In habits they are very similar to the preceding family. The adults are often found at flowers. The eggs of some braconids give rise to more than one wasp. Such eggs are said to be polyembryonic.

YOUNG: In general, very much like those of ichneumon wasps.

IMPORTANCE: Almost as important as the ichneumons as destroyers of the larvae or pupae of moths and butterflies, other Hymenóptera, and, to a lesser extent, beetles. Being smaller, some of these insects can parasitize such tiny hosts as aphids; bloated, dead aphids with round holes cut in the top of their abdomens once contained these little wasps.

EXAMPLE: Braconid Wasp   *Macrocéntrus ancylivorus*

Widely distributed. This native, very useful little wasp attacks many kinds of lepidopterous larvae. It is known especially as a parasite of the oriental fruit moth (*Graphólitha molésta*) and the strawberry leaf roller (*Áncylis comptàna*).

The life cycle of this insect can be completed in 25 to 30 days, so in much of its range there are 3 generations a year. A single female can produce as many as 500 eggs during her lifetime, and very little arithmetic will show how the parasite population might increase in the presence of abundant host material.

127 Gall Wasps — *Family Cynípidae*

ADULTS: Very small or minute insects, responsible for most of the galls on the leaves and twigs of oak trees, rose, and plants of the thistle family (*Compósitae*). Their abdomens are laterally compressed or rather globular, and both thorax and abdomen, when viewed from the side, are circular in outline. The head is attached at a point almost underneath the thorax. The antennae are short and 11- to 16-segmented. The wings normally are well developed, but in some species those of the females are absent or vestigial. The ovipositor arises at the approximate center of the underside of the abdomen and is mostly coiled within the body. The eggs are laid singly in plant tissue, chiefly in the leaves and stems. In a few species, a parthenogenetic generation alternates with a bisexual one.

YOUNG: The almost colorless larvae are legless, with small heads and much-reduced antennae and palps. The plant gall does not commence to form until the larva has hatched. Some substance given off by the developing larva, or introduced with the egg, perhaps even a fungus or bacterium, seems to promote the formation of the characteristic swellings and malformations of the host plant which we term galls. In some cases, however, no gall is formed, the larva developing inside a cyst in the plant stem. The entire developmental period of these insects is spent inside the tissue of the host plant.

IMPORTANCE: Some of the galls produced by cynipids are rather unsightly, especially when very numerous, but in general they do little harm. The host plant is never killed, and no plants of agricultural importance are attacked. A honeydew-like substance is secreted by some of the galls, and this is collected by various other hymenopterons, notably ants. Squirrels eat many kinds of cynipid galls.

EXAMPLE: Oak Apple Gall Wasp
                    Amphíbolips confluéntus

Widespread on oak. These galls are rich in tannins. Certain oak galls of southeastern Europe and the Near East have been used for centuries in the manufacture of permanent inks.

128 Chalcid Wasps   *Family Chalcídidae*

ADULTS: Minute or very small, short-bodied insects with a head as wide or wider than the large, dorsally rounded thorax. Dull black or brown, sometimes with lighter markings. The head is short, with a wide indentation between the eyes. The ocelli are in a straight row between the eyes. The surfaces of both head and thorax are coarsely or finely pitted. The wings are almost veinless. The legs are short, the hind femora being very much enlarged and toothed below. Chalcids can hop as well as crawl and fly. All are parasites, chiefly upon the larvae of beetles, moths, butterflies, and flies, and are sometimes secondary parasites, preying upon the tachinid or ichneumonid parasites of coleopterous and lepidopterous larvae. The eggs are laid singly in or on the host insect.

YOUNG: The tiny larvae may feed either inside or upon the host insect. Although more than 1 egg may be placed on a host, only 1 parasite ever reaches maturity. There are 5 larval stages and 1 to 8 generations a year, depending upon the species of chalcid and the availability of hosts.

IMPORTANCE: The members of this rather small family are of secondary importance as control factors upon economic species of insects.

EXAMPLE 128a: Chalcid Wasp   *Spilochálcis nórtoni*

Widely distributed in the eastern United States south and west to Virginia and Texas. A parasite of lepidopterous caterpillars.

EXAMPLE 128b: Chalcid Wasp   *Spilochálcis delúmbis*

Recorded for most of the United States with the exception of the northwestern states. A solitary, internal parasite of the immature stages of leaf beetles.

129   Torymid Wasps   *Family Torýmidae*

ADULTS: This is a large family of very small wasps called the "beautiful parasites" because of their striking metallic green colors. They seldom exceed ⅛ inch in length. They are longer-bodied than the wasps of the preceding two families and neither the hind femora nor coxae are greatly enlarged. Most of them are parasitic upon insects living inside plant tissue, such as the larvae of gall wasps (*127*) and of wasps and flies living in seeds, stems, and leaf mines, and upon mantid eggs. The plant feeders infest the seeds of a great variety of plants.

YOUNG: The larvae are mostly external primary parasites, but some are internal parasites and a few are both primary and secondary parasites. In some species, several eggs are laid upon the same host insect and all may develop into adults.

IMPORTANCE: The life histories of these beautiful little insects for the most part are incompletely known if known at all. They are probably important natural control factors for many insects, for they are quite abundant. One torymid is a solitary external parasite of the wheat jointworm larva (*130*), another is a gregarious internal parasite of the gypsy moth (*76*), and both sometimes become secondary parasites, attacking almost any of the primary parasites of the original host. The Douglas fir seed chalcid (*Megastigmus spermótrophus*) and several other species of that genus infest the seeds of conifers.

EXAMPLE: Apple Seed Chalcid   *Tórymus drupàrum*

Widespread in our region and in Europe. The larvae live in apple seeds.

This family is closely related to the fig wasp family, Agaóntidae. The fig wasp develops in galled, infertile flowers on the anther-bearing caprifig trees and pollinates the exclusively female flowers of the Smyrna fig trees, which would not otherwise set fruit. The male wasps are wingless and do not leave the caprifigs in which they developed. This insect was imported from the Middle East into the fig plantations of California, where it has become established.

130 Eurytomid Wasps *Family Eurytómidae*

ADULTS: Very small, much like the preceding in size and general appearance, but almost always metallic black, never green. The legs are rather long and slender, with greatly enlarged hind coxae. The abdomen of the female is wedge-shaped as viewed from the side, gradually tapering to the pointed extremity. The ovipositor leaves the body near the center of the lower side of the abdomen. Many species are external parasites on the larval stages of gall wasps and other insects that feed inside plant tissue; others live as larvae inside seeds, or in the galls which they have caused to develop inside the stems of grasses and other plants.

YOUNG: Five larval stages appear to be the rule. Development occurs upon the body of the host or inside plant tissues. In a few species the insects are parasites in the early stages and plant feeders later on. There is usually one generation a year, but in some species the life cycle requires little more than 2 weeks and so several generations may occur. The winter is passed as a larva or pupa.

IMPORTANCE: This family is a strange mixture of beneficial and pest species. The widely distributed clover seed chalcid destroys much clover and alfalfa seed; the wheat straw-worm, a close relative of our example, is a 2-generationed species whose larvae destroy or stunt young wheat in the spring and stunt or weaken the stems of maturing plants. Too little is known of eurytomid life histories to appraise their value as parasites of pest insects. Some of them are secondary parasites, attacking the natural insect enemies of certain noxious species. One interesting form is predacious on the eggs of the snowy tree cricket (*11b*), tunneling through the pith of plant stems to reach one egg after another.

EXAMPLE: Wheat Jointworm *Harmolìta trítici*

One of the most important pests of wheat in the states east of the Mississippi River. The eggs are laid singly or in small groups inside the stems just above the first to third basal joints of wheat and a few other wild grasses. The galls, stimulated to growth by the presence of the larvae, swell out into the hollow centers of the wheat stems, often causing them to twist or bend or become so brittle that they will be broken by the wind.

131 Trichogrammatid Wasps
Family Trichogrammátidae

ADULTS: These minute wasps, all of them parasites inside the eggs of other insects, are less than 1/32 inch long and are not likely to be collected or seen except as a result of caging parasitized host eggs and observing them with a lens. They are black, brown, or yellow in color. The tarsi have only 3 segments and the antennae are prominent, being short, very heavy, and hairy. The wings are fringed with hairs, the hind pair being very narrow, the fore pair broad. The greatest width of the body is at the eyes. The ovipositor is short. One to 5 eggs are ordinarily placed in the host egg, which preferably is freshly laid. A European and an Australian species actually swim underwater in order to place their eggs in those of aquatic insects.

YOUNG: There seems to be some variation in the number of larval stages; some have 3, some 5, and some perhaps fewer. The entire immature life is passed within the host egg. A parasitized egg often can be recognized by its darker color. The life cycle may require only 7 to 10 days in hot weather, and there may be many generations in a year.

IMPORTANCE: Several species have been used extensively in attempts to control various lepidopterous pests. They are sometimes very effective because of their potentially tremendous rate of increase.

EXAMPLE: Trichogrammatid Wasp
Trichográmma minùtum

This insect, although native and widely distributed in our region, at various times has been bred in large numbers by commercial, state, and federal entomologists to supply farmers and orchardists. Mass liberations of the parasite did not result in sufficient reductions in codling moth larvae and other lepidopterous pests to warrant their continuance. The recorded host insects belong to 15 families of Lepidóptera, 4 of Hymenóptera, and 1 or 2 each of Neuróptera, Díptera, and Coleóptera.

132 Scelionid Wasps   *Family Scelionidae*

ADULTS: Another family of egg parasites, averaging somewhat
   larger than the preceding and sometimes reaching a length of
   $\frac{3}{16}$ inch. They are black or brown in color and in a few species
   are wingless. The normally 12-segmented antennae are
   elbowed. The wings are very narrow and fringed. The female,
   in most species, oviposits but once in a host egg. Scelionids are
   more restricted in their selection of hosts, most of which belong to the orders Orthóptera, Hemíptera, Lepidóptera, and
   Díptera. The eggs of spiders and certain beetles and lacewings
   are attacked. The adult females of some species attach themselves to the bodies or wings of a grasshopper, mantid, or
   moth, and ride about on it (a habit called "phoresy"); they
   even shed their own wings. The wasp, if adhering to a host of
   like sex, eventually oviposits in the eggs of her mount. There
   may be 8 or 9 generations a year in some species.

YOUNG: The 4 or 5 larval stages all are passed within the host
   egg. The early ones, if seen under high magnification, would
   probably not be recognized as insects at all by anyone but a
   specialist.

IMPORTANCE: In general, a useful family of parasites, since
   most of the host insects are not beneficial. The eggs of Mormon crickets and grasshoppers are sometimes heavily parasitized by scelionids. Of course those which parasitize the eggs
   of mantids and other useful predators are not rendering a
   service.

   EXAMPLE: Scelionid Wasp   *Scèlio caloptèni*

   Widely distributed in the United States and southern Canada. A parasite of the eggs of the lesser migratory grasshopper (*Melánoplus mexicànus mexicànus*) and other grasshoppers.

133 Pelecinid Wasps   *Family Pelecínidae*

ADULTS: A very small family of slender, shining black, long-
   bodied wasps, with only one representative in our region. The
   fore wings have few veins, and the hind wings, which are very
   much smaller, are veinless. The thread-like antennae are
   about as long as the fore wings. The females have an exceed-

ingly long abdomen, which may be 2½ inches long and about five-sixths of the total length of the insect. The males, which have short, club-like abdomens, are seldom collected; it is thought, in fact, that perhaps they are unnecessary to reproduction in our species. These insects are found in open woods. They are known to lay their eggs in the root-feeding larvae of scarab beetles (*114*), but not all the host relationships are understood.

YOUNG: The immature stages have not been thoroughly studied. The larvae are internal parasites but pupate outside the body of the host.

IMPORTANCE: Our species is not abundant enough to be of any importance as a natural control factor.

EXAMPLE: Pelecinid Wasp　　*Pelecìnus polyturàtor*

In woodlands almost everywhere in our region and southward over much of South America.

134　Ants　　　　　　*Family Formícidae*

ADULTS: Our species are minute to small insects, and it isn't likely that they need description. However, the winged, sexual forms which are produced once a year might be mistaken for wasps or flying termites, and the wingless forms are sometimes confused with worker termites. Ants are easily distinguished from termites by the much-constricted abdomen which gives them a "waist," and from other hymenopterons by the fact that the dorsal side of the 1 or 2 constricted segments of the abdomen (pedicel) bears an upright projection or hump, instead of being simple and perhaps concealed. Ants are black, brown, reddish, or yellowish, and either naked or somewhat hairy. The females, including all types of workers and soldiers, which are really infertile females, have elbowed antennae, the basal halves of which consist of one long segment; males often appear to have straight antennae because the basal segment may be about the size of the others. Eyes are almost always present, although in some species they may be mere vestiges. For the most part workers lack ocelli.

All ants are gregarious, living in small or very large colonies of from dozens of individuals to half a million or more. Our species live in a system of galleries in the soil, often under a dome of soil, sand, or debris of considerable proportions; in galleries in dead wood or in cavities in living plant tissue (including insect galls); in papery nests attached to twigs or rocks; and in buildings and even ships.

The ants in a single colony are of 3 principal kinds: (a) the fertile females or queens, (b) the males, short-lived insects which die shortly after the annual mating flight, (c) the infertile females—the workers and soldiers and some other specialized castes. Sometimes queens must depend upon workers of the same or even of other species to assist them in establishing new colonies, but more often a single fertilized female establishes an ant colony. She bites or scrapes off her wings, excavates a chamber in the soil, and rears a brood which she tends to maturity and feeds from her own mouth. These first, innumerable offspring then take over the care of the queen and the enlarging colony. A queen need mate only once to be able to lay fertile eggs continuously for the rest of her life—which may be 10 to 15 or more years.

Ants are herbivorous, carnivorous, or omnivorous. They are especially fond of the honeydew exuded by aphids, and some species tend aphids as man does cattle. The honeydew of many other kinds of homopterons is also sought. The Texas leaf-cutting ant feeds upon a fungus, among other things, which it cultivates on macerated leaf tissue in "gardens" located in their sometimes vast nests. Slave-making occurs among ants, who undoubtedly adopted this labor-saving device long before man did. The intended slaves are seized usually while still larvae or pupae by parties of raiders and become useful servants in the colonies of the master species.

In the world at large there are several thousand different species of insects which have become adapted to living in ant colonies. Some of these outwardly appear very like the ants with which they live. They may be scavengers, thieves, or actual predators upon weak or even healthy ants. There are "ant-loving" crickets, roaches, and rove beetles that live on secretions they remove from the bodies of ants. There are species of beetles which are tended inside colonies for the sake of savory secretions which the ants glean from tufts of special hairs on their bodies.

YOUNG: Ant larvae are white, curved, and legless, with the body gradually tapering toward the very small head which lacks ocelli. Most of these helpless insects, like squabs, are fed with partly digested food from the mouths of the tending workers, which, in turn, sometimes derive nourishment from glandular secretions of their charges. The pupae may be naked or enclosed in a thin, papery cocoon.

IMPORTANCE: Very important and the most abundant of all insects; truly the dominant family in point of numbers of individuals. It is fortunate, therefore, that so few are pest species. The many predatory kinds, those that feed upon larvae and pupae of insects in the soil and in or upon plants, are important assets to man and have not received the study and appreciation that they undoubtedly deserve. The primary pest ants are those that enter houses to steal bits of food and gnaw holes in fabrics; those that tend injurious homopterons (mealybugs, aphids, etc.) on field crops and orchard trees, corn and citrus, for example; and those ants which injure seedling plants and flowers, cut leaves, steal seeds from seed beds, or cover lawns and cultivated plants with their mounds of soil or sand. Some ants, like the fire ant of the southeastern United States, are pests of wild nestlings and young poultry, which they sting to death and devour. Several species are notable stingers and biters and some damage structural timbers, telephone poles, and fence posts.

Ant pupae in cocoons, mistakenly called ant eggs, are collected in large numbers and sold as fish and bird food. An ant of the southwestern United States, the so-called honey ant (*Myrmecocystus*), collects the honeydew secreted from a cynipid wasp gall on oak leaves and fills the stomachs of certain specialized individuals, whose abdomens gradually distend until they are balls of sweet liquid the size of a large pea. These creatures cling to the top of an underground chamber and give or receive honey as their more shapely sisters demand. The Indians of our Southwest and Mexico use these insects for "sweetening." Ant larvae and pupae are eaten by men in various parts of the world.

Ants are eaten by bears, many kinds of birds (notably the

flicker), lizards, amphibians, and insects, especially the ant-lion. Winged ants, when swarming, may fall into streams and lakes in large numbers and be devoured by fishes. They are used as models for various dry flies by anglers.

EXAMPLE: Black Carpenter Ant
Camponòtus herculeànus pennsylvánicus

Our largest ant, a common species throughout the eastern half of the United States. It lives in the galleries it constructs in dead trees, logs, fence posts, telephone poles, and the timbers of buildings, and is sometimes quite destructive; this ant does not consume the wood itself. Carpenter ants sometimes enter houses in search of sweet foods.

135 Cuckoo Wasps *Family Chrysídidae*

ADULTS: These beautiful insects often are called "jewel wasps" because of the brilliant green, blue, red, or purple of their bodies, the surfaces of which may be smooth or pitted. The name "cuckoo wasps" refers to their practice of laying eggs in the "nests" of bees and of other wasps. Our species, so far as is known, are solitary, external parasites. Cuckoo wasps are mostly small insects, seldom exceeding ½ inch in length. When in danger they may fold the abdomen flat against the underside of the head and thorax and remain immobile, giving excellent protection to the more vulnerable parts of the body. These insects appear to be recognized for what they are by the adult hosts and are subject to deadly attacks. They are therefore rather furtive, endeavoring to enter the host dwellings in the absence of the owners.

YOUNG: There are 5 larval stages in the species whose life histories have been studied. The egg is sometimes laid in the cell of a bee or wasp when the host larva is very small or perhaps even before the egg has been placed, but feeding usually does not start until the host is a mature or nearly mature larva. Pupation occurs in a cocoon outside the body of the host. There is a single generation annually in most species. The winter is passed as a larva in the host cell or cocoon.

IMPORTANCE: Cuckoo wasps are not of known importance. While they certainly destroy some beneficial pollinating insects, they themselves are visitors at flowers and are probably good pollinators in their own right. An Asiatic species parasitizes the mature larvae of the oriental fruit moth.

EXAMPLE: Cuckoo Wasp   *Chrȳsis nitídula*

This species is thought to be a parasite of solitary wasps. It is widely distributed in our region. There is a European wasp of the same name which may or may not be identical.

136 Velvet Ants   *Family Mutillidae*

ADULTS: The females do resemble ants (*134*) because they are wingless and superficially formed like them. But the "waist" is without upward projections and the antennae are never elbowed (in the females the tips have a backward hook). The bodies of our species are covered with usually short, dense hairs. The females are mostly red or yellowish, with bands and other patterns of white, black, or brownish. The males, which are almost all winged, are predominantly black, with orange or reddish markings on the abdomens; their antennae are straight. Mating sometimes is accomplished in the air, the males carrying their mates about while copulating.

Mutillids are parasites of wasps and bees, especially the burrowing species, and so the females should be looked for on barren, gravelly, sandy, or clayey spots, which the host insects would be likely to choose for their nest building. The females have powerful ovipositors with which they can deliver death to their victims and a very painful sting to incautious collectors. The females enter the burrows of the host to oviposit upon the larvae and pupae or, at times, to attack the adult and gorge on its body fluids.

YOUNG: Very little is known of the early stages of mutillids. They are external parasites, and some species develop on the young of beetles and flies as well as on those of wasps and bees. The cocoon is spun by the larva near the remains of the host in cell, cocoon, or puparium, as the case may be.

IMPORTANCE: These interesting insects are not beneficial, but usually they are not abundant enough to be of appreciable importance. Many of the host insects upon which the larvae develop are beneficial predatory species, and the adults have been found killing honeybees as well as other hymenopterons.

EXAMPLE 136a: North American Cow-killer
Dasymutílla occidentàlis

Rather common in its habitat throughout the southeastern quarter of the United States. This is one of our largest mutillids; its sting is quite severe, as the writer can testify, but is not fatal to large animals.

EXAMPLE 136b: Velvet Ant   *Dasymutílla nígripes*

Widely distributed in the United States east of the Rocky Mountains. Nothing at present seems to be known of its biology.

137 Tiphiid Wasps   *Family Tiphìidae*

ADULTS: Mostly small, slender insects, with elongate abdomens, sparsely haired. They are black, or black marked with white, yellow, or red. The females of some species are wingless. Our known tiphiids are parasitic on white grubs (*114f*) and some other scarabaeid larvae. The female of our example, a rather typical species, enters the soil to reach the host, a white grub in the third stage of development. After stinging it, to render it quiet, she massages the lower surface of its abdomen with her mouth parts, rasps the crease between 2 segments, and places a single egg there. To top it off, she will likely snip away part of a leg of the grub and take a nourishing drink of fresh blood. At some later time she may be found sipping nectar from flowers of goldenrod or of plants of the parsley family or drinking honeydew.

YOUNG: The larva perforates the skin of its host at the oviposition site and feeds there, externally, until mature. The host larva does not die until the parasite is in its last developmental stage. The dead grub is almost completely eaten by the now large parasite larva, which finally spins a cocoon and pupates in the soil cell of its host.

IMPORTANCE: These insects are important checks on the larval populations of certain scarab beetles.

EXAMPLE: Tiphiid Wasp   *Típhia popilliávora*

A Japanese species, which has been introduced into the United States and established as one of the more important factors in the biological control of the Japanese beetle.

A closely related family of wasps, the Scoliidae, which we have not illustrated, contains generally larger, very hairy species. They are mostly black, spotted or banded with red or yellow, and are likewise parasites of scarabaeid larvae.

138 Spider Wasps *Family Pompílidae*

ADULTS: Our better-known species are medium-sized to large insects with dark blue, black, or brownish bodies. The wings are sometimes purplish and may be orange or red. The slender legs are very long and the abdomen is comparatively short. The antennae of the male are straight, those of the female curved back at the tips. These wasps nest in burrows in the soil, in mud cells, and in holes and cracks in trees, rocks, and buildings. They stock their nests with spiders, including the very largest kinds, and with insects, which they have paralyzed by stinging and upon which they have placed an egg. Apparently only one host spider or other insect is placed in a nest. Some species are said to use beetles and orthopterons as food for their young. Sometimes the nest built by a spider is taken over by a wasp as a home for its developing young. The adults often visit flowers.

YOUNG: The larvae feed externally upon the provender supplied them.

IMPORTANCE: Since spiders are chiefly beneficial, it may be assumed that these insects which feed upon them are not so. However, they do not appear to threaten the existence of our spiders.

EXAMPLE: Tarantula-hawk *Pépsis formòsa*

This very large and beautiful species lives in the southwestern United States. It stings and paralyzes tarantulas and places them in its burrows as food for its young. There is a large fly of the Southwest, *Mÿdas luteipénnis* (family Mydàidae), which bears a strong superficial resemblance to the tarantula-hawk and, in flight, might be confused with it.

139 Potter Wasps, Hornets, and Allies
Family Véspidae

ADULTS: A large family of (a) social insects—the hornets, yellowjackets, and other paper wasps, which construct nests of coarse paper made from wood fiber, and (b) solitary, or un-social, insects—the potter wasps and a lesser number of bur-rowing species. All are medium to large-sized insects, often brightly marked with white, yellow, or red. The wings are folded longitudinally when not in use.

The potter wasps build cells of earth, sand, or chewed foliage, sometimes in the form of beautifully fashioned vases and globes attached to twigs. Some species utilize hollow twigs and stems as nests, partitioning the space off into cells. All species, including those that nest in the soil, collect the larvae of lepidopterons or of some other insects to provision the cells, each of which will receive a single egg. The victims are permanently paralyzed by stinging.

The paper wasps construct sometimes massive nests, which may be suspended from the branches of trees, eaves, and barn roofs, or placed in cavities in trees or in the ground. They have a caste system, which is not as complex as that of ants, certain bees, or termites. The large, fertile females are the queens, each of which may found a new nest. She lays eggs which, if unfertilized, will produce only males (drones) or, if fertilized, females, which may turn out to be future queens or infertile workers, according to the amount of food the larvae are supplied during their development. The more poorly nourished workers, which usually are completely sterile, sometimes produce eggs which give rise to sterile and useless drones. The workers relieve the queen mother of the care of the nest, enlarging it and gathering food, chiefly lepidopterous larvae, for the young.

YOUNG: Potter wasp larvae are solitary in their mud cells. In most species the food necessary for their complete develop-ment is in the cell at the time of oviposition. Paper wasp larvae are fed by workers or queens with chewed portions of insects, especially caterpillars, and sometimes with honey-dew, the nectar of flowers or fruit juices. The mature larva is sealed up in its cell to pupate; no cocoon is made.

IMPORTANCE: Most of these insects are beneficial, since the in-sects they feed their larvae are mostly injurious or at least not useful species. Some of the paper wasps are annoying because of their liking for fruit juices. They may collect where canning of fruit is being done or may do injury to ripe fruit on the tree or after it is picked. Hornets and yellow-jackets are respected for their short tempers and stinging abilities.

EXAMPLE 139a: Potter Wasp   *Eùmenes fratérnus*

Abundant in eastern North America. It makes cells of clay on the twigs of trees and fills them with paralyzed canker-worms (*78a*) for its young to eat.

EXAMPLE 139b: Bald-faced Hornet
Dolichovéspula maculàta

One of the paper wasps, a widely distributed hornet that suspends its large, globular, covered nest from the branch of a tree or bush. A. T. Gaul recently has distinguished 4 forms or castes in addition to the ordinary queens, males, and workers in certain hornets of the genera *Dolichovéspula* and *Véspula:* wingless (or nearly wingless) queens which can mate and lay eggs but probably cannot found new colonies; diminutive workers, the first brood of a new queen; fertile workers whose eggs produce males only; workers of normal size, but wingless except for short stalks.

EXAMPLE 139c: Paper Wasp   *Polístes fuscàtus*

The wasps of the genus *Polístes* do not enclose the cells of their nests in a paper wrapper. The nests of our example, a very common paper wasp, distributed throughout the United States and southern Canada, are suspended from the branches of trees, shrubs, and the eaves and ceilings of outbuildings. The illustration shows 2 opened cells with their contents, a larval and a pupal wasp.

140 Sphecid Wasps   *Family Sphécidae*

ADULTS: Small to large, mostly medium-sized wasps. Several major subgroups, including the one represented by our example (*140b*), have long-stemmed (petiolate) abdomens; others do not. Sphecids are solitary or colonial in habit, sometimes nesting in close proximity to other members of the same species. The adult tunnels in soil or wood; utilizes the hollow stems of grasses or constructs chambers in pithy stems or twigs; or builds cells of mud, either singly or in groups, in sheltered sites on buildings, trees, and rocks. The cells or chambers are usually stocked with an assortment of insects or spiders that have been captured by the adult female and paralyzed or stung to death, to serve as food for the young. Spiders, grasshoppers, and other orthopterons, caterpillars, aphids, bugs, and flies are the prey usually chosen for the larder. The egg of the wasp usually is laid upon one of the paralyzed or dead victims and the entrance to the cell closed up, but in some species the young are fed daily with insects that have been partly chewed by the parent.

YOUNG: The young are hearty eaters. After completing their development they spin a cocoon in which to pupate. The winter is passed as a larva or pupa in this cocoon.

IMPORTANCE: These are beneficial insects, since most of the prey consists of injurious insect species.

EXAMPLE 140a: Sand Wasp   *Bémbix spínolae*

Distributed from eastern Canada and the Dakotas south to Florida and Texas. One of a group of burrowing species, feeding its young daily upon all sorts of flies. The insects live in small colonies.

EXAMPLE 140b: Blue Mud Wasp   *Chalýbion caerùleum*

Widely distributed in our region. Until Phil Rau published his interesting observations in 1928, this wasp was thought to be a true mud dauber, a builder of mud cells. Actually, it nests in the cells of mud daubers, especially those of the sphecid, *Scéliphron caementàrium*. The female imbibes large quantities of water, which she uses to soften the wall of a mud dauber cell. After an opening has been made she removes the contents of the cell and then fills it with spiders which she has paralyzed by stinging. An egg is affixed on the last spider to go into the cell. Finally the opening is sealed with mud taken from another part of the same host nest, or perhaps from a neighboring one. The mud nest shown in the illustration is that of *S. caementàrium*.

EXAMPLE 140c: Giant Cicada-killer   *Sphècius speciòsus*

Widely distributed. One of our very largest wasps; as the name suggests, it hunts cicadas. It gives its victim a paralyzing sting, then takes it to its large, sometimes branched, burrow in the soil. This difficult task, with so large a burden, is performed by dragging the cicada up a tree to gain altitude and then gliding off on rigid wings, a process which may be repeated several times before the wasp reaches its burrow. One, sometimes 2, paralyzed cicadas are placed in the chamber at the end of the burrow. The female wasp places an egg near the base of a middle leg of the cicada. The wasp larva feeds upon the cicada from the outside and, when fully grown, constructs a cocoon in which it spends the winter and later pupates. There is only 1 generation a year.

141 Colletid Bees   *Family Collétidae*

This and the remaining families of the order Hymenóptera are set off as a group (the superfamily Apoìdea) known as bees by their possession of dilated hind tarsi, typically equipped with a "pollen basket" of stiff hairs, and a usually dense coat of feathery hairs on head and thorax. The primitive bees of the family Prosópidae lack pollen baskets, are black, marked with yellow, and have shorter hairs than the colletids to which they are most closely related.

ADULTS: Small insects, black, densely covered with long hairs, and with short, slightly bilobed tongues. The 3 ocelli are almost in a line across the "forehead." The legs are hairy and relatively short, the hind ones fitted with pollen baskets. The nests are burrows, up to 28 inches long, in clay, sand, or rotting masonry, which the bees line with a thin, gelatinous film, probably from the salivary glands. These burrows are partitioned off into from 5 to 8 cells or may have lateral branches with a cell at the end of each. Each cell contains a liquid or pasty mass of honey and pollen and receives an egg.

YOUNG: Legless, robust, C-shaped, sluggish larvae with nothing to do but eat the sweets provided by the parents.

IMPORTANCE: The adults of this very small family are important pollinators of many plants of agricultural value. The young are parasitized by certain blister beetle larvae (*108*).

EXAMPLE: Colletid Bee   *Collètes compáctus*

Occurs throughout much of the United States east of the Rocky Mountains. This species builds a low mound about the mouth of its steeply descending burrow which averages more than 20 inches in depth and has 2 to 4 side branches.

142 Mining Bees   *Family Andrénidae*

ADULTS: Insects of medium size, usually black with reddish or yellow markings. The head, thorax, and legs are densely hairy; the tongue is short and pointed. There are many species, most of them very difficult to separate. The hind tarsi are equipped with pollen baskets. They live in tunnels that may be solitary or, in some species, clustered together in colonies which are often very large. At or near the bottom of the burrow are cells in which they place a pasty mass of pollen and an egg. There are 1 or 2 generations a year. The adults overwinter in the burrows.

YOUNG: Typical bee larvae.

IMPORTANCE: The andrenids are very important pollinators of a wide variety of cultivated plants.

EXAMPLE: Mining Bee   *Andrèna cárlini*

Found east of the Rocky Mountains in the United States.

143 Sweat Bees   *Family Halíctidae*

ADULTS: Mostly very small insects, black (which may be iridescent), occasionally with red or yellow markings. The tongue is short and sharp-pointed. All of the species live in the ground, some in colonies with a common entrance and many side tunnels belonging to individual females. The cells opening off these family tunnels are provided with both nectar and pollen for the nourishment of the young. The adults, of course, are flower visitors and some are nocturnal. They do alight frequently on perspiring human skin—thence their popular name. Some halictids are social parasites, laying their eggs in the nests of other species.

YOUNG: Typical bee larvae.

IMPORTANCE: Valuable pollinators, especially of fruit trees.

EXAMPLE: Sweat Bee   *Halíctus farinòsus*

This species is found from New Mexico to California and north to Montana and British Columbia.

144 Leafcutting Bees
Family Megachilidae

ADULTS: Medium-sized or large hairy bees, usually black or metallic blue, green, or purple. The short antennae are elbowed; the ocelli form a triangle. The tongue is long and slender and the mandibles quite large. The legs are long and are not equipped with pollen baskets; pollen is carried on brushes under the abdomen. These are solitary bees nesting in burrows in the soil, dead wood, hollow stems of plants, and old masonry. They cut large disks from leaves of certain plants, oval ones for linings of the burrows, round ones for cell partitions. Rose foliage is especially desirable for this purpose, and there is scarcely a reader who will not remember seeing rose leaves with dime-size holes in them and probably wondering how they were cut out so perfectly. A typical burrow has 10 or 12 cells, each with a sticky mass of nectar and pollen topped with an egg.

YOUNG: Typical bee larvae.

IMPORTANCE: These are all flower visitors and important pollinators. The family numbers some social parasites of its own members as well as those of other closely related families.

EXAMPLE: Leafcutting Bee *Megachìle latimànus*

Occurs in the United States east of the Rocky Mountains. It is one of the outstanding pollinators of the various cultivated clovers.

145 Carpenter, Bumble, Honey Bees and Allies
Family Ápidae

This is by far the largest family of bees, and justice could hardly be done it even if this book were devoted solely to its exposition. It includes some of our best-known insects—the bumble and honey bees—and, in fact, all of the larger bees that do not have the leaf-cutting habit.

ADULTS: These bees are small- to medium-sized insects and may be social, solitary, or parasitic in habit. Their tongues are long. The social species have complicated caste systems which are explained in some detail in the discussions of our examples. The parasitic species live in the nests of other bees and feed upon the food stored up by the hosts for their own progeny; such bees do not have the pollen-gathering apparatus which characterizes the free-living members of the family.

YOUNG: The robust, legless larvae live in cells on food supplied by the adults. The nature of the food given the young of the honey bee determines its caste.

IMPORTANCE: Honey bees really are more valuable as pollinators of cultivated plants than as producers of honey and beeswax. In many orchards and fields they take the place of the badly depleted wild bee populations. Native pollinating insects of importance, especially the solitary bees, have suffered greatly from the destruction of their nesting places by certain of our agricultural practices, and honey bees are now the dominant insect pollinators. Some species of clovers and other plants with long-tubed corollas must be pollinated by bumble bees or other long-tongued bees. Insecticidal sprays and dusts have played havoc with bees throughout our region, and increasing attention must be given to methods of eliminating noxious insects while safeguarding the lives of the beneficial ones. Carpenter bees are occasionally destructive to fence posts and the timbers of outbuildings.

EXAMPLE 145a: Hairy Flower Bee
Anthóphora occidentàlis

A species distributed throughout the Great Plains of North America. This bee will represent a large subfamily of the Ápidae, containing numerous hairy flower bees, cuckoo bees, and related species. They are all rather large and hairy, some approaching the size of the bumble bees. The hairy flower bees nest in tunnels in clay banks, sometimes in large colonies. The entrances to these tunnels sometimes are protected by short "chimneys," which curve downward at the ends. The young are fed with a mixture of pollen and nectar. The adults are valuable pollinators of flowers having long corollas. The cuckoo bees, as the name implies, lay their eggs in the nests of other bees so the young may parasitize the host larvae or devour the food intended for them.

EXAMPLE 145b: Great Carpenter Bee
Xylócopa virgínica

Widely distributed in eastern and southern North America. This is one of a group of wood-boring species resembling bumble bees in general appearance but not as densely hairy and not as robust, being considerably flatter in outline. Carpenter bees nest in dead wood, sometimes in hollow stems. Occasionally they severely damage fence posts and building timbers. The large burrows, which may exceed a foot in length, are divided off into a number of separate cells by partitions of cemented wood chips, each cell containing a mass of honey-pollen paste and an egg.

EXAMPLE 145c: Bumble Bee   *Bómbus americanòrum*

Found throughout the United States and southern Canada; especially abundant in the central Mississippi Valley. The various members of the genus *Bómbus* are the bumble bees. These insects average larger than the other bees of this family and are more densely hairy. The color of the coat is black with yellow, orange, or red markings. The outer surfaces of the hind tibae and the first tarsal segments in the females are smooth and edged with long, curved stiff hairs, forming "baskets" in which pollen is carried to the nest. They live in large underground colonies, which are often placed in abandoned rodent burrows. They construct waxen "combs," sometimes of several stories, in the cells of which they lay their eggs, store pollen and nectar, and make honey. The caste system of the bumble bees is very like that of the honey bee, which follows. However, only fertilized female bumble bees who will become colony queens the next season survive the winter. Their tongues are very long, and because of this bumble bees are the only insects which can pollinate certain red clovers. Bumble bee nests are often dug up and their contents devoured by badgers, bears, mice, and foxes.

The "cuckoo" bumble bees of the genus *Psithyrus,* which strongly resemble the ordinary bumble bees in appearance, are parasites in the nests of our example and in those of other species of *Bómbus*. There is no worker caste among these parasites, and the females lack pollen baskets on the hind legs. In some instances the parasite remains in the nest with the host queen, apparently without conflict; in others, the prospective host or her workers will drive her out or kill her.

Sometimes 2 or more of the parasite females will dwell in the same host nest.

EXAMPLE 145d: Honey Bee   *Apis mellifera*

Naturalized from Europe throughout our region except in the extreme North. Apples, almonds, cherries, plums, pears, raspberries, clovers, cantaloupes—all need the honey bees' good offices to set fruit. Honey bees are represented in our region by several races of a single species, which has lived in domestication with man for more than 4000 years. There are 3 castes. The ordinary visitor at dandelions and other flowers is a worker, an infertile female, whose task is to build the colony, clean it, defend it, and care for the queen and her progeny. The queen is a fertile female, considerably larger than the workers and having a pointed abdomen. She lays fertile eggs which produce workers (and queens on occasion) and infertile eggs which produce drones (males). She has a sting with which to kill rival queens in struggles over hive supremacy. Old queens swarm out with part of a colony each year to found a new one. The drone is stingless and sooner or later, after the mating flight, is driven off or destroyed by the workers. A colony of honey bees may number 30 to 50 thousand individuals and may live in hives provided for them by apiarists (beekeepers) or may build their combs in hollow trees in the woods. In the 300 years or so since honey bees were introduced into our region they have become well established outside of domestication. The "honeycomb" is made of wax secreted from "wax pockets" between the abdominal segments. The eggs which produce queens and workers are alike, but the cell containing an egg designated to become a queen is large and cylindrical rather than hexagonal, like the others, and stretches over the face of the comb. The queen larva is fed royal jelly from the mouths of nurse bees until she pupates, while worker larvae get this type of food only during the first 3 days of larval life.

FLIES
Order Díptera

Flies differ from most other adult insects in having but a single pair of wings—some Mayflies and the males of certain scale insects and strepsipterons being the chief exceptions. These wings are membranous and, in most species, unpigmented. Hind wings are represented by small vestigial organs called "halteres," mere knobs on short stalks, which cannot function like wings at all but do have an important balancing action during flight. There are some wingless flies. The eyes are usually very large, sometimes touching, and as a rule there are 3 ocelli. The antennae are mostly inconspicuous and variable in shape. The mouth parts are for piercing and sucking, lapping, sponging, or may be reduced and functionless. The order contains the swiftest of all insects as well as numerous slow-flying species. The body is fragile and has a thin, soft covering usually beset with bristles and hairs.

The larvae, called maggots, are legless and usually cylindrical. In the more primitive families, the head is rather well developed and the mouth parts move in the horizontal plane; in the higher ones, the head is very much reduced and a pair of "mouth hooks" (not true mandibles), which work forward and backward in the vertical plane, are used to tear plant or animal tissues so the liquid contents can flow into the mouth. Metamorphosis is complete, with the pupal stage frequently passed inside the last larval skin, which is called a puparium.

This is one of the 4 largest orders of insects, with many species yet to be named in our region. In the small state of Connecticut alone, almost 3000 different species of flies have been recorded, and more than 80,000 have been described from the entire world. Flies are extremely useful as scavengers and as parasites or predators upon noxious insects, but among them are practically all the insect vectors of human diseases. Mosquitoes, house flies, sand flies, deer flies, gnats, and others have given the order Díptera a pretty bad name. Flies have never been popular as collectors' items, largely because of their relatively small size and generally rather drab appearance. However, some are quite attractive on close inspection, and the life histories of most species invite further study.

146 Crane Flies   *Family Tipùlidae*

This family and those that follow, through the gall midges (*152*), are characterized by antennae as long as or longer than the thorax and consisting of from 6 to many segments. The pupae of these flies are not enclosed in puparia formed of the last larval skins.

ADULTS: Very small to large insects, with extremely long, slender legs and narrow wings. The better-known species suggest giant mosquitoes; they are most numerous in wet meadows and damp woods near streams or other bodies of water. The legs break off almost without provocation, and a crane fly with a full complement is almost unknown in the collections of beginners. Serious collectors usually pin crane flies in the field, before they become too dangerously brittle, and carry them home in a cork-bottomed box. A distinctive feature of crane flies is a usually conspicuous V-shaped suture atop the second thoracic segment. The halteres or balancers are prominent. The antennae of the females are thread-like, while those of the males may be feathery or saw-toothed and are longer. There are no ocelli. Crane flies lay their eggs in the soil or upon plants.

YOUNG: The larvae have diverse habits—some are leaf miners; some live in damp soil, feeding upon the roots and lower stems of plants or upon decaying vegetation. Aquatic forms, of which there are many, may live on decaying plants or prey upon the larvae of midges (*150*), worms, and other small invertebrates. The appendages of the pupa are free of the body.

IMPORTANCE: Not very important economically. The larvae of some of the aquatic species are the food of fishes; others occasionally injure lawns by feeding on the roots of grasses.

EXAMPLE: Crane Fly   *Típula trivittàta*

One of the commonest species of *Típula* (our largest crane fly genus) in the area from South Carolina, Tennessee, and Iowa northward to Newfoundland and Quebec. To the angler, crane flies are known as "spinners" and serve as models for dry flies.

147 Moth Flies   *Family Psychódidae*

ADULTS: Minute insects, rarely exceeding ⅛ inch in length. In the more typical species the relatively large, usually rounded wings, opaque because of their coat of minute hairs and scales, are held roof-like over the body, giving them a somewhat moth-like appearance. The small head lacks ocelli. The antennae are half the length of the body. Moth flies dart about erratically "on all six," with many abrupt halts, and fly only weakly. They are seen about sinks and lavatories, having come out of the drainpipes in the surface films and traps of which they breed. Other species will be found out of doors in damp situations—on decaying vegetable matter, the bark of trees, and rocks. The eggs of some species are laid, 20 to 100 at a time, in a gelatinous mass.

YOUNG: The tiny larvae live in water, sewage, dung, and decaying vegetable matter. The traps in drainpipes may support large populations of the species that occur in houses.

IMPORTANCE: Our species are of practically no importance, seldom becoming a nuisance even in houses. In the Old World and in tropical and subtropical areas outside of the region covered by this book several species of the genus *Phlebótomus* are disease carriers, and others are suspected of being such.

EXAMPLE: Moth Fly   *Psychòda alternàta*

Widely distributed and cosmopolitan. A common species on sewage filter beds and in houses, where it breeds in drainpipes.

148 Mosquitoes   *Family Culicidae*

ADULTS: Small or very small, long-legged insects, usually
with some scales on legs and body. The females of most
species have piercing-sucking mouth parts; the males may
have an elongated "beak" or proboscis, but it is not fitted for
piercing. Only females can "sing," and this they do by vibrating thin chitinous processes lying across the thoracic spiracles.
The narrow wings are folded flat across the back when the
insect is resting; they have scales along the veins and the hind
margins. The halteres are prominent. The 15-segmented antennae are thread-like, encircled with many whorls of hairs
which are short in the females and quite long in the males—
giving a brushy appearance. The adults lay very tiny eggs
either singly or in floating clusters or "rafts" on the surface
of stagnant, fresh, or brackish water or upon soil or even snow
and ice. The females of most species apparently must feed at
least once upon the blood of some warm-blooded animal
before their eggs can develop properly. In any case, it is this
requirement which makes them a nuisance to man and many
other animals, and it is at the time of these blood meals that
they may either acquire or transmit the protozoan parasites
which cause malaria, the virus of yellow fever (eradicated
from our region), the nematodes responsible for filariasis in
tropical regions, and some other disease organisms. The mosquitoes of the North Temperate Zone and colder areas are not
as dangerous from the disease standpoint, although they have
been established as vectors of human encephalitis. Mosquitoes
have become adapted to an extreme range of climate, and
some species occur in tremendous numbers far north of the
Arctic Circle. The winter usually is passed either in the egg
or as an adult, according to species and latitude; some winter
as larvae frozen in the ice.

YOUNG: Aquatic, so eggs laid upon soil do not hatch until rains
or melting snow or ice provide sufficient moisture. The tiniest
puddle or water-filled depression can provide a suitable habitat. These larvae are called "wrigglers" from their method of
traveling through the water. Except in the genus *Anópheles,*
there is a siphon or short breathing tube near the end of the

body, and to use it the larva makes frequent trips to the surface. There are also 4 small tracheal gills on the last abdominal segment which may function to maintain salt balance rather than to extract additional oxygen from the water. The mouth parts are of the chewing type; the food consists of microscopic animal and plant life—algae, protozoa, etc. There are usually 4 larval stages.

The pupae, called "tumblers," are strange-looking creatures with 2 large body divisions—a head and large thorax combined as one large unit and a thin, 9-segmented abdomen which ends in a pair of small paddles. The pupa moves actively about by lashing its tail-like abdomen. It takes no food but makes frequent trips to the water surface to take in air through a pair of short breathing tubes atop the thorax. The entire life cycle of the summer generations of some mosquitoes may require only 2 or 3 weeks. There are several generations a year in some species, but many have only one.

IMPORTANCE: Mosquitoes are of great moment in the tropics and warmer regions of the world for the part they play in transmitting certain human diseases. All adult females are pests because of their often painful, somewhat poisonous bites. The adults form a large part of the diet of dragonflies, damselflies, and such birds as swallows, swifts, nighthawks, and flycatchers, while the larvae and pupae are devoured in great quantities by small fishes and aquatic insects, especially the young of dragonflies and damselflies. Adult mosquitoes, like crane flies, are models for the dry flies which fishermen call "spinners."

EXAMPLE: Salt Marsh Mosquito   *Aèdes sollìcitans*

This is the famous "New Jersey mosquito" which breeds in the salt marshes of our Atlantic and Gulf coasts; it is very abundant, difficult to control, and a major pest species, but does not carry disease organisms.

149 Buffalo Gnats   *Family Simulìidae*

ADULTS: Very small or minute insects with big round eyes, humped backs, and short, piercing-sucking mouth parts. The wings are broad and without hairs or scales. The females are bloodsuckers, attacking many kinds of wild or domesticated birds and mammals and man. The bites are painful, often accompanied by swellings. These insects are often called "black flies," a rather meaningless name. The eggs, ranging from black to yellow, are laid in great single-layered masses upon wet rocks, logs, or upon the plants that protrude from or grow near rushing streams; sometimes they are actually submerged.

YOUNG: The little black or dark gray larvae, which are equipped with a suction disk with marginal hooked hairs at each end of the body, swarm over submerged rocks and vegetation or stand on their tails. They are usually in swift, churning waters, never in perfectly still water. A thread spun from the mouth enables them to cling more securely. The food consists of microscopic plant and animal life swept into the mouth, which is of the chewing type, by means of 2 large food brushes, or scoops. Three short posterior blood gills are the breathing organs. There are said to be 6 larval stages. The larvae (those that do not live over winter) pupate in a few weeks inside a silken cocoon attached to a sunken rock or water plant and open at the free end. After a few days or weeks the adult, enclosed in an air bubble, pops to the water surface and flies away.

IMPORTANCE: During severe infestations of black flies, poultry, horses, cattle, sheep, and many other farm animals may suffer severely and even be bitten to death, sometimes in large numbers; humans may be rendered very uncomfortable, although they usually can find means of protecting themselves. These insects are especially worrisome for a brief season in the high mountains and in the northern coniferous forests, as campers and fishermen can attest. Some species are abundant in Alaska. The larvae of buffalo gnats sometimes are heavily parasitized by nematodes of the genus *Mérmis* and by Protozòa.

EXAMPLE: Turkey Gnat   *Simùlium meridionàle*

Widespread in the southern United States, attacking many kinds of warm-blooded animals.

150 Midges *Family Tendipédidae*

ADULTS: Minute to small fragile insects with long legs, slender wings and bodies, and short beaks. They resemble mosquitoes in appearance and frequently are confused with them. There are a few distinct longitudinal veins near the anterior margins of the wings and 1 or 2 cross veins; the few others are quite faint. The long antennae are plumose in the males. Adults of aquatic species often assemble in vast numbers, usually over or near water, and dance to the accompaniment of a distinct, sometimes loud, humming sound. The eggs are laid in gelatinous bands in water or on damp, rotting vegetation.

YOUNG: Cylindrical, green, red, or white; on or in damp organic matter, dung; under bark; or aquatic, in mud or bottom debris. Some are red from the hemoglobin they contain and are called "bloodworms." Some species live in salt lakes and some are marine. So far, only a single marine form, *Clùnio marshálli*, has been described from our region. Most are probably free-living, but some build cases of silk and sand or organic debris attached to rocks. Pupae may be active, like those of mosquitoes, or inactive inside the last larval skin, which is split and does not constitute a puparium in the strict sense.

IMPORTANCE: Both the adults and young are important fish food. The former are jumped for as they dance over water, the latter are taken from the bottom mud. Midges in all stages are said to be the largest single food item in the diets of most small- and medium-sized trout in mountain lakes. The immature forms also are eaten by larger aquatic insects, which in turn are eaten by fishes. Birds and bats take many of the adults. Some larval midges are predacious, consuming mites, aphids, and probably other insects.

EXAMPLE: Midge *Téndipes decòrus*

An abundant species, widespread through our region. The larvae are aquatic, inhabiting both lakes and streams.

There is a family of flies, the Mycetophílidae, known as the "fungus gnats" because their larvae live chiefly in fungi and decaying vegetation. We have not figured a fungus gnat but make mention of them at this point because of their similarity to the midges, from which they differ in lacking halteres and in having thread-like antennae. Their slender, white larvae have distinct, usually black, chitinized heads. The larva of a North Carolina species is luminous and spins a web to entrap the small insects on which it feeds.

151 Biting Midges   *Family Heleïdae*

ADULTS: Mostly minute insects whose presence is felt but seldom seen. The Indians called the several species which annoy man "No-see-ums." Somewhat less appropriate but more widely used names are "sand flies" and "punkies." They breed in damp or watery habitats. The adults have mouth parts adapted for piercing the skin of mammals and other insects and sucking their blood. Certain species ride the wings of dragonflies, lacewings, and probably other insects, drinking blood from the veins of their hosts.

YOUNG: Aquatic, or almost so, living in fresh, brackish, or even strongly salt water, in damp places under bark, and in moist soil. The water-dwelling species are said to feed on the very young larvae of flies and caddisflies.

IMPORTANCE: We appreciate these insects only as pests. Their bites, coming without warning and sometimes in scores of places at once, cause intense although temporary burning. Ordinary mosquito screens do not keep sand flies out. A tropical American species is an intermediate host for a filarial worm, *Mansonélla ozzárdi,* which it can transmit to man. One species, *Forcipomyia èques,* in the adult stage, is a parasite of green lacewings (55), riding upon the host and sucking the blood from the wing veins.

EXAMPLE: Common Sand Fly   *Culicoïdes guttipénnis*

A pest in the eastern and southern parts of the United States.

152 Gall Midges   *Family Itonídidae*

ADULTS: Small, long-legged, humpbacked flies with long an-tennae which are encircled by many rings of short bristles but are never plumose. The wings are rather broad and traversed by 3 to 5 longitudinal veins. There is a single distinct cross vein or none.

YOUNG: The larvae taper anteriorly or at both ends and vary in color from white and yellow to red, many common species being salmon-colored. Their habits are diverse—some are predators upon mites, aphids, and mealybugs on plant surfaces, or upon the larvae of bark beetles under the bark of trees; others consume decaying vegetable matter, fungi, and dung. The most important and interesting, however, are the plant feeders. These live inside plant tissue, in rolled leaves, or in galls which they cause in the stems, roots, leaves, and flowers of grasses, composites, and willows. Several species live in the pitch oozing from wounds in the bark of pine trees, where they feed on the plant cells. The pupae are in single- or double-walled cocoons which may be silken or formed of a resinous exudate. The larvae of some gall midges, rarely even the pupae, are able to produce living young. This very unusual type of parthenogenetic reproduction is called "paedogenesis."

IMPORTANCE: There are many, many species of itonidids, with more to be named. Most are of slight importance. The Hessian fly, our example, on the contrary, is an especially destructive pest of wheat. The chrysanthemum gall midge (*Diarthronomẏia hypogaèa*) blights the flower heads and foliage of chrysanthemums with many small galls. Other midges develop in the seeds of sorghum, clovers, and numerous cultivated composites and grasses.

EXAMPLE: Hessian Fly   *Phytóphaga destrúctor*

This pest was brought to the United States in the bedding straw of Hessian soldiers during the Revolutionary War. All wheat-growing areas of North America east of the Rocky Mountains are now infested. The larvae live between the stem and leaf sheaths of the wheat plant and rasp the stem in order to feed upon the exuding juices. The stems may be killed or may be broken by the wind as a result of the feeding. Infestations always lower the yields of grain, sometimes quite severely. Shrews and mice eat a considerable number of the larvae and puparia. There is a small family of tiny wasps, the Platygastéridae, whose members are chiefly parasites of gall midges, several of them laying their eggs in either the larvae or eggs of the Hessian fly. The Platygastéridae, like the Bracónidae (*126*) and 2 other families of parasitic wasps, contain species which can lay polyembryonic eggs; that is, single eggs which give rise to more than one insect.

153 Soldier Flies   *Family Stratiomyidae*

In this family and in all that follow, the antennae are shorter than the thorax and never have more than 4 segments, usually 3, although the third sometimes is divided into subsegments or may bear a long bristle (arista).

ADULTS: Mostly small, flat-bodied insects with abdomens short and wide or elongate and tapered. The head, which bears large eyes and 3 ocelli, is usually wider than the thorax. The body surface in most species is naked or covered with inconspicuous short hairs. Some are brightly marked with red, green, white, or yellow. It appears to have been the gaudy species which were originally called "soldier flies" in reference to the often dazzling uniforms warriors wore long ago. The short antennae are extremely variable. The wing venation, as shown in the illustration of our example, is the most useful characteristic in identification. These insects are commonly found on flowers. They place their eggs in water, mud, decaying vegetation, or dung.

YOUNG: Elongate, tough-skinned, and legless, with flattened or cylindrical bodies. The aquatic forms may have a short, terminal breathing tube edged with hairs, which are held in the surface film and keep the insects floating head downward. Their food consists of microscopic plants and animals or decaying organic matter. They are unique in their habit of secreting a limy coating over their bodies. The terrestrial species feed upon rotting plant material and dung and possibly on the larvae of certain dung-inhabiting insects. Some live under bark and feed on other insects. The pupa remains inside the last larval skin from which the adult escapes by a T-shaped slit in the thoracic region.

IMPORTANCE: Insignificant economically. The aquatic larvae, of course, are eaten by fishes. The larvae of one common species, in rare instances, have been found living in the intestine of man.

Example: Soldier Fly   *Stratiomys unilimbata*

Widely distributed in the northern United States and southern Canada.

154 Horse Flies and Allies   *Family Tabánidae*

Adults: Some of the tabanids are very large flies, almost an inch long, and the rest are at least of medium size, mostly exceeding ⅜ inch in length. The surface of the large head is mainly occupied by the eyes, which are separated by some space in the females but are touching in the males of most species. Ocelli may or may not be present. The short mouth parts are for piercing and sucking. The females drink the blood of horses, cattle, deer, and other large wild and domesticated animals, and some of them annoy man; they also may take nectar or, if blood is scarce, even puncture succulent plant stems and drink the juices. The males consume only plant sap or nectar. Deer flies of the genus *Chrysops* have been found to transmit tularemia (rabbit fever) to man in the West, and it is thought they may spread some diseases of horses. Tabanids are active only by day; they are swift flyers, and some of them, at least, can keep up with or outdistance the fastest horses. The females are attracted to large moving objects, such as automobiles and trains, which they will follow tenaciously, evidently mistaking them for possible hosts. They are especially numerous in low wet situations, for the larvae are aquatic or semi-aquatic, and the eggs, long and spindle-shaped, are laid in clusters of as many as 100 on foliage overhanging water. Each egg stands on end, firmly cemented to the leaf surface and to neighboring eggs; there may be one or several tiers of eggs in a cluster.

Young: Aquatic or nearly so, living in damp earth or rotting wood. Long, rather robust, hard-bodied, and tapered at each end. There is a raised ring bearing tiny tubercles about each segment to aid in moving through mud and soil. Some attain a length of 2 inches. They eat the larvae of other insects and arthropods they encounter as well as earthworms and snails. The larvae may require more than a year to complete development. The older ones seek drier soil, above water level, in which to pupate. The pupa is naked—not enclosed in the last larval skin—and each of its abdominal segments has a ring of spines by means of which it works its way to the soil surface just before the adult emerges.

IMPORTANCE: Adult tabanids are pests of horses and cattle and many other wild and domesticated animals. Their bites, in addition to causing an appreciable loss of blood, are painful and maddening and may result in loss of weight or physical injuries because of nervousness and reckless running in vain attempts to escape the flies. Harnessed animals must be protected from horse flies to avoid accident to the driver and other persons.

EXAMPLE 154a: Black Horse Fly   *Tabànus atràtus*

Throughout eastern North America. The larvae live through 1 or, often, 2 winters before completing their development.

EXAMPLE 154b: Deer Fly   *Chrỳsops cállidas*

Generally distributed east of the Rocky Mountains and reported from Washington and British Columbia on the Pacific coast. The larvae have been found in mud and decaying leaves at the edges of pools.

155 Snipe Flies   *Family Rhagiónidae*

ADULTS: Many of these look like smaller editions of robber flies (*157*). The head is rather small with large round eyes and, in some species, with a distinct proboscis which is presumed to give the insects a bird-like appearance. The thorax is large with long legs, and the abdomen is long and tapering. They sit head downward upon the leaves or trunks of trees and spring upon passing insects, chiefly other adult flies. A few species are rather fierce biters and bloodsuckers and may attack man. The eggs are laid in large masses in dust, dung, rotten wood, damp soil, or on branches, bridges, and other objects overhanging water.

YOUNG: The land-dwelling larvae are usually cylindrical, sometimes with pseudopods (false prolegs) on some or all abdominal segments. They are all predacious, chiefly upon the immature forms of other insects. Some species called "worm-lions," common in western North America, dig conical pits in the dry sand or dust under rocky ledges and in other protected sites. These pits, like those of antlions (56) which they resemble, trap small insects, chiefly ants. The aquatic larvae are flat with a pair of long tail filaments and 2 retractile blood gills on the terminal segment. The pupa is naked.

IMPORTANCE: Probably more useful than otherwise, although many of the ants trapped and devoured by worm-lions are themselves useful predators. It has been said that the egg masses laid by congregating thousands of the aquatic species upon branches and rocks overhanging water were once gathered by Indians, cooked, and eaten. A few bloodsucking species occasionally are annoying to man.

EXAMPLE: Snipe Fly   *Rhàgio vertebràta*

This species is recorded from most parts of our region but seems to be most abundant in eastern North America.

156 Bee Flies   *Family Bombyliidae*

ADULTS: These attractive, fuzzy flies, when short and robust, resemble bees, and, when elongate and slender, resemble wasps. The eyes are large, the legs long and slender. The proboscis may be quite long. The wings are sometimes marked with dark opaque areas; at rest, they are usually held out at the sides, never folded over the back. Bee flies are swift flyers, often stopping to hover in mid-air like sparrow hawks. They frequently visit flowers for nectar, are active only by day, and prefer the warmest, sunniest sites, usually choosing to rest on the ground, a stone, or a twig. The eggs are placed on the ground near the nests of bees and wasps or the egg pods of grasshoppers.

YOUNG: Some of the larvae are parasites upon or inside the bodies of a wide range of larval and pupal wasps, bees, moths, butterflies, and beetles; others are predators inside the egg pods of short-horned grasshoppers. The larvae have been found feeding upon the young of blister beetles, which are themselves predators upon grasshopper eggs. They are occasionally secondary parasites, attacking the young of other bee flies or of certain parasitic wasps. The pupa is not enclosed in a puparium and may be somewhat spiny on head and thorax.

IMPORTANCE: It is rather difficult to judge the importance of the bee flies as a group. Numerous species predacious upon grasshoppers' eggs are definitely beneficial, although not recognized as significant checks upon host populations. Most of the parasitic species, unfortunately, attack insects which are either parasites or predators.

EXAMPLE: Large Bee Fly   *Bombýlius màjor*

Widely distributed in our region and in Europe and Asia. A parasite of the larvae of various species of colletid, mining, and sweat bees.

157 Robber Flies   *Family Asílidae*

ADULTS: Our commoner asilids are large flies not likely to be confused with any others when seen at close range. The head and thorax are large; the stout "beak" is a piercing-sucking organ. The abdomen is long, narrower than the thorax, and tapering to the rear. The wings are large, mostly clear, and are held folded flat over the body. The legs are quite long and are held and manipulated much like those of the dragonflies, for robber flies, likewise, capture their prey on the wing. They prey on all sorts of flying insects and will attack species almost as large as themselves. When in flight, certain asilids could be mistaken for bees or wasps. Some of them make a buzzing or droning noise while flying, and some are densely hairy, like bumble and some other bees; certain species appear to mimic bees and wasps.

YOUNG: The larvae live in soil, rotten wood, and vegetable mold, feeding upon the larvae of other insects. The pupae are free—not enclosed in a puparium.

IMPORTANCE: Adult asilids show definite food preferences. Hymenopterous insects probably form the bulk of their diet, and the honey bee is particularly sought after by some of the larger species. Flies, beetles, butterflies, moths, and even spiders are also consumed. Other robber flies, including adults of the same species, are frequently eaten.

EXAMPLE: Robber Fly   *Asìlus prairiénsis*

This species inhabits the Great Plains area of the United States.

The mydas flies of the family Mydàidae are rather closely related to the robber flies and, like them, are large species; the larvae are predacious and usually inhabit rotting wood. Mydas flies constitute a very small family in number of species. Little is known of their life histories and habits. Perhaps the best-known species in our region is the large one that appears to mimic the wasp we call the "tarantula-hawk" (*138*) in the southwestern United States.

158 Humpbacked Flies   *Family Phóridae*

These flies and all that follow pupate inside the last larval skin, which forms a hard, protecting case called a puparium. The adults escape through a hole at one end made by forcing off a circular section of the puparium wall by means of a remarkable bladder-like organ (the ptilinum), which is inflated and thrust through a semicircular suture on the front of the face, just above the antennal bases.

ADULTS: Very small or minute, dark-colored, with thorax conspicuously humped. The legs are fairly long. These drab little flies are commonly found on windowpanes in buildings, at flowers, or resting on leaves. The strongly tapered abdomen curves downward slightly. The head is small, but the eyes are very large. The antennae are short, 3-segmented; the terminal segment, which bears an arista, sometimes covers one or both of the other 2 segments. The wings are distinctive in having, near the front margins, 2 heavy, longitudinal veins running only half of the way or less to the tips, and in having only 4 or 5 very light, transverse veins. There are some wingless species. The eggs are laid in a great variety of situations, according to the habits of the larvae.

YOUNG: The tiny larvae may live in decaying vegetable matter, carrion, or dung, or may be "guests" in ant, bee, and termite nests. Some of the comparatively few species whose life histories have been recorded are borderline parasites—that is, they develop in a dead host insect or may attack one that is injured or weak.

IMPORTANCE: So far as known, the phorids are principally scavengers on both plant and animal matter and so are beneficial.

EXAMPLE: Humpbacked Fly   *Diploneùra nitídula*

Occurs throughout the United States; a scavenging species.

159 Syrphid Flies   *Family Sýrphidae*

ADULTS: Often called flower flies because of their habit of feeding upon the nectar of flowers. They are also attracted to tree sap and fermenting fruit. As regular visitors to flowers they are more important than most flies in cross-pollination. The majority of species taken by the collector at flowers bear at least a superficial resemblance to bees—some of them being considered bee mimics. Many are marked with orange or cream white. As a group these are probably the showiest and most attractive of our flies.

YOUNG: Syrphid larvae are of 4 principal types: those living on feces in ant nests are tough-skinned and limpet-shaped; those living submerged in liquid decaying vegetation, carcasses, and filth may have a long posterior respiratory tube from once to several times the length of the body and are called rat-tailed maggots; a third type has a pair of short posterior respiratory tubes; the fourth type, the common aphid- and mealybug-eating larva, has a broad, blunt posterior with inconspicuous spiracular tubes, and a body tapering strongly toward the head.

IMPORTANCE: Adult syrphids may rank next in importance to bees as cross-pollinators of flowers. The larvae are important checks on aphid and mealybug populations.

EXAMPLE 159a: Syrphid Fly   *Milèsia virginiénsis*

Occurs rather generally in the eastern United States.

EXAMPLE 159b: Narcissus Bulb Fly *Lampètia equéstris*

A European species frequently intercepted in shipments of narcissus, hyacinth, and other bulbs from Holland. It is now well established in western Canada and at scattered points in the United States, chiefly in large commercial bulb plantings.

160 Big-headed Flies   *Family Dorilàidae*

ADULTS: Very small flies with great globular heads, which are
considerably wider than the thorax and almost completely
covered by the eyes. These features are sufficient to distinguish the family from all other flies. Our species are believed
to be solitary parasites in the bodies of nymphal leafhoppers,
spittlebugs, and related homopterons. One hundred and seven-
teen species and subspecies have been described from our
region. In the few instances where egg laying has been observed, the insects picked up the prospective host nymphs and
flew with them while inserting the egg between the abdominal
segments.

YOUNG: The larva develops wholly within the body of its host,
which it eventually kills. The mature larva leaves the host
cadaver and pupates inside a puparium in the soil or upon
plant foliage.

IMPORTANCE: These are all useful as parasites of homopterons.
In the western United States, 2 species attack the beet leafhopper (*Eutéttix tenéllus*). None is recognized as important
in the control of pest insects in our region.

EXAMPLE: Big-headed Fly   *Dòrilas àter*

Widely distributed in the United States and southern Canada.
Also occurs in Europe, where it was originally described. A
parasite of several species of leafhoppers.

161 Pictured-wing Flies   *Family Otítidae*

ADULTS: Small- or medium-sized flies with wings variously
mottled with brown or black. These insects frequent sunny
spots on foliage and tree trunks and appear to be strutting
and exhibiting their beautiful wings and metallic-hued bodies
to an admiring world—hence they have been called "peacock
flies." They can be confused with fruit flies, the distinguishing
features of which are given in the succeeding family discussion.

YOUNG: Most of the larvae live in decaying plant and animal
matter, but some invade healthy plant tissues.

IMPORTANCE: Little or none, economically. The young are mostly useful scavengers.

EXAMPLE: Pictured-wing Fly   *Delphínia pícta*

Common throughout the eastern United States.

162 Fruit Flies   *Family Tephrítidae*

ADULTS: Very small insects, with large, wide heads and large, iridescent greenish eyes. The legs and bodies are rather hairy and the bristles of the head and thorax may be long and heavy. The wings are fairly large, quite variable in shape, and usually prettily mottled with brown or black. The bodies of the flies may be marked with various combinations of orange, brown, and black. To distinguish fruit flies from the pictured-wing flies of the preceding family, which they resemble very closely, note the first longitudinal vein paralleling the front wing margin. If this vein curves forward and distinctly meets the margin, then the insect probably is a pictured-wing fly; if it becomes quite indistinct and cannot be traced to the wing margin, then the insect probably is a fruit fly. The eggs, white and spindle-shaped, are laid in small clusters in cavities hollowed out by the often large ovipositor of the female in the host plant tissue.

YOUNG: Leaf miners in plants of the parsley family (Umbellíferae), borers and gall-makers in the stems and feeders in the flower and seed heads of plants of the thistle family (Compósitae), also feeding in the pods and husks of various seeds and nuts, and in the pulps of many kinds of fruits and the tissues of vegetables. To prevent the entrance of devastating members of the fruit fly family into our citrus plantings, it is necessary to prohibit the importation from other lands of the fruits of many of their wild and cultivated host plants.

IMPORTANCE: One of the most important of all insect families from the quarantine standpoint. The Mediterranean fruit fly (*Ceratìtis capitàta*) and the Mexican fruit fly (*Anástrepha lùdens*) pose serious threats to the citrus industry in the United States. The former species once became established in Florida but was successfully eradicated at great expense. A constant war is waged against the Mexican fruit fly in the Rio Grande Valley of Texas. Blueberries, cherries, and apples commonly are heavily damaged by various species of fruit flies.

EXAMPLE: Cherry Fruit Fly   *Rhagolètis cingulàta*

Occurs in the central and eastern parts of the United States and Canada and in the cherry-growing regions of the northwestern states. The eggs are laid under surfaces of fruit skins. Larvae penetrate to the centers of fruits, where they remain until mature. Puparia overwinter in the soil.

163 Vinegar Flies   *Family Drosophilidae*

ADULTS: Very small or minute insects, abundant everywhere that fruits and other plant materials are fermenting or decaying. They are also attracted to flowing sap and to fungi. The bristles of the antennae are long and plume-like. A generation is completed in about 10 days at summer temperatures, so there may be many during the course of a year. Although these insects lay their eggs on the contents of garbage pails and fruits decaying on the ground in the shade of orchard trees, they are strongly attracted to light and are frequently seen on windowpanes.

YOUNG: The whitish larvae live in fermenting and decaying vegetable matter, feeding largely upon yeasts and other fungi. They come to the surface of the semi-liquid mass to pupate in a drier situation. The puparium has a pair of short "horns" or respiratory tubes at one end.

IMPORTANCE: Vinegar flies are annoying in dwellings and vegetable or fruit markets by their mere presence; however, their scavenging habits are actually useful. Because of the ease and rapidity with which they can be cultured in captivity the fly chosen as an example of the family is famous as an experimental subject for geneticists; also, the very large chromosomes of the cells in the salivary glands are much used in studies of genes as inheritance factors. That grapes readily ferment without artificial inoculation with yeasts is due in large part to the agency of these flies which carry the spores on their bodies and contaminate the fruit as they feed and oviposit.

Example: Common Vinegar Fly
Drosóphila melanogáster

Common everywhere in our region. Cosmopolitan.

164 Leaf- and Stem-mining Flies *Family Agromýzidae*

Adults: Very small or minute insects, less than ³⁄₁₆ inch long, and usually dark-colored. About 100 species of this family are known from our region. These little flies are often taken in sweep nets from low vegetation, but it is easier to rear them from the larval "mines" in the leaves of plants. The adults may insert their eggs singly into the tissue of a leaf and then drink the sap exuding from the egg puncture; they have been observed to puncture leaves with their ovipositors and drink sap without laying an egg.

Young: The cavities made by the tiny larvae in the narrow spaces between the upper and lower surfaces of leaves usually show distinctly and are often unsightly on the foliage of garden flowers. The shapes of the mines are usually characteristic for each species and are roughly classified as linear, serpentine, blotch, trumpet, digitate, etc., according to their general outline. The puparium usually is found at the center of a blotch mine or in a blister-like chamber at the end of a gradually enlarging serpentine mine. In some species, development from egg to adult is completed in a very few days. Miners may leave their tunnels in the fall to enter the ground or secrete themselves under surface litter before pupating, in order to pass the winter in a more protected situation.

Importance: Comparatively small, the host plants seldom being seriously injured by the mines of the fly larvae. A species which tunnels in the cambium layer of birch trees causes a discoloration of finished lumber known as "pith-ray flecks." An Australian species, *Cryptochaètum icèryae,* an internal parasite of the cottony-cushion scale *(47b),* was introduced into the California citrus groves in 1888. Because of its economic importance, the life history of this agromyzid is better known than most. Probably our most important pest species is the asparagus miner *(Melanagromỳza símplex),* whose larval tunnels sometimes girdle the stems of the host plants. Leaf miners, as larvae, would seem to be rather well protected from natural enemies; however, mites have been found attacking them and a small, predacious flower bug (*31*) has been seen to stab its beak through the leaf epidermis to feed upon the miners in their tunnels; they are attacked by numerous parasitic wasps.

EXAMPLE: Serpentine Leaf Miner   *Liriomy̆za pusílla*

Originally described from Europe; widespread in our region. This species, one of the commonest of leaf miners, is shining black with yellow markings; it tunnels in the leaves of many different plants, including cotton, potato, various wild and cultivated species of crucifers, clovers, and other legumes. At the latitude of New York City there are 5 or 6 generations annually. No less than 28 species of parasitic wasps attack this insect in its mines.

165 Grass Flies   *Family Chlorópidae*

ADULTS: Very small or minute, mostly ⅛ inch or less in length, dark to yellowish in color, with bare heads and bodies and with the 3 ocelli situated on a very large triangular plate between the eyes. The eye gnats of the genus *Hippelàtes* probably are the best-known members of the family; they cluster about the eyes of domesticated animals such as cattle and dogs and are quite annoying to man, who is better prepared to defend himself against them. A gnat in the eye is rather painful.

YOUNG: The larvae are thought to be chiefly scavenging, but many are borers or gall-makers in the stems of grasses; some are leaf miners, and a few are predacious upon other arthropods.

IMPORTANCE: The family includes some pests of cereal grasses, of which our example is one of the most important. The frit fly (*Oscinélla frít*) destroys much grain as a borer in developing plants. "Pink eye" of humans is thought to be transmitted at least occasionally by the eye gnats, as are several other epidemic eye diseases. Among the predacious species there is one, *Thaumatomy̆ia glàbra,* whose larvae are valuable checks on the increase of a sugar beet root aphid, and another whose larvae feed on the contents of black widow spider egg sacs.

EXAMPLE: Wheat Stem Maggot   *Meromỹza americàna*

A native pest of rather minor importance, distributed throughout the United States east of the Rocky Mountains. The
larvae winter as borers in the crowns of rye, oats, barley,
winter wheat, and other wild or cultivated grasses. An early
summer generation of larvae tunnel the stems under the
sheaths and cause the young heads of wheat or other food
plants to whiten and die.

166 House and Stable Flies and Allies
Family Múscidae

ADULTS: Our species are mostly insects of small or very small
size. It is interesting to consider that the common house fly,
a nearly average-sized fly, which we are accustomed to regard as a rather tiny creature, is very close to the average size
for the entire animal kingdom—from the smallest one-celled
species (Protozòa) to the largest whales. The house fly, which
needs no description, is representative of the family in general appearance, muscids being rather robust and short-
bodied, with a relatively large, bristly thorax and a wide head
with large eyes which are usually well separated. A few
species have mouth parts adapted for piercing the skins of
animals and sucking blood. The eggs are whitish and spindle-
shaped and are laid singly or in small clusters in or near the
food of the larvae.

YOUNG: Typical maggots, living in decaying plant and animal
matter and dung as scavengers, and also living in or feeding
upon growing plant tissue. Some of the latter are leaf miners,
borers in stems of cruciferous plants and grasses or feeders
upon the roots of many different cultivated plants.

IMPORTANCE: The house flies are probably next in importance
to the mosquitoes as pests of man. The adults are said to be
capable of transmitting 30 to 40 different diseases, including
typhoid fever, cholera, and tuberculosis. The passing of the
horse from the streets and generally improved sanitation
methods have greatly reduced the house fly population in the
modern city and town, and several new insecticides will make
it possible to control or eliminate them altogether from barns
and poultry houses. Great losses to sprouting corn are suffered

in wet springs because of the seed-corn maggot. The stable fly and horn fly are fierce biters and pests of livestock.

EXAMPLE 166a: Seed-corn Maggot   *Hylèmya cilicrùra*

Widespread in our region and in Europe, its native home. The larvae feed in rotting plant material as well as on sprouting corn and beans, and damage sprouting potatoes and spinach alone to the extent of several millions of dollars annually. Related species have damaged the seeds of conifers in plantings.

EXAMPLE 166b: House Fly   *Músca doméstica*

Cosmopolitan. Found in all the inhabited regions of the earth.

EXAMPLE 166c: Stable Fly   *Stomóxys cálcitrans*

The larvae breed in dung, fermenting hay, sea wrack, and other souring plant material. The bloodsucking adults are commoner about barns than houses, but they do attack humans and seem especially vicious before summer thunderstorms, when they are most likely to enter houses. This has given rise to the erroneous belief that house flies, with which this species is sometimes confused, bite before approaching storms.

The tsetse flies of Africa, transmitters of sleeping sickness and some other trypanosomic diseases of man and wild and domesticated animals, belong to the genus *Glossìna* in the family Glossínidae, which is closely related to the Múscidae. None of these insects occurs in our hemisphere.

167 Horse Bot Flies   *Family Gasterophílidae*

ADULTS: Mostly medium-sized insects, sometimes exceeding an inch in length. They are robust and hairy, but without bristles, and are found only in the vicinity of horses, mules, or donkeys, on whose hairs the females glue their eggs or "nits." The abdomen of the female is elongate, pointed, and curved forward under the body, while that of the male is short and bluntly tipped. We have 4 species, 3 of them widely distributed. Our example, the common horse bot fly, lays its eggs almost anywhere on the body that can be reached by the host's mouth, but favors the inner side of the knee as an oviposition site. The throat bot fly (*Gasteróphilus nasàlis*) oviposits on the throat, the nose bot fly (*G. haemorrhoidàlis*) on the lips.

YOUNG: The spiny, robust larvae, reaching ⅔ inch in length, have 2 pairs of mouth hooks with which to cling to the lining of the alimentary tract of the host. The larvae of the horse bot fly hatch upon being removed from their moorings by the lips or tongue of the host. After a brief period of burrowing in the mouth membranes, the bots travel to the stomach, where they fasten themselves and feed, at least to some extent, upon blood until the following spring, when they loose their hold and drop to the ground with the feces. Pupation occurs in the soil, and the flies emerge from 3 to 10 weeks later, depending upon the temperature. The larvae of the throat bot fly find attachment in the pyloric end of the stomach and in the duodenum (the first section of the small intestine), otherwise the life history is much like that of the preceding. The nose bot fly larvae attach first to the walls of the stomach, then the rectum, and finally, just before dropping to the ground, the anus.

IMPORTANCE: Bot larvae are sometimes numerous enough on the walls of stomach and duodenum to interfere with digestion. A considerable number of animals have died or been seriously weakened by bot infestations. However, it is possible to eliminate them from individual animals, and complete control and even eventual eradication seem distinct possibilities.

EXAMPLE: Horse Bot Fly   *Gasteróphilus intestinàlis*
Distributed throughout our region.

168 Warble Flies   *Family Hypodermátidae*

ADULTS: Large, swift-flying, hairy flies whose robust forms suggest bumble bees. They are parasitic in many different mammals, including cattle, deer, and bison. The tiny, elongate eggs are glued singly or side by side in series to the hairs of the host. The adults of some species make a buzzing sound in flight. The northern cattle grub or "bomb fly" (*Hypodérma bòvis*) frightens cattle into blind flight and follows them as they run, darting in with a loud buzz from time to time to lay eggs.

Young: The larvae of the cattle warbles penetrate the skin of the host immediately upon hatching and migrate about in the connective tissues for a period of several months, causing considerable irritation and resultant loss in weight and milk production. They finally settle under the skin of the back and grow into plump maggots about an inch long. The larva cuts a breathing hole through the skin and orients itself so the posterior spiracles lie next it. The host tissues form a tough fibrous cyst about the parasite, which appears to live upon exudates from the irritated cyst wall. After the winter months have been spent in the host, the warbles leave their cysts through the breathing hole and drop to the ground, in which they pupate.

Importance: Infested cattle do not gain weight properly, produce less milk, and give a leather seriously damaged in its more valuable parts by the burrows and breathing punctures of the warble larvae. In cold winter weather starlings have been seen alighting on the backs of cattle to remove warbles and, to probe hungrily, somewhat farther into the warm flesh. Magpies are said to do the same thing. These and other birds that may follow cattle in the early spring feed upon the fat warbles as they drop from the backs of their hosts as well as upon the insects routed out of the grass by the hoofs of the animals.

Example: Common Cattle Grub *Hypodérma lineàtum*

Originally from the Old World, now abundant throughout our region.

169 Bot Flies   *Family Oéstridae*

Adults: We have a very few species in North America, and our example is the only one of importance. It is a typical bot fly, robust, yellowish gray, hairy, and about ½ inch long, an insidious parasite of sheep, goats, and, very rarely, man. The females skillfully place their larvae in the nostrils of sheep without actually alighting upon their terrified hosts. Sheep are instinctively afraid of these flies and do all they can to prevent them from getting near their noses. Some of the apparently most exaggerated claims for the flight speeds of insects have been made on behalf of deer bot flies, since they are known to be able to deposit their larvae in the nostrils of animals running at top speed. It is thought by most entomologists that the fastest bot fly probably does not fly more than 50 miles an hour.

YOUNG: The tiny whitish larvae, which have a pair of large mouth hooks, work up into the nasal passages, sinuses, and other cavities in the bones of the head and develop into fat, black-banded maggots, flat on one side and almost an inch long. In adult hosts, about 10 months are required to complete larval development, so the next spring or summer the mature grubs leave the sheep through the nostrils and pupate in the ground.

IMPORTANCE: The sheep bot fly is a serious pest of sheep, causing loss of weight through irritation, symptoms called "blind staggers." Infestations may result in death to the hosts. The family is better represented in the Old World, where camels, elephants, horses, mules, donkeys, and deer are afflicted by various bots.

EXAMPLE: Sheep Bot Fly   *Oéstrus òvis*

A native of the Old World, now occurring in our region wherever sheep are grown.

170 Robust Bot Flies   *Family Cuterébridae*

A small family containing less than 50 known species at present.

ADULTS: Insects of medium or even large size; among our biggest fly species. The large eyes are separated in both sexes, and the abdomen is covered with short hairs, which lie flat against the body. These flies are seldom taken as adults, and their life histories are not well known. One species lays its eggs near the entrances to the nests of pack rats, the young of which are its hosts.

YOUNG: The larvae are larger and more robust than those of bots of the preceding 2 families. They cause great swellings under the skin of rabbits, pack rats, and other rodents, but do not bring death or even noticeable discomfort to their hosts.

IMPORTANCE: Practically none, economically, in our region, but a Central and South American species, the human bot (*Der-*

matòbia hóminis), is a serious pest of cattle and frequently attacks man, dogs, and other animals. This amazing fly attaches its eggs to bloodsucking mosquitoes, and thus contact with a mammalian host is fairly well assured.

EXAMPLE: Robust Bot Fly   *Cutérebra approximàta*

A species of the West. Apparently ranging from British Columbia and Nebraska south to Arizona and New Mexico.

171 Blow Flies   *Family Calliphóridae*

ADULTS: Mostly small or very small insects, resembling house flies in body shape, but usually metallic blue or green in color. The brilliant species are called bluebottle and greenbottle flies. The eggs are laid upon the material in which the larvae will feed—this may include decaying flesh or the open wounds of wild and domesticated animals.

YOUNG: Largely scavengers, especially in decaying flesh. The screw-worm (*Callitròga americàna*) develops in the cuts and sores of farm animals, many wild mammals, and even man. They invade the living tissue and, if unattended, may cause death. At least one species is an internal parasite of various earthworms.

IMPORTANCE: The calliphorids render a valuable service as scavengers. The screw-worm, however, causes great suffering and innumerable deaths among cattle and other domesticated and game animals, especially in the South. Several other species, however, seem to promote the healing of certain wounds by consuming dead tissue and giving off salutary substances. *Phoenícia sericàta* and some other species were used in the treatment of osteomyelitis for a time, but more effective and less objectionable methods have been discovered.

EXAMPLE: Bluebottle Fly   *Callíphora vicìna*

Widely distributed in our region. A very abundant scavenger.

172 Flesh Flies and Allies   *Family Sarcophágidae*

ADULTS: These insects superficially resemble the house fly and its allies even more so than the calliphorids, for, excepting the red eyes, they are drab-colored. Most of them can be distinguished from the house fly or muscid family by the fact that the apical half (more or less) of the antennal bristle is bare, not plumose to the tips as is typical of the Múscidae, and that there are 3 black stripes on the thorax, rather than usually 2 or 4. The young hatch within the bodies of the mother and are deposited as maggots upon the food material—which may be a grasshopper in flight.

YOUNG: Similar to house fly larvae but with various habits. Some scavenge in decaying flesh and the dead bodies of invertebrates; some live in wounds or tunnel under the skin of mammals, including man, and of turtles and tortoises. Some are internal parasites of insects and other arthropods or predacious upon their eggs. Locusts and grasshoppers and many kinds of wasps and bees are parasitized. Development from egg to adult requires 16 to 30 days.

IMPORTANCE: Mostly a useful group of scavengers and parasites of injurious insects.

EXAMPLE: Flesh Fly   *Sarcóphaga latistérna*

An abundant species in the eastern half of our region and occurring in some numbers on the Pacific coast. Evidently both scavenging and parasitic in lepidopterous pupae.

173 Tachina Flies   *Family Larvaevóridae*

This large family, which includes many useful insect parasites, has long gone by the name of Tachínidae, and even though we must now use another scientific family designation, it is likely that the insects will be called tachina flies for some time to come.

ADULTS: Bristly, usually somber-colored flies of small or medium size of the house fly type. The antennal bristle typically is clothed with very short hairs or is naked, differing in this respect from the Múscidae and Sarcophágidae with which they could be confused. The eggs usually hatch within the bodies of the females. Several thousand offspring may be produced by a single tachina fly. The unfertilized females of some species produce only male progeny. The eggs or larvae are placed upon or within the host insect or upon vegetation which will be consumed by the host. Frequently visitors at flowers.

Young: Of the house fly or muscid type; internal parasites of other insects of many different orders, especially of the moths, butterflies, beetles, grasshoppers, and wasps. The larvae breathe through an opening in the integument of the host or through a connection with one of the air tubes (tracheae) inside its body. The larval and pupal stages of the moths and butterflies are preferred hosts. Usually only a single tachina fly develops in one host insect. Some are restricted to a single or a few host species; others have a wide range. The parasite of a moth larva frequently devours its host completely, save for the head capsule and perhaps a fragment of skin, before forming a brown puparium inside the cocoon or pupal cell.

Importance: Our debt to the tachina flies as natural checks upon the populations of injurious insects is impossible to estimate with our present knowledge, but it is undoubtedly large. Numerous species have been imported into the United States or Canada as natural enemies of the Japanese beetle, European earwig, and gypsy, brown-tail, and codling moths. Even the aquatic larvae of crane flies and certain moths are parasitized by tachina flies.

Example: Tachina Fly   *Compsilùra concinnàta*

This remarkable fly, best known as a parasite of the gypsy and brown-tail moths, was introduced into New England from Europe in 1906. It parasitizes about 100 different species of insects, mostly moths and butterflies of some 18 different families. The eggs are laid underneath the skin of the host larva, and the winter is passed as a larva inside the hibernating stage of the host. From 1 to 5 parasites may develop in a single host.

174 Louse Flies   *Family Hippobóscidae*

This is 1 of 3 families of bloodsucking flies which have a unique way of reproducing—they bear mature larvae rather than eggs or first-stage larvae. The few known species of the families Nycteribìidae and Stréblidae are external parasites of bats and are called bat flies.

Adults: Resembling in habits and appearance the sucking lice of the order Anoplùra, though larger. They are small to minute insects, flat, with thorax considerably narrower than the abdomen, which is covered with short, sparse, spine-like hairs. The head, almost completely hidden in a recess of the thorax, bears large eyes and a proboscis fitted for piercing the skin of various warm-blooded vertebrates and sucking blood. Wings may or may not be present. They never leave the host during their life. The eggs of these remarkable insects hatch inside the body of the mother and there develop into mature larvae. At birth the larva is glued to a hair or feather of the host.

YOUNG: Within a few hours after birth the larva forms a puparium of its last larval skin and pupates within it. A few weeks later it emerges as an adult.

IMPORTANCE: The so-called sheep-tick, one of our examples, injures its host by setting up an irritation which induces scratching, biting, and nervousness and results in great loss of weight. There is a perceptible loss of blood in heavy infestations, and the wool is soiled by the excrement and puparia of the insects. Some louse flies transmit diseases to their hosts.

EXAMPLE 174a: Sheep-tick *Melóphagus ovìnus*

Occurs on sheep everywhere.

EXAMPLE 174b: Louse Fly *Pseudolýnchia brúnnea*

A widespread New World pest of nighthawks, whippoor-wills, and related birds.

A strange little fly, quite wingless and much like the louse fly in general appearance, is *Braùla coèca,* the bee-louse, an external parasite of honey bees. It is the only member of the family Braùlidae and is an Old World species which has become established locally in our region. The bee-louse lays eggs, and the larvae tunnel among the brood cells in beehives. The adults ride about on the bodies of bees and are said to obtain food from the mouths of their hosts.

FLEAS
Order Siphonáptera

This last order is represented in our region by 5 families of about 200 species. If they had not inspired an occasional humorous song or poem, it would be next to impossible to think of any good thing to say of fleas. The characters and habits of the order are represented sufficiently in the family we have chosen as an example.

175 Common Fleas   *Family Pulicidae*

ADULTS: Agile jumpers with long, powerful legs fitted with very large coxae, 5-jointed tarsi, and large claws. They are minute, exceedingly narrow-bodied and wingless—ideally suited for moving through the feathers or hair of the birds and mammals they parasitize. The piercing-sucking mouth parts are used to penetrate the skin and draw out the blood of the host, the only food of adult fleas. The eyes are relatively large in this family but are reduced to a simple unit (not faceted); there are no ocelli. The antennae, which at low magnification are apparently 3-jointed, fit into grooves at the sides of the head. The white or yellowish eggs are round or oval, quite smooth, and are laid singly; they at once drop off the host to the ground or into the nesting or bedding place.

YOUNG: In the dust or debris into which the egg has fallen the legless, eyeless, bristly larva, bearing a strong superficial resemblance to an active fly maggot, feeds on organic material, passes through 3 developmental stages, then spins a silken cocoon in which to pupate. The life cycle can be completed in a month, more or less, depending upon the temperature.

IMPORTANCE: The dog, cat, and human fleas, all of them at least occasional pests of man, belong to this family. The human flea actually is commoner on other animals—hogs, for example—than on man. The dog and cat fleas frequently exchange hosts and are not easily distinguished. In the Old World, bubonic plague is transmitted from rats to man by the tropical rat flea (*Xenopsýlla cheòpis*), a foreign species, which now occurs sparingly in the United States. In western North America fleas cause epidemics of bubonic plague in rodent hosts, especially ground squirrels. Fleas can transmit typhus from rats to man and probably tularemia from rabbits and other hosts to man.

EXAMPLE: Dog Flea   *Ctenocephálides cànis*

Almost cosmopolitan. Occurring on dogs, cats, and gray foxes throughout most of North America, but apparently absent in the Rocky Mountains and intermountain areas. House infestations are common and may become so severe that suppressive measures must be taken.

Collecting, Preserving, and Studying Insects

COLLECTING

Some kind of insect can be found in almost every conceivable type of environment, as a reading of the habitat information in this book will show; it is necessary only to look in order to find. Collecting is especially enjoyable when it takes one away from cities and towns and into areas of great natural beauty, but remember, there is no lawn or vacant lot without insects to watch or collect. In general there are no restrictions against the collection and killing of insects; on the contrary, a collector intent on "cornering the market" in insects might find public opinion decidedly, if somewhat mistakenly, behind him. Only in certain parks, where in order to protect either or both the showier butterflies and the flowers upon which they might alight, is the collection of insects prohibited or discouraged. While there are many rare species, especially among the moths and butterflies, their scarcity is not due to the efforts of collectors. Unless, for example, the cocoons of some moth that leaves large ones in exposed places are systematically gathered, it isn't likely that your take of insects will affect the population of desirable species at all, even in a very small area.

Free-flying, delicate insects, such as butterflies, moths, and dragonflies, are caught in nets of wide-mesh, light material (marquisette or fine netting) on long handles. The ability to capture insects in flight requires a skill that comes only with practice. Leaf-feeding insects, if not simply picked off their food plants, usually are caught in beating or sweeping nets. The former are of stout cloth—heavy muslin will do—and are struck against branches and plant stems to dislodge insects. Sweeping can be done with a beating net or a butterfly net, but a so-called general-purpose net of medium strength (unbleached muslin) is more appropriate. In sweeping, the net is passed back and forth so that its lower rim brushes over the upper portions of the stems of weeds and grasses. The insects, dislodged or startled into flight, fall into the net. Aquatic forms must usually be captured in nets, and since the greater number is to be found at or just below the bottom of a pond, lake, or stream, and it is often desirable to bring up some of the debris or mud in the net, cloth of considerable strength, such as heavy scrim, is required. The rim of an aquatic net should be flat on the side opposite the handle.

Everyone has observed that at night lights attract many insects. Indeed, on a summer evening one may make a nice collection of screen-penetrating insects from the pages of the book he is reading under a lamp indoors. If there are not too many nearby lights to compete with, a porch light may be used to draw a wide variety of insects within comfortable collecting range. More effective light traps, equipped with killing chambers, may be made or purchased.

Insects are baited in various ways. Leave the carcass of a small animal such as a rabbit or bird on the ground, protected under a screen of chicken wire (to prevent its being carried off or devoured by dogs or coyotes). As the bait putrifies an interesting series of insects comes to inhabit it, commencing with the sexton beetles, that may try to bury it, and ending with the skin beetles and dermestids, that will work on the skin and sinews.

Moths may be baited with a less offensive lure concocted of crushed banana or peach, with sugar water or molasses, all somewhat fermented. This ambrosia, when daubed on the bark of an occasional tree along a woodland trail or about a lawn, and visited with flashlight and killing bottles at intervals during the night, yields a rich harvest of nocturnal moths and some other sweet-loving insects.

Turning over stones and fallen limbs or logs (and then considerately turning them back into their original positions) is the way to find many beetles, ants, termites, and lots of interesting animals besides insects. Peeling the bark from dead trees or logs or deadened areas of trees will reveal beetles in all stages of development, particularly bark beetles, clerids, and cerambycids. The piles of drift along the water's edge at the bend of a stream are a good source of insects—both those that have been carried there by high water (an extremely varied group of insects that must be collected soon after they are deposited) and those insects which choose the heap of debris as living quarters. Insects may be sifted or otherwise separated from sod, forest litter, and soil.

Tiny, delicate, jumping insects, such as springtails, the smaller leafhoppers, and many other insects as well, are most conveniently collected in a suction bottle or "aspirator." This apparatus, which has been illustrated, is operated by gently placing the glass or plastic intake tube about ½ inch from the insect and sucking sharply on the mouth tube or, in a modification, by squeezing a rubber bulb.

Insects usually are killed in wide-mouthed, stout glass or plastic vials and bottles containing potassium or sodium cyanide, *very dangerous poisons*. The crystalline compound is embedded in a little sawdust and covered with a ¼- to ½-inch layer of plaster of Paris. A cyanide killing bottle should be labeled "Poison" and kept tightly corked except when insects are being introduced or extracted. The contents of old or broken cyanide jars must be burned or buried. Satisfactory killing jars are made by placing a few drops of carbon tetrachloride (carbona) or chloroform in a wad of cotton covered by a disk of cardboard. Such a jar must be "strengthened" before each collecting trip. A killing bottle, both safe and relatively long-lasting, can be made as follows: Pour about an inch of plaster of Paris in a jar and, after it is quite dry, saturate it with ethyl acetate. Such a bottle is easily recharged. Several strips or light wads of tissue paper should be kept in every bottle to prevent the rattling about of the contents. Because of the ease with which scales come off their wings, butterflies and moths should be killed in a separate bottle and never placed in a jar with other insects. Many collectors pinch the thorax of a moth or butterfly to stun it before dropping it into the killing bottle, so that it will not injure its own wings in attempts to escape. Others prefer to add a few drops of quick-acting chloroform to the cyanide bottle before each collecting trip.

After losing a variable number of desirable specimens, the amateur collector will learn how to transfer active flying, jumping, or running insects from the net to the killing bottle. With the exception of certain aquatic nets, the bag is always long enough to fold over the rim and hang down when the net is held horizontally, mouth downward. The insects in the end of the bag thus are trapped, at least until the stronger ones have had time to force their way between the two layers of cloth. This gives the collector opportunity to remove the top from his killing bottle, work it into the bag of the net, and place its mouth over the insects as they cling to the cloth. The lid is usually held over the bottle for a few seconds while it is still inside the net until the insects are at least partially overcome by the fumes.

Insects should be removed from the killing bottle as soon as they are certainly dead and placed between layers of cellucotton in pillboxes or other small containers. Butterflies, moths, and dragonflies are usually placed in paper envelopes or the more economical "triangles" made out of rectangular pieces of paper. (See following diagrams.) Specimens will dry out in these containers and may be preserved indefinitely if kept in a dry place and subjected to the fumes of paradichlorobenzene frequently enough to deter dermestids and booklice.

Insects which are going to be kept in preserving fluids may be dropped into vials of alcohol, etc., as collected.

Collecting equipment can be made or purchased. Most of the firms specializing in such items and in all the various supplies needed by amateur or professional entomologists advertise in the *Naturalists' Directory* and in the various entomological periodicals (see References). On pages 222 and 223 are sketches of insect-collecting equipment, pinning and display methods, and rearing cages; it is hoped that these illustrations with their labels will explain themselves sufficiently to the reader and be of some help to the novice.

PRESERVING

We would not discourage anyone from starting a collection of insects, but would warn that an insect collection, at least one to take pride in, demands considerable care and some cash outlay. The indispensable rustproof pins must be obtained from an entomological supply house, and the insects must be protected from mice, dermestids, mold, and breakage. For handling small or delicate specimens a pair of light forceps is necessary. Excellent descriptions of insect-mounting methods are given in the publications which are listed in the References under the heading, "About collecting, rearing, and preserving insects." Briefly, insects are mounted on pins or between a plate of glass and a cotton or plaster of Paris backing. The specimen is either pierced directly by the pin or is glued to a small triangle of paper which itself is pierced by the pin. Insects with large wings, such as moths, butterflies, and dragonflies, are usually pinned and then allowed to dry out on a spreading board, so that the wings harden in an outstretched position. Insects are also preserved in liquids, such as 70 per cent alcohol, 5 per cent formalin, or certain special mixtures; minute ones are mounted on glass slides after being embedded in Canada balsam or other mounting medium. Embedding in transparent plastics is probably the newest way to make attractive mounts of insects.

Dried insects are brittle and cannot be pinned or otherwise manipulated until they have been "relaxed." A relaxing jar is any sort of glass jar or crock with tight-fitting lid, containing about 2 inches of clean, water-saturated sand, to which a few drops of carbolic acid have been added to prevent the growth of molds. A few blocks of wood and a disk or square of glass will serve as a platform to hold the insects off the wet sand. A period of 1 to 3 days in the relaxing chamber will soften up most insects so they can be mounted.

Adult insects which become greasy after death because of the breakdown of the large amounts of fat in their bodies may be degreased before or after pinning by immersing them for a few hours in chloroform, benzene, xylene, or some other solvent.

In pinning insects, it is good practice to allow ⅜ inch between the top of the pin and the insect or the paper triangle to which the insect is glued. Pin labels showing place and date of collection of the specimen, name of collector, and the name of the insect are spaced below the specimen by using a "pinning block" of the sort illustrated in the preceding diagrams. Collec-

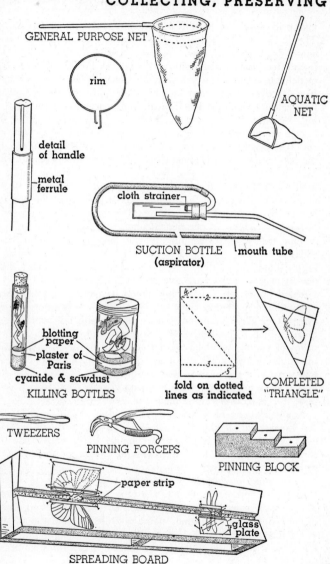

COLLECTING, PRESERVING

GENERAL PURPOSE NET

rim

AQUATIC NET

detail of handle

metal ferrule

cloth strainer

SUCTION BOTTLE (aspirator)   mouth tube

blotting paper

plaster of Paris

cyanide & sawdust

KILLING BOTTLES

fold on dotted lines as indicated

COMPLETED "TRIANGLE"

TWEEZERS

PINNING FORCEPS

PINNING BLOCK

paper strip

glass plate

SPREADING BOARD

AND STUDYING INSECTS

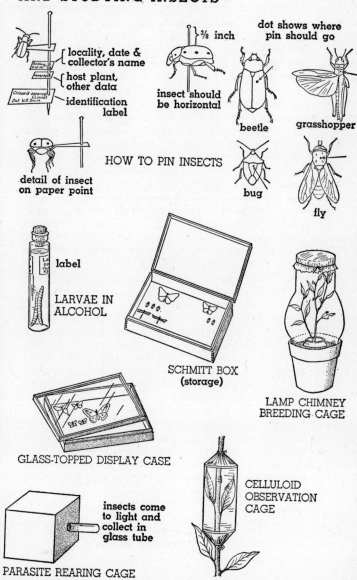

locality, date & collector's name

host plant, other data

identification label

detail of insect on paper point

HOW TO PIN INSECTS

³/₈ inch

insect should be horizontal

dot shows where pin should go

beetle

grasshopper

bug

fly

label

LARVAE IN ALCOHOL

SCHMITT BOX (storage)

LAMP CHIMNEY BREEDING CAGE

GLASS-TOPPED DISPLAY CASE

CELLULOID OBSERVATION CAGE

insects come to light and collect in glass tube

PARASITE REARING CAGE

tion site and date and collector's name can be written or printed on a single label.

The immature stages of insects usually are killed in boiling water and preserved in 70 per cent alcohol or other liquid preservative. For exhibition purposes, the showy caterpillars of certain butterflies and moths may be inflated and dried after expressing the body contents through the anal opening by rolling the insects with a round object such as a pencil. A glass tube, drawn to a point, is inserted into the anal opening and the skin fixed to the glass with a thread or spring clamp; the caterpillar is then distended to normal size by blowing through the tube (or by using the steady air pressure from a double-bulb apparatus) and is held in an oven over a source of heat until quite dry. Lastly the dried skin is carefully removed from the glass tube and mounted as desired. Naked larvae, whose colors may vanish when emptied of their body contents, can be filled with molten wax of the proper color and their natural appearance preserved. The wax is introduced into the caterpillars with the same apparatus used to inflate them with air, but the glass tube must be judiciously warmed with a small flame so the quick-hardening wax will flow into the insects.

A homemade display box can be made of various materials and in various styles. A good box must be tight enough to contain the fumes of paradichlorobenzene, and a large pinch of "PDB" crystals should be wrapped in a square of cloth and pinned securely in a corner of every insect box. Loosely fitting boxes require more care to guard against dermestids. Cork makes the best lining for a box, but corrugated paper and some composition boards can be used.

In preparing pinned insects for shipment through the mails, fix the pins very securely in a small cork-bottomed box (special pinning forceps will be of assistance). Then wrap the box in paper and place it in a carton lined with a 2- to 4-inch layer of excelsior or shredded paper, packed firmly but not too tightly. Vials of alcoholic specimens should be wrapped individually with paper before packing in excelsior.

STUDYING

To study insects is to enjoy them. Many are so beautiful in color and form that just contemplating them in a display case or in an artistic arrangement of their bodies or wing fragments gives pleasure. They make excellent subjects for amateur photographers. From ancient times, insects or insect forms have been used as ornaments and in designs for decorating man's dwellings, garments, etc. The living insect, however, is more interesting than the dead or the facsimile, and for most of us the greatest enjoyment comes from observing them out of doors in their natural surroundings. But for convenience, and in order to see certain activities which cannot readily be observed in nature, insects may be confined or even reared in cages of simple design.

The caterpillars of butterflies and moths make interesting subjects for rearing. Placed in a cage with some of the foliage upon which they were captured, they will usually complete their feeding, spin their cocoons or form chrysalids, and eventually emerge as adults. Fresh foliage must be supplied from time to time if the larvae are not almost ready to pupate when caged. Usually it is best to have an inch or 2 of soil in the bottom of the cage, since so many insects, even among those that feed upon the leaves and stems of plants as larvae, enter the soil to pupate. You may find it more fun to experiment with jars, screen cages, terraria, and aquaria than to follow written instructions and diagrams, but among the references we have given you will find many well-tested schemes for keeping insects alive and comfortable in confinement.

Many students of insects, including the writer, have found pleasure in associating themselves with local groups or national organizations devoted wholly or partially to insect study, or in themselves forming groups for the purpose. New members and contributors as well as subscribers to their periodicals are welcomed by the larger organizations of entomologists.

Public displays of living insects, a field successfully pioneered by Brayton Eddy of the New York Zoological Society at Bronx Park, are becoming increasingly popular in zoological gardens. We venture to predict that all first-rate zoos eventually will have living insect exhibits and that in popularity they will vie with the snakes and monkeys.

Special projects in insect study pay big dividends in knowledge and satisfaction. Try collecting all of the insects you find feeding on a particular plant species, rearing out parasites from selected host insects, working out the complete life cycle of some insect that interests you; concentrate on a subject such as protective coloration, mimicry, adaptation to certain environments, and make specialized collections of both insects and publications to assist you in your study. The more serious student will keep careful notes on his observations.

Serious study, however, is not essential to the enjoyment of insects, and you may take what we have said on the subject of study as lightly as you please. We shall be satisfied if the general reader, in rambling through the pictures and pages of this little book, finds the answers to some of his long-standing questions about insects, or if he learns, as effortlessly as possible, to distinguish ants from termites and bugs from beetles. If benefits beyond these should be derived, then we shall be more than satisfied—we shall be pleased beyond measure.

References

Keys to insect orders and families

How to Know the Insects, by H. E. Jaques, published by the author, Mount Pleasant, Ia., 1937.

A Key to the Principal Orders and Families of Insects, by Z. P. and C. L. Metcalf, published by the authors, North Carolina State College, Raleigh, N.C., 1928.

Classification of Insects, by C. T. Brues and A. L. Melander, published by Harvard University Press, Cambridge, Mass., 1945.

General textbooks (classification and biology)

General Entomology, by S. W. Frost, published by McGraw-Hill Book Co., New York, N.Y., 1942.

College Entomology, by E. O. Essig, published by Macmillan Co., New York, N.Y., 1942.

An Introduction to Entomology, by J. H. Comstock, published by Comstock Publishing Co., Ithaca, N.Y., 1940.

Fieldbook of Insects, by F. E. Lutz, published by G. P. Putnam's Sons, New York, N.Y., 1935.

About particular kinds of insects (classification and biology)

PROTURONS: *The Protura of North America,* by H. E. Ewing, published in the *Annals of the Entomological Society of America,* Vol. 33, pp. 495–551, 1940.

SPRINGTAILS: *A Monograph of the Collembola of Iowa,* by H. B. Mills, published by Collegiate Press, Ames, Ia., 1934.

ROACHES, GRASSHOPPERS, CRICKETS, AND ALLIES: *Orthoptera of Northeastern America,* by W. S. Blatchley, published by Nature Publishing Co., Indianapolis, Ind., 1920.

The Grasshoppers and Other Orthoptera of Arizona, by E. D. Ball, et al., published by the University of Arizona Agricultural Experiment Station in Tech. Bull. 93, pp. 255–373, 1942.

The Dermaptera and Orthoptera of Illinois, by M. Hebard, published by the Illinois Natural History Survey in Bull. 20, pp. 125–279, 1934.

STONEFLIES: *A Monograph of the Plecoptera or Stoneflies of America North of Mexico,* by J. G. Needham and P. W. Claassen, published by the Thomas Say Foundation, Springfield, Ill., 1925.

The Stoneflies, or Plecoptera, of Illinois, by T. H. Frison, published by the Illinois Natural History Survey in Bull. 20, pp. 281–471, 1935.

TERMITES: *A Revision of the Nearctic Termites, with Notes on their Biology and Geographical Distribution,* by N. Banks and T. E. Snyder, published by the U. S. National Museum, as Bull. 108, 1920.

EMBIIDS: *A Revision of the Embioptera, or Web-spinners, of the New World,* by E. S. Ross, published in the *Proceedings of the U. S. National Museum,* Vol. 94, pp. 401–504, 1944.

PSOCIDS: *Corrodentia of the United States of America,* by P. J. Chapman, published in the *Journal of the New York Entomological Society,* Vol. 38, pp. 219–90; 319–403, 1930.

ZORAPTERONS: *A Synopsis of the Order Zoraptera, with Notes on the Biology of Zorotypus hubbardi Caudell,* by A. B. Gurney, published in *Proceedings of the Entomological Society of Washington,* Vol. 40, pp. 57–87, 1938.

BITING AND SUCKING LICE: *A Manual of External Parasites,* by H. E. Ewing, published by Thomas, Baltimore, Md., 1929.

THRIPS: *Synopsis and Catalogue of the Thysanoptera of North America,* by J. R. Watson, published by the University of Florida Agricultural Experiment Station as Bull. 168, 1923.

BUGS, APHIDS, SCALES, AND ALLIES: *Catalogue of the Hemiptera of America North of Mexico,* by E. P. Van Duzee, published by University of California as Bull. 2 (technical ento-mological), 1917.

The Hemiptera or Sucking Insects of Connecticut, by W. E. Britton, et al., published by the State of Connecticut Geological and Natural History Survey, Hartford, Conn., as Bull. 34, 1923.

Heteroptera of Eastern North America, by W. S. Blatchley, published by the Nature Publishing Co., Indianapolis, Ind., 1926.

The Plant Bugs, or Miridae, of Illinois, by H. H. Knight, published by the Illinois Natural History Survey in Bull. 22, pp. 1–234, 1941.

The Plant Lice or Aphididae of Illinois, by F. C. Hottes and T. H. Frison, published by Illinois Natural History Survey in Bull. 19, pp. 121–447, 1931.

Atlas of the Scale Insects of North America, by G. F. Ferris, published by Stanford University Press, 1938.

MAYFLIES: *The Biology of May Flies with a Systematic Account of North American Species,* by J. G. Needham, J. R. Traver, and Y. H. Hsu, published by Comstock Publishing Co., Ithaca, N.Y., 1935.

DAMSELFLIES AND DRAGONFLIES: *Handbook of Dragonflies of North America,* by J. G. Needham and H. B. Heywood, published by Thomas, Baltimore, Md. 1929.

The Odonata or Dragonflies of Connecticut, by P. Garman, published by the Connecticut Geological and Natural History Survey as Bull. 39, 1927.

SCORPIONFLIES: *Revision of the Nearctic Mecoptera,* by F. M. Carpenter, published by the Museum of Comparative Zoology (Harvard University) in Bull. 72, pp. 205–77, 1931.

CADDISFLIES: *The Caddis Flies, or Trichoptera, of Illinois,* by H. H. Ross, published by the Illinois Natural History Survey, Urbana, Ill., in Bull. 23, pp. 1–326, 1944.

The Caddis Flies or Trichoptera of New York State, by C. Betten, published by the New York State Museum, Albany, N.Y., as Bull. 292, 1934.

MOTHS AND BUTTERFLIES: *The Butterflies of North America,* by W. H. Edwards, published by the American Entomological Society, 1868–72. Reprinted by Houghton Mifflin, Boston, 1897. (3 vols.)

The Moth Book, by W. J. Holland, published by Doubleday, New York, N.Y., 1913.

The Butterfly Book, by W. J. Holland, published by Doubleday, New York, N.Y., 1931.

The Lepidoptera of New York and Neighboring States, by W. T. M. Forbes (covering most of the moth families), published by Cornell University Agricultural Experiment Station as Memoir 68, 1923.

How to Know the Butterflies, by J. H. and A. B. Comstock, published by the Comstock Publishing Co., Ithaca, N.Y., 1936.

The Classification of Lepidopterous Larvae, by S. B. Fracker, published by the Illinois Natural History Survey, Urbana, Ill., in Ill. Biological Monograph 2, pp. 1–161, 1915.

Caterpillars and their Moths, by I. M. Eliot and C. G. Soule, published by Century Co., New York, N.Y., 1902.

BEETLES: *Catalogue of the Coleoptera of North America,* by C. W. Leng, published by Sherman, Mount Vernon, N.Y., 1920. (Supplement, with A. J. Mutchler, 1927, and Supplements 2 and 3, 1925–32. Supplement 4, by R. E. Blackwelder, 1939.)

A Manual of the Genera of Beetles of America, North of Mexico, by J. C. Bradley, published by Daw, Illston and Co., Ithaca, N.Y., 1930.

Coleoptera of Indiana, by W. S. Blatchley, published by Nature Publishing Co., Indianapolis, Ind., 1910.

The Bark and Timber Beetles of North America, by W. J. Chamberlin, published by O. S. C. Cooperative Assn., Corvallis, Ore., 1939. (Lithographed.)

The Rhyncophora or Weevils of Northeastern America, by W. S. Blatchley and C. W. Leng, published by Nature Publishing Co., Indianapolis, Ind., 1916.

An Illustrated Synopsis of the Principal Larval Forms of the Order Coleoptera, by A. G. Böving, and F. C. Craighead, published by the Brooklyn Entomological Society, 1931.

WASPS, ANTS, AND BEES: *The Hymenoptera or Wasp-like Insects of Connecticut,* by H. L. Viereck, A. D. MacGillivray, C. T. Brues, W. M. Wheeler, and S. A. Rohwer, published by the State of Connecticut Geological and Natural History Survey, Hartford, Conn., as Bull. 22, 1916.

A Generic Classification of the Nearctic Sawflies, by H. H.

Ross, published by the Illinois Natural History Survey, Urbana, Ill., in Ill. Biological Monograph 15, pp. 1–173, 1937.

Ants, Their Structure, Development and Behavior, by W. M. Wheeler, published by Columbia University Press, New York, N.Y., 1910.

A Generic and Subgeneric Synopsis of the United States Ants, based on the Workers, by M. R. Smith, published in the *American Midland Naturalist,* Vol. 37, pp. 521–647, 1947.

Wasps, Social and Solitary, by G. W. and E. G. Peckham, published by Riverside Press, Cambridge, Mass., 1905.

Comparative External Morphology, Phylogeny, and a Classification of the Bees, by C. D. Michener, published by the American Museum of Natural History as Bull. 82, 1944.

FLIES: *A Catalogue of North American Diptera,* by J. M. Aldrich, published by the Smithsonian Institution as Misc. Coll. Bull. 46, 1905.

The Families and Genera of North American Diptera, by C. H. Curran, published by Ballou, New York, N.Y., 1934.

Tanyderidae, Ptychopteridae, Trichoceridae, Anisopodidae, and Tipulidae of Connecticut, by C. P. Alexander, published by the Connecticut Geological and Natural History Survey in Bull. 64, pp. 183–509, 1942.

Handbook of the Mosquitoes of North America, by R. Matheson, published by the Comstock Publishing Co., Ithaca, N.Y., 1944.

Aquatic Diptera (covers larvae and pupae), by O. A. Johansen, published as Cornell University Agricultural Experiment Station as Memoirs 164, 177, 205, and 210, 1934–37.

FLEAS: *Fleas of the Eastern United States,* by I. Fox, published by Iowa State College Press, Ames, Ia., 1940.

Fleas of Western North America, by C. A. Hubbard, published by Iowa State College Press, Ames, Ia., 1947.

INSECTS OTHER THAN MOTHS, BUTTERFLIES, AND BEETLES: *The Insect Book,* by L. O. Howard, published by Doubleday, Page and Co., Garden City, N.Y., 1923.

About insects of particular habits or habitats

AQUATIC INSECTS: *The Life of Inland Waters,* by J. G. Needham and J. T. Lloyd, published by Comstock Publishing Co., Ithaca, N.Y., 1916.

Field Book of Ponds and Streams, by A. H. Morgan, published by G. P. Putnam's Sons, New York, N.Y., 1930.

CAVE INSECTS: *Animal Life of Carlsbad Cavern,* by V. Bailey, published by Williams and Wilkins Co., Baltimore, Md., 1928.

GALL INSECTS: *Plant Galls and Gall Makers,* by E. P. Felt, published by Comstock Publishing Co., Ithaca, N.Y., 1940.

LEAF-MINING INSECTS: *Leaf-mining Insects,* by J. G. Needham, et al., published by Williams and Wilkins Co., Baltimore, Md., 1928.

PARASITIC AND PREDACIOUS INSECTS: *The Biological Control of Insects,* by H. L. Sweetman, Comstock Publishing Co., Ithaca, N.Y., 1936.

The Bionomics of Entomophagous Insects, by W. V. Balduf, published by John S. Swift and Co., St. Louis, Mo., 1939.

The Bionomics of Entomophagous Coleoptera, by W. V. Balduf, published by John S. Swift and Co., St. Louis, Mo., 1935.

Entomophagous Insects, by C. P. Clausen, published by Mc-Graw-Hill Book Co., New York, N.Y., 1940.

About insects of economic importance and their control or culture

Destructive and Useful Insects, by C. L. Metcalf and W. P. Flint, published by McGraw-Hill Book Co., New York, N.Y., 1939.

The Gardener's Bug Book, by C. Westcott, published by American Garden Guild and Doubleday and Co., Garden City, N.Y., 1946.

Handbook on Insect Enemies of Flowers and Shrubs, by C. A. Weigel and L. G. Baumhofer, published by the U. S. Department of Agriculture as Misc. Publication 626, 1948.

The Chemistry and Toxicology of Insecticides, by H. H. Shepard, published by Burgess Publishing Co., Minneapolis, Minn., 1939.

Principles of Forest Entomology, by S. A. Graham, published by McGraw-Hill Book Co., New York, N.Y., 1939.

Insects of Citrus and Other Subtropical Fruits, by H. J. Quale, published by Comstock Publishing Co., Ithaca, N.Y., 1938.

202 Common Household Pests of North America, by H. Hartnack, published by Hartnack Publishing Co., Chicago, Ill., 1939.

The Biological Control of Insects, by H. L. Sweetman, published by Comstock Publishing Co., Ithaca, N.Y., 1936.

A Manual of External Parasites, by H. E. Ewing, published by Thomas, Baltimore, Md., 1929.

Medical Entomology, by W. B. Hermes, published by Macmillan Co., New York, N.Y., 1939.

Beekeeping, by E. F. Phillips, published by Macmillan Co., New York, N.Y., 1928.

Also innumerable bulletins, circulars, and leaflets of the U. S. Department of Agriculture and of state colleges and experiment stations.

About insect anatomy, physiology, and food habits

Principles of Insect Morphology, by R. E. Snodgrass, published by McGraw-Hill Book Co., New York, N.Y., 1935.

A Glossary of Entomology, by J. R. de la Torre-Bueno, published by Science Press, Lancaster, Pa., 1937.

The Principles of Insect Physiology, by V. B. Wigglesworth, published by E. P. Dutton and Co., New York, N.Y., 1939.

Insect Dietary, an Account of the Food Habits of Insects, by C. T. Brues, published by Harvard University Press, Cambridge, Mass., 1946.

Insect microbiology

Insect Microbiology, by E. A. Steinhaus, published by Comstock Publishing Co., Ithaca, N.Y., 1946.

Insect Transmission of Plant Diseases, by J. G. Leach, published by McGraw-Hill Book Co., New York, N.Y., 1940.

More popular books about insects

Insects, by G. Pickwell, C. D. Duncan, K. S. Hazeltine, and E. Smith, published by Suttonhouse, Los Angeles, Cal., 1933.

Near Horizons, by E. W. Teale, published by Dodd, Mead and Co., New York, N.Y., 1942.

How Insects Live, by W. H. Wellhouse, published by Macmillan Co., New York, N.Y., 1926.

Wasp Studies Afield, by P. Rau and N. Rau, published by Princeton University Press, Princeton, N.J., 1918.

Especially for younger people

Hexapod Stories, by E. M. Patch, published by Little, Brown and Co., Boston, Mass., 1930.

The Boys' Book of Insects, by E. W. Teale, published by Blakiston Co., Philadelphia, Pa., 1943.

Insect Adventures, by J. H. Fabre, published by Dodd, Mead and Co., New York, N.Y., 1929.

Insect Life, by E. W. Teale, published by the Boy Scouts of America, New York, N.Y., 1944.

4-H Club Insect Manual, by M. P. Jones, published by the U. S. Dept. of Agriculture as Misc. Publication No. 318, 1943.

Periodicals wholly or partially devoted to entomology

Journal of Economic Entomology, published by the American Association of Economic Entomologists at Menasha, Wis.

Entomological News, published by the American Entomological Society and the Philadelphia Academy of Natural Sciences at Lancaster, Pa.

Annals of the Entomological Society of America, published by the Society at Columbus, Ohio.

The Canadian Entomologist, published at Guelph, Ontario.

Biological Abstracts, published by the Union of American Biological Societies at Philadelphia, Pa. (Abstracts of papers.)

About collecting, rearing, and preserving insects

How to Make an Insect Collection, published by Ward's Natural Science Establishment, Rochester, N.Y., 1945.

Collection and Preservation of Insects, P. W. Oman and A. D. Cushman, published by the U. S. Department of Agriculture as Misc. Publication 601, 1946.

A Manual of Entomological Equipment and Methods, by A. M. Peterson, published by Edwards Bros., Ann Arbor, Mich. (Part I), 1934, and by John S. Swift and Co., St. Louis, Mo. (Part II), 1937.

Culture Methods for Invertebrate Animals, by J. G. Needham, et al., published by Comstock Publishing Co., Ithaca, N.Y., 1937.

About the locations and interests of other insect enthusiasts and specialists

The Naturalists' Directory, published by the Cassino Press, Salem, Mass., 35th edition, 1948. (Includes lists of natural history museums, scientific periodicals and societies, and sellers of entomological equipment.)

American Men of Science, published by Science Press, Lancaster, Pa., 7th ed., 1944.

The literature on insects is very large. The references given here would be entirely inadequate if it were not that many of these books and pamphlets themselves contain bibliographies and lists of references further to guide the determined seeker for published facts about insects.

Index

INDEX

NUMBERS IN BOLD-FACE TYPE REFER TO ILLUSTRATION
AND FAMILY NUMBERS.

ORDER	EXAMPLES	DEVELOP-MENT	WING
THRIPS (Thysanoptera)		Gradual	Four
BUGS, LEAF-HOPPERS, SCALES, AND ALLIES (Hemiptera)		Gradual	Four (or none two in m scales
MAYFLIES (Ephemeroptera)		Gradual	Four
DAMSELFLIES AND DRAGONFLIES (Odonata)		Gradual	Four
NERVE-WINGED INSECTS (Neuroptera)		Complex	Four
SCORPION-FLIES (Mecoptera)		Complex	Four
CADDISFLIES (Trichoptera)		Complex	Four
MOTHS AND BUTTERFLIES (Lepidoptera)		Complex	Four (none ir some fema
BEETLES (Coleoptera)		Complex	Four
STREPSIPTERONS (Strepsiptera)		Complex	None in fem two, hind in males
WASPS, ANTS, BEES, AND ALLIES (Hymenoptera)		Complex	Four (or none
FLIES (Diptera)		Complex	Two (for (or none
FLEAS (Siphonaptera)		Complex	None